SACRED
SCOTLAND

The Travelle

D0686446

The Traveller's Guide to

SACRED SCOTLAND

A Guide to Scotland's
Ancient Sites and Sacred Places

MARIANNA LINES

Gothic Image PUBLICATIONS

Many masks merge in an island face,
Pict, Norseman, Scot,
Salt wanderers, tremulous first-comers
After the ice broke.
Face of the countryman, strength of loam in it.
Faces of the fishermen, sailor: the eyes
Level as horizons.

by George Mackay Brown

First published by Gothic Image Publications in 2014,
7 High Street, Glastonbury, Somerset BA6 9DP, England
www.gothicimage.co.uk
Copyright © Marianna Lines 2014.
All rights reserved.

ISBN 978 0 906362 76 1
0 90632 76 8

A CIP catalogue record for this book is available
from the British Library.

Cover photograph:
Aurora Borealis at Ring of Brodgar © by Michael Sharpe

Design, mapping, layout:
Bernard Chandler [graffik], Glastonbury

Printed by Gutenberg Press Ltd,
Gudja Road, Tarxien, GXQ 2902, Malta

CONTENTS

ACKNOWLEDGEMENTS

Thanks go to... well, nearly everyone I have ever known in Scotland in the field of archaeology and history and the arts! Official bodies whose members have provided great service include the Pictish Arts Society, National Museums of Scotland, Royal Commission on the Ancient and Historical Monuments of Scotland and the National Monuments Record, the National Trust for Scotland, Historic Scotland, Falkland Centre for Stewardship and Living Lomonds Landscape project, Claire Herbert of Aberdeenshire Council Archaeology Service, Val Turner of Shetland Amenity Trust, Nick Card of Orkney Research Centre for Archaeology (ORCA), National Library of Scotland Edinburgh, HER Highland Council, Comhairle Nan Eilean Siar, Isle of Lewis (Western Isles Council), WOSAS West of Scotland Archaeological Service, Caithness Broch Project.

So many individuals have assisted in so many ways. A starter list includes: Jim Allan of Capercailzie Graphics, Niall Robertson, Norman Atkinson, David Henry, Peter Barz, Pete Kinnear, Simon Taylor, Mark Hall, David Strachan, Derek Hall, Derek Alexander (NTS), Graeme Cruickshank, Dot Clark, Mairi MacArthur, Bob Pegg, Peter Yeoman (HS), John Borland (RCAHMS), Adam Welfare (RCAHMS), Douglas Speirs (Fife Council Archaeology), Margaret Elphinstone, Terry Myers, Kathleen Cochrane, Helen Speed Jenkins, Jane Christie, David Ritchie, Bob Brydon (RIP), Lindsay Brydon, Alastair McIntosh, Susan Lynch, Lynda McGugan (Meigle Museum), Iain Grimston, Paula Benhaddad, Leona Graham, Jane Yolen, Robert D. Galbraith, and to all at Pillars of Hercules organic café in Falkland, the inspiration of Fife.

Photographic contributions from friends and colleagues is one of the greatest offerings toward the creation of this book. Contributors include: Gordon Thomson, Bob Henery, Ingrid Haas, Tess Darwin, Heather Richard, David McGovern, Ruari Halford-MacLeod, Kate Hajducka, Salli Shand of Glasgow, Evelyn Roe, Alice Simpson, Jannette MacDonald & Stewart Danks, Helen and Bob Pass, Fiona Docherty, Marion Leigh, Margaret Bennett & Gonzalo Mazzei, Michael Sharpe, Iain Maclean, Niall Robertson, Mhairi MacMillan, Malcolm Irving (HS), Ian Scrivener-Lindley (HER), Deborah Anderson (cnc-siar, Stornoway, Isle of Lewis), William Kempen (Belgium), Walter Baxter (Geograph) and all the many others that may be nameless, including the Pictish spirits and guides that surround this land and this laptop.

Finally, this would not have been possible without the constant support, guidance and brilliant editorship of Frances Howard Gordon of Gothic Image Publications, to Jamie George who is the inspiration behind the whole Sacred Stones tours, and to the impeccable 'Holy Grail' designer Bernard Chandler in Glastonbury.

TIMELINE FOR THE MAKING OF THE SACRED LANDSCAPE

BC

*c.*12000 BC   Earliest archaeological evidence of human habitation in Scotland.

*c.*8500 BC   MESOLITHIC (middle Stone Age): hunters and gatherers inhabit Scotland.

*c.*3500 BC   NEOLITHIC (new Stone Age): introduction of agriculture, pottery, polished stone tools, monumental architecture, henges, cursuses, chambered tombs, standing stones, cup and ring marked stones.

*c.*2500 BC   BRONZE AGE: introduction of metallurgy (copper alloy, gold). Evidence for warfare. Individuals rather than communities buried in monumental tombs.

*c.*700 BC   IRON AGE: introduction of iron working. Scotland split into tribal kingdoms. Hillforts, brochs, duns and crannogs built.

AD

81   Invasion of Caledonia by Romans under Agricola.

83   Battle of Mons Graupius in which Romans defeated Caledonians.

90   Abandonment of Roman positions north of the Forth.

122–36   Building of Hadrian's Wall.

*c.*143   Building of Antonine Wall.

*c.*154   Abandonment of Antonine Wall.

297   First recorded mention of the Picti (painted people), by Eumenius.

*c.*420   Bishopric of Whithorn founded by St Ninian (Nynia), the first recorded Christian missionary.

470   Votadini tribe form Kingdom of Gododdin in region north of River Tweed.

*c.*500   Emergence of the Kingdoms of the Picts and the Dál Riata.

503   Traditional date of the move of the kings of Dál Riata from Ireland to Scotland.

563   Arrival of Colum Cille (St Columba) on Iona. Monastery of Iona founded.

574   Aedán mac Gábráin begins reign over Gaelic kingdom of Dál Riata.

597   Death of Colum Cille.

638   Northumbrians (Angles) capture Din Eidyn (Edinburgh) from Gododdin.

685 Battle of Nechtansmere/Dún Nechtáin:
Pictish King Bruide mac Bili defeats Ecgfrith of
Northumbria, thus halting the northern expansion
of Northumbria.

747 First mention of Cennrígmonaid (St Andrews).

795 First recorded Viking raids in Scotland.

802, 806 Viking attacks on Iona.

843 Kenneth mac Alpin the King of Dál Riata takes
over Pictland: traditional date of the union of Picts
and Scots.

849 Kenneth mac Alpin king of Picts and Scots establishes shrine of St Columba's relics at Dunkeld.

878 Death of Áed, son of Kenneth mac Alpin, last to
be called King of Picts.

880 Norse Earldom of Orkney established.

900 Death of Donald II, first to be called King of Alba.

1018 Malcolm II established Scottish control over
southeast Scotland.

1040–57 Reign of Macbethad mac Findlaíg (Macbeth).
About this time, the Gaelic language reached its
widest extent.

1058–93 Reign of Malcolm III Ceann Mór (Canmore), and
St Margaret of Hungary. Beginning of Norman
influence in Scotland.

1098 Norwegian overlordship over the Western Isles and
the Isle of Man.

1124–53 Reign of David I. Many abbeys and burghs founded.

1157 Scotland loses Cumbria. Border with England on
present line.

1266 Treaty of Perth. Scottish control of Western Isles
recognised by Norway.

1296–1328 Scottish wars of independence.

1412 Foundation of St Andrews University.

1468 Marriage of James II and Margaret of Denmark.
Orkney and Shetland come to Scotland as part of
her dowry.

1493 Lordship of the Isles suppressed by James IV.

1559 Reformation in Scotland. Religious houses and
cathedrals attacked.

1560 'Reformation' Parliament officially establishes
Protestantism.

NOTE: All dates which are rounded are estimates. All early
dating is approximate as written records did not exist until the
late Middle Ages and current accepted opinion on early history changes all the time. So this timeline is only a guideline.

GLOSSARY OF TERMS

BARROW – an earthen mound covering a burial.

BARP – a Hebridean word that means cairn, or stones piled to make a mound to cover chambers, a burial or a stone lined burial cist. Common usage on the Uists in Outer Hebrides for cairn sites such as Barpa Langais.

BEAKER – early Bronze Age drinking cup, the first time that pottery vessels were produced for individual consumption.

BLACKHOUSE – a thick-walled, thatched oblong house with rounded corners and no chimney or windows, fire in the middle with hole in roof and cows kept in one end, sleeping accommodation in the other.

BOTHY – a simple shelter or hut.

BRONZE AGE – an age that began with metalworking, the smelting of copper and tin to make bronze. Introduced into Scotland circa 2000 BC.

BROCH – a circular drystone defensive tower-like structure of the Iron Age with features of architectural sophistication such as intramural galleries and cells. The etymology is related to Old Norse: *borg*, castle.

CAILLEACH –an old woman or hag from the Scottish Gaelic, derived from an Old Gaelic term meaning 'veiled one'. The Cailleach is such a strong concept in Scottish folklore that she lives in many place names and landscape features, and is considered the goddess of winter. She is the wise woman of the triple goddess set, also known as 'carlin', or witch.

CAIRN – a mound of small stones, often placed over a grave site in conical form, sometimes covering a system of tunnels or passageways underground, such as a passage grave or megalithic tomb.

CIST – a slab-built box or grave, from the Scots word for chest or box *kist*.

CRANNOG – an artificial offshore island comprising a timber or timber and stone superstructure, usually found in lochs rather than in the sea around Scotland. Gaelic *crann* = wood or beam.

CROFT – a small plot of land held by a single tenant used for subsistence farming, generally found in Western and outer isles.

CROP-MARK – a land feature mostly visible from the air: a difference in crop growth owing to buried features or variations in soil water retention that makes structures and shapes stand out beneath the soil.

CUP-MARK, CUP AND RING MARKINGS – small pecked hollows in natural rock surfaces, in some cases surrounded by single or multiple rings. Also to be found on standing stones in upright position dating from late Neolithic to Bronze Age.

DÁLRIADA/ DÁL RIATA – an ancient Gaelic kingdom on the western seaboard of Scotland with some territory on the northern coasts of Ireland. In the late sixth to early seventh century it encompassed most of Argyll, Bute and Lochaber in Scotland and County Antrim in Northern Ireland.

DATING – there is no final set dating for most of prehistory or early medieval history, and many dates are virtually apocryphal. It is only reasonable to give approximate dating, which continues to be argued over by academics and historians. Archaeology with its use of carbon dating is overturning past dating constantly, so history moves with the times.

DUN – drystone fortification of Iron Age or Early Historic date representing a single homestead. Gaelic *dun* = fort/fortification.

GLEN – a valley, typically long, deep and often U-shaped or with a watercourse running through it. Gaelic *gleann* = glen.

HAAR – Scottish mist, a special kind of Scottish fog that envelops everything, comes in from the sea and makes it all cold and clammy. It can be hot and sunny one moment, then the *haar* comes in and changes the climate completely. Never fear. It will go away.

HENGE – a Neolithic earthwork monument consisting of a ditch and external bank with one or two entrances, sometimes enclosing circles of stone or timber uprights. Generally circular or oval in form.

HILLFORT – a type of fortified refuge or defended settlement located to exploit a rise in elevation for defensive advantage. Typically found European wide, they date from the Bronze Age and Iron Age.

HOGBACK – a massive gravestone carved with an arched ridge and roof tiles (*tegulae*), often with animal ornament, dating to the tenth to eleventh centuries reflecting Scandinavian styles.

IRON AGE – the period during which tools and weapons were primarily made of iron or steel, replacing bronze. This began in Scotland around 800 BC.

KELP – large brown seaweed suitable for use as manure. Calcined or burnt ashes also used to make glass and soap on remote islands.

KELPIE – a water demon in the form of a horse, which is said to haunt rivers and fords and to lure the unwary to their watery deaths. Also used in Scottish folklore as a shape-shifter transformational symbol, possibly even on Pictish symbol stones. Derived from the Gaelic *cailpeach / colpach* meaning bullock or colt.

LAZY-BED – cultivation strips appearing as striped or 'corrugated' patches of land.

MACHAIR – coastal plains formed by wind-blown calcareous shell-sand from around 3000 BC onwards. Most popular in Hebrides such as Iona, the machair supports cultivation and biodiversity.

MEGALITH – a large stone which has been used to build a structure or monument either singly or together with other stones. Megalithic means structures made of such large stones, often utilizing an interlocking system without the use of mortar. Dates from 4500 to 1500 BC.

MIDDEN – a heap of household rubbish, often full of animal bones and shells that can date back to the Bronze Age or earlier, and a great source of archaeological information.

MOTTE – earthen mound on which a timber castle was built in the eleventh to twelfth century.

MULTIVALLATE – a descriptive term for Iron Age forts which have several concentric lines of defence.

NEMETON – a sacred or ritual space in pagan Celtic religion associated with shrines or temples. Nemetons or nemeta appear to have been situated primarily in nature areas, often centred around trees and described as sacred groves. Nemeton relates to the name of the Nemates tribe on the Rhine, the goddess Nemetona, and to place names which incorporate the word, often in much distorted form, such as Roseneath, Navity, Newtyle, Dalnavie, Inshnavie, Newmore. Root word in Gaelic is *neimheadh*, Old Gaelic *neimed*, meaning 'church-land, glebe, consecrated ground'; Gaulish *nemeton.*

NEOLITHIC – sometimes referred to as the New Stone Age, the Neolithic period in the development of human technology began around 4000 BC in Scotland, the last period of the Stone Age. The Neolithic people were farmers who domesticated plants and animals, created pottery and wove textiles. They built numerous constructions including dolmens, stone circles, henges, and erected standing stones.

OGHAM – an alphabet consisting of straight strokes on either side of a central line which was invented in Ireland by the second century AD for ease of cutting in wood and stone. The Picts adapted this written alphabet for their sculptured stones during the fifth or sixth centuries onward, but the transliteration is altered from the Irish style.

ORTHOSTAT – an archaeological term for a stone set upright.

PASSAGE TOMB – A megalithic site dating to the Neolithic period, these have either simple single chambers or sub-chambers leading off the main chamber entered via a covered stone passageway. Although called tombs, they served ceremonial and ritual purposes as well.

PICTS – the descendants of the Celtic tribes whom the Romans encountered north of the Antonine Wall in the early centuries AD. The word Pict is derived from Latin: *picti* = the Painted Ones.

PICTISH STONES – dated into three general types:
Class I consists of incised symbols, but not crosses, carved into unshaped stone slabs or boulders. 6th–8th century.
Class II includes stones carved in relief, usually on both faces of dressed stone slabs. One face always includes a Christian cross, the other may have Pictish symbols, biblical scenes or other motifs. 8th–9th century.
Class III Early Christian monuments without Pictish symbols. This limited definition has since been revised; the Picts created a wide range of carvings in this period. 8th–9th century.

RUNES – an angular alphabet used by the Norse and other Germanic tribal people that was invented before the second century AD.

SCOTS – people from Ulster, County Antrim in Northern Ireland who settled in Argyll in the fifth to sixth centuries AD. Latin *Scotti* = Irishmen.

SHEELA-NA-GIG – figurative carvings of naked women displaying exaggerated genitalia, found on churches, castles and other buildings dating from the eleventh to sixteenth centuries. More prevalent in Ireland, they tend to be found mostly in the western areas of Scotland and the islands and are associated with the symbol of fertility.

SHIELING – a roughly constructed hut for summer pastoral use usually found on high ground.

SOUTERRAIN – An underground chamber thought to be for storage and / or for ceremonial purposes. Used in Scotland from about 800 BC to AD 200 they were lined with stone and roofed either with stone lintels or with a timber frame projecting above ground. French *souterrain* = below ground.

VALLUM – a wall or rampart of earth, sods or stone erected as a line of defence. Latin *vallus* = stake, palisade.

VOE – a Shetland term for sea-loch.

WHEELHOUSE – a stone-built circular house with internal radial subdivisions resembling a spoked wheel on plan dating from the Iron Age. Also called an 'aisled house'.

INTRODUCTION

TRAVELLING around Scotland for over a quarter of a century has drawn me to a dazzling array of ancient and sacred sites. Many of these are touched upon in this book, as I have spent much of my life studying the carved stones of the ancient Picts, the stone circles of the keepers of ancient wisdom, and the various mysterious symbols of the past. All of these pursuits in search of the pulse of the past has brought me to this point in print in which I have attempted to portray and illustrate what treasures are wrought in this Sacred Scotland which is intended for the traveller to discover anew.

From the Border lands of the reivers, the crossing point of many a tribal people, we find the legends that weave Thomas the Rhymer with the enlightened times in both fact and fiction. Southwest Scotland adds another colour to the palette, with great white stone settings in dramatic landscapes and cup-marked stones in great diversity of patterns and ley points. Central Scotland, the settled land where civilisation strengthens its mark, leaves further traces of the ancient people and their tribes, while the West coast, the Western Isles and the Highlands enhance the unique archaeology that defines the landscape of sea and mountains.

Once we reach the far north and the islands beyond to Orkney and Shetland we find another world that is not just surprising to the visitor, but startling in its magnitude, depth – and immeasurable entrancing beauty. There may be nowhere else on earth that has the expansive and diverse wealth of ancient sites that Scotland gathers together over its 6000-odd years of human history. Yet the power of these sites is impossible to perceive without going there.

I have searched from one end of Scotland's long and meandering path of stones to the other to illuminate and make more accessible the messages in stone that have faded and often disappeared. I have touched ancient layers of prehistoric images which have virtually disappeared from view but still resound with a message, still beating with a heart deep within the stone.

Through art and through words these images return to an unrecognisable world of the post-modern era. To reveal the past and bring it back into full colour is what I seek to share.

The spiral revolves and evolves.

Touchstones of the past, beacons of the future.

Marianna Lines
August 2014
Collessie, Fife

WHO WERE THE PICTS?

THE HISTORY OF THE PICTS is a mystery story with few clues and no proper ending. Their origins are misty. They were first mentioned by the Romans in the third century, then did a disappearing act in the early tenth century. Several centuries of glorious stone carving is hardly a period of 'Dark Ages' as it is often misleadingly termed. Their 'nom de guerre' was the Picti, the painted people. This was a new power grouping north of the Forth/Clyde line and bordering on the Mounth, perhaps an amalgamation of twelve tribes who were indigenous to Caledonia, the Caledoni and the Maeatae who lived beyond the Antonine Wall. The mountainous landforms of the Mounth, a ridge from the Grampians to the North Sea coast, form a barrier dividing the northeast of Scotland from the Lowlands. The Venerable Bede, writing his *Chronicles* in the eighth century, distinguishes between the 'Northern Picts' who were a pagan people first touched by St Columba in his mission up the Great Glen, and the 'Southern Picts', who had been converted to Christianity a few centuries earlier by Ninian, the Galloway saint.

A mature medieval kingdom emerged from the five centuries of Pictish rule, a period of migrations when differing tribal people – Picts, Scots, Angles, Britons and Scandinavians – inhabited the mainland of Scotland and displaced or mingled with each other. A warrior aristocracy can be read in the stories on the stones, the culture of the elite. It was considered by some to be a matrilinear society, the lineage descending from the mother line. Thus the Pictish symbols seem to be appropriated to either gender on the stones, often selectively when shown with a dynastic family scene. Many kings and centuries later, the Dalriadic King Kenneth mac Alpin became king of both countries between AD 843 and 848. Pictish kings such as Nechtan and Bridei left their mark. The Cruithne, Gaelic for Pict and another name adopted for these people, left an uneasy yet powerful legacy that has been at the heart of Scottish nationalism ever since.

Within the first few generations of the mac Alpin kings the entire culture of the Pictish people who dominated Scotland for so long was subsumed by the Gaels in the formation of the new Alba. Their distinctive culture lives on. The best evidence is the sculptured stones that are found over the whole of the mainland and islands, east to west. The broad common heritage of Irish and Northumbrian art on Pictish art and sculpture seen on many of the stones depending on their location and time period makes the study all the more fascinating. There was a constant flow between Pictland, Ireland and North-umbria, which reflects in the culture. The Irish Sea and the firths around Scotland were just another M1 motorway in those days. The haunting images of Pictish art, the corpus of symbols, the lost meanings and lost language, only leave questions, never answers. Their real history may have been obscured, but the stones remain to inspire.

As Robert Louis Stevenson, one of Scotland's favourite writers, wrote in his tale of *Heather Ale*:

> *From the bonny bells of heather*
> *They brewed a drink long-syne*
> *Was sweeter far than honey*
> *Was stronger far than wine*
> *They brewed it and they drank it*
> *And lay in a blessed swound*
> *In their dwellings underground.*

SACRED SCOTLAND

BOOK SECTION GUIDE

1 SCOTTISH BORDERS
2 DUMFRIES & GALLOWAY
3 WEST & CENTRAL MAIN
4 FIFE
5 PERTHSHIRE AND KINROSS
6 ANGUS
7 ABERDEENSHIRE
8 MORAYSHIRE
9 THE HIGHLANDS
10 NORTHERN ISLES
11 WESTERN ISLES,
   ARRAN AND BUTE

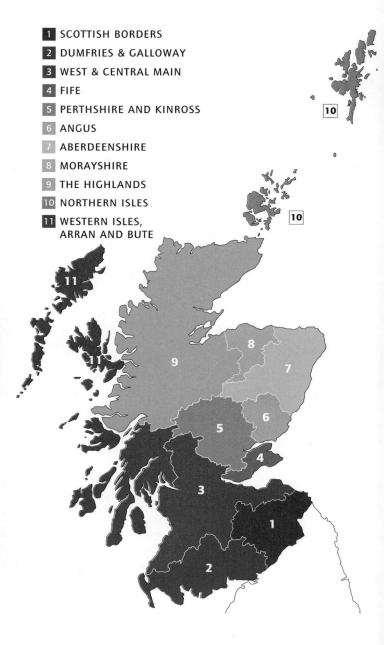

HOW TO USE THIS BOOK

Historically Scotland has been divided into 34 counties or shires. Scotland is also divided into 32 council areas for local government purposes. It gets rather complicated so we have decided to use the counties and shires as they work geographically and culturally which is fine for our purposes.

We start with the Scottish Borders and travel anti-clockwise to Aberdeenshire, west to the Highlands, then to the Northern Isles, the Western Isles, ending at the isles of Arran and Bute.

There is a map of each county or shire at the beginning of the appropriate section. There is basic road and physical feature information on the maps. These will help you with the general location of a site and a quick visual reference for their general distribution. Block figures (numbers) in a list on the map pages refer to site locations in the map and entries in the text. Any sites not numbered on the maps have either not been included for the sake of clarity, or do not warrant a number of their own.

Ordnance Survey map references are clearly shown below the site headings. They are mainly displayed as eight-figure references, accurate to 10 metres, eg: Ormaig Rock Art NM 8222 0270. Many mobile phones have navigation apps which show map references to this degree of accuracy. As many sites are low-lying in open country, they can be easily missed or confused with features which lie within the 100 metre square of six-figure references. Some sites of larger areas do have six figure references, eg: Kilmartin Glen NR 835 989, or even just four, which indicate an area of 1 kilometre square.

In the text horizontal distances are given as imperial and metric values: feet/metres, yards/metres or miles/kilometres, and occasionally inches/centimetres. Heights are given in feet/metres. Decimalised values are given to both values throughout for clarity and all values are approximate.

Major cities are not included in this guide, not because there are not sacred places there, but because this information is already easily available. Go to any tourist office or bookshop in Edinburgh or Glasgow and you will find plenty of guidebooks and histories. For the most part, the sacred places of the cities have been created by human endeavour in historical times and their stories are well documented.

THE SCOTTISH BORDERS

1

Scottish
Borders

THE
SCOTTISH BORDERS
PRINCIPAL SITES

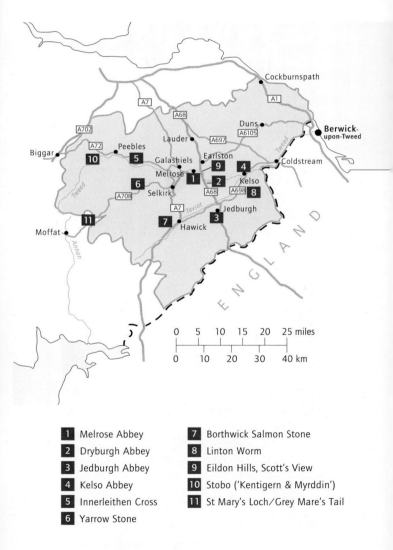

1 Melrose Abbey		**7** Borthwick Salmon Stone	
2 Dryburgh Abbey		**8** Linton Worm	
3 Jedburgh Abbey		**9** Eildon Hills, Scott's View	
4 Kelso Abbey		**10** Stobo ('Kentigern & Myrddin')	
5 Innerleithen Cross		**11** St Mary's Loch/Grey Mare's Tail	
6 Yarrow Stone			

Previous page: Melrose Abbey by J.M.W. Turner.

Scottish
Borders

THE SCOTTISH BORDERS

THE ROLLING HILLS OF THE BORDERS is the theme tune for many a favourite Scottish song. It describes the wild beauty of the many lush valleys in the rich Borderlands of Scotland from the Yarrow Valley to the Tweed, Ettrick Water, Teviotdale and Liddesdale. The romantic Lammermuir Hills form part of the border with England and are the inspiration for an opera and Walter Scott's novel *Bride of Lammermoor*. The Lammermuirs form a natural boundary between the Lothians and Berwickshire where Lady John Scott, née Alicia Anne Spottiswoode, another famous nineteenth century Scots poet and composer, lived at Spottiswoode by Lauder. She wrote many memorable songs and ballads including *Annie Laurie*. Ruined abbeys and tales of wizards and mystics set the scene for the dramatic story of the Borders. King Arthur himself has a foothold in the Borderlands as many believe this area is the true origin of Arthurian legends. Merlin too is linked in legend with Upper Tweeddale.

Bernard Chandler

The Tweed valley by Melrose, looking east.

St Abb's Head on the jagged cliffs of the Berwickshire coast is a great haven for wildlife and location of one of the many Thomas Stevenson lighthouses. Besides the brilliant bird life of the Borders, salmon in the Tweed is another nature highlight of the region.

Ancient sites flow back in time as far as the rivers, with the triple volcanic peaks of the Eildon Hills creating sacred sites and legends. Carved stones and four great medieval abbeys as well as many holy wells are found throughout the old shires of Berwick, Roxburgh, Selkirk and Peebles.

The Romans, the Scots and the Anglo-Saxons all spent much time and energy fighting over Border territory. The legacy of these conflicts are the many forts which have been uncovered by dedicated archaeologists. At a glance there are at least seventeen major forts, two brochs, several cairns and traces of Roman roads. While the valleys may be famous for the medieval abbeys and castles, the hills of the Borders take the traveller back into prehistoric times when Celtic tribesmen fortified almost every hilltop. Roman engineers laid out the great arterial Dere Street at Sutra across the hills and moors between the two Roman Walls of Hadrian and Antonine. Well-preserved camps and forts line the way to mark the army's progress.

The pilgrim seeks the sacred, the historian favours the facts and the more bloody history while the dreamer among us looks to the magic of the legends to recreate the places that we inhabit, even momentarily on our path.

There may be a bit of us in all three of these seekers.

MEDIEVAL ABBEYS

MELROSE ABBEY

NT 548 341

Melrose Abbey is by far the finest of the Border abbeys, located in the heart of the Tweed valley between the river and the gorse-laden Eildon Hills. Pink sandstone ruins illuminate the first Cistercian settlement in Scotland founded in 1136 by King David I. Melrose is famous for being the location of the heart of Robert the Bruce (1329). What was a legend turned into fact when a heart cask was exhumed in 1997 with a plaque to mark the spot located in the chapter house.

The present remains date mostly from extensive rebuilding after medieval raids razed the original simple foundations. The elaborate Gothic style of northern English abbeys created a new fifteenth century Abbey at Melrose. The Abbey Church gleams with its magnificent window arches, chapels, stone '*pulpitum*' or screen, and presbytery of capitals and vaulting as

Bernard Chandler

The ruined abbey at Melrose.

well as superb carving. Sculptural details almost on a scale with Rosslyn Chapel include cornices with angels playing instruments and gargoyles of crouching beasts with a pig playing the bagpipes. Columns carved with curly kale capitals and delicate foliate tracery throughout make Melrose as beautiful now as it ever must have been.

DRYBURGH ABBEY

NT 5913 3169

Evan Nelson, Wikimedia Commons

Dryburgh Abbey.

The setting for one of the great Borders abbeys, Dryburgh, is idyllic. Located near St Boswell's the ancient cedars, redwoods, beech and lime trees frame the rosy ochre-tinted ecclesiastical ruins. Founded by the Premonstratensians/ White Canons in the twelfth century, the Gothic remains leave much to the imagination. Only the cloisters and the barrel-vaulted Chapter

House are complete with low stone benches, interlaced arcading, and a lovely sacred atmosphere that pervades the space.

JEDBURGH ABBEY

NT 6503 2044

'Mrsinna' Wikimedia Commons

Jedburgh Abbey.

The stately remains of Jedburgh Abbey dominate the frontier town that is only ten miles north of the English border with the Cheviot Hills to the south. Like its sister abbeys, Jedburgh was founded by David I in the twelfth century as an Augustinian priory. It is the best preserved of all the four, having continued in use as the parish church for another three centuries. Built in red, yellow and grey sandstone, the vast church towers over a sloping site in the centre of town. The Jedburgh comb is its claim to fame, a treasured archaeological find from the 1100 period, carved from walrus ivory and decorated with a griffin and a dragon. The architecture is a good example of transition Romanesque to Gothic design, with pointed window arches surmounted by round-headed arches leading up to lancets in the clerestory.

* * *

KELSO ABBEY
NT 7284 3381

Kelso Abbey.

Postdlf, Wikimedia Commons

The fourth of the Border abbeys in the market town of Kelso was once the richest and most powerful of the group but was severely ravaged by the English in the sixteenth century. There is little to see today compared to the others, although it is impressive in its own special setting.

CARVED STONES

INNERLEITHEN CROSS
NT 3320 3694

A unique piece of sculpture is found in the Tweed valley town of Innerleithen at the parish kirk where a cross-shaft sits by the wall. The carving appears to be linked cup and ring shapes, all four sides showing a regular design of interlinking dumb-bell patterns done in the early technique of pecking. It is dated around the ninth century and thought to be of the Anglian school of carving, meaning Anglo-Saxon, south of the Border and non-Pictish. Yet none of this is proven or understood so best to enjoy the simplicity and naivety of this most unusual

Early Christian stone. It could even be a throwback to a prehistoric stone.

The stone is part of a local ritual on St Ronan's Day known as the Cleikum Ceremony which celebrates the patron saint of St Ronan's Well in Innerleithen. Starting at this old Runic Cross, a relic of antiquity held in much veneration, a procession passes by the well where the holy waters are used as a blessing. It then culminates in a bonfire on Caerlee Hill where St Ronan, portrayed as a novice schoolboy, sets alight an effigy of the 'Deil'. The ceremony arises from a legend that the saint had an encounter with the Devil when he visited Innerleithen in the eighth century when he 'cleekit the Deil by his hint hoof with his Cleikum', or crosier staff, thereby banishing the archetype of evil.

This is another fire festival of purification to add to the expanding number that take place throughout Scotland. This 'victory over evil' is held in mid August at the Lammas time of harvest. Such ritual doings certainly bring an old stone to life.

From 'Sacred Stones, Sacred Places' by Marianna Lines

Innerleithen Cross.

* * *

YARROW STONE

NT 3480 2744

Oliver Dixon

The Yarrow Stone is one of the most important physical testimonies to Early Christianity in Scotland. Located on its original site on a field track near Yarrow in the tranquil Yarrow Valley, it displays an inscription from the sixth century in Latin in crude lettering that reads:

"*In this place lie the most famous princes Nudas andDumnogenus. In this tomb lie the two sons of Liberalis.*" It commemorates a British ruling dynasty which was a Christian family, perhaps due to the missionary efforts of Whithorn.

BORTHWICK SALMON STONE

NT 4372 1411

Marianna Lines

Mhairi MacMillan

Previous page – Pictish symbol stone on the banks of the Borthwick at Roberton depicting a Salmon, indicating that "the annual spawning, bringing large fish into shallow water in the Autumn must have been of major importance for winter food supplies since the start of human settlement in the area after the Ice Age". [Campbell, 2006]
Left: An interpretation of the Borthwick Salmon Stone by Marianna Lines.

A rather fine salmon is incised on a pillar stone beside the Borthwick Water at Borthwick Mains, along St Cuthbert's Way near to Hawick and the spiritual retreat centre of Chisholme House. The figure of an upright fish with tail downwards is cut into the stone, standing 5ft/1.5m high with pecked lines, and a hole at the top suggests it was once used as a gatepost. Local legend tells that it originally stood in the river to mark the height of the water for safe crossing. While some suggest it's an early Pictish symbol stone, others say that it is more likely to be a marker denoting fishing rights on the River Teviot erected by local Britons imitating the Picts. The fish is a powerful Early Christian symbol and is used throughout the western world in this symbology.

LINTON WORM

NT 7732 2622

Linton Parish Kirk, east of Jedburgh in Roxburghshire, crowns the hillock of an ancient site with a round kirkyard. The *Linton Worm*, an historic Northumberland dragon motif, is found within a tympanum carving over the doorway. Curious and unique in Scotland, the Linton Worm is a variation on the earth serpent, the dragon.

Paul Buxton

Linton Parish Kirk, near Jedburgh.

In a Borders legend that dates from the twelfth century, the Linton Worm is a mythical beast, *wyrm* being Old English for serpent. It was said to be "in length three Scots yards and bigger than an ordinary man's leg". The monster lived in a hollow on the northeast side of Linton Hill, a spot known today as 'the Worm's Den'. Emerging from its lair at dusk and dawn to ravage the countryside, it was invulnerable to any weapon. The story continues and eventually the Laird of Lariston, Wm. de Somerville, managed to slay it. The writhing death throes of the great worm created the curious topography of the hills of the region, and the hero was memorialised with the carved stone described at Linton Kirk. The myth is similar to that of the famous Lambton Worm, but that is another story for another day.

Kirk Yetholm is a short distance from Linton in the Cheviots near the English border, famed for being the home of the Scottish Gypsies. Kings and queens of the Romani people were crowned in Yetholm (*yett* in Scots means gate) and the former Gypsy Palace can be seen today just off the Green. It's tiny. This picturesque settlement has a colourful past.

FOLKLORE AND LEGENDS

THE EILDON HILLS

North: NT 555 328

Any visit to the Eildons, the crown of the Borders at Melrose, should begin with Scott's View (NT 5938 3429), named after Sir Walter Scott's favourite spot, to get a sense of the entire magical landscape below and beyond. Included in the view are the meandering Tweed, the promontory where the original Melrose Abbey stood in St Cuthbert's day, and the three peaks of the Eildon Hills where the fortress of Trimontium (*Three Hills*) was built by the Romans in AD 80. Above it all, the great Iron Age fort (NT 555 328) on the northernmost summit

The Eildon Hills from Scott's View.

indicates a site of occupation since the Bronze Age. This ancient sacred site has given rise to much human history along with a great corpus of lore and literature.

Myth is as much a part of history as hard facts, and in Irish archaeology the two go together as the mythology forms the basis of much of the ancient world's mind and the building of their sacred sites, such as Tara.

The Eildon Hills are true to this premise. Eildon is believed to be a 'hollow hill', noted in the legend of Thomas the Rhymer who went under and inside the hill himself. Sir Walter Scott, the great Scots writer who put the Borders on the map, tells a tale of a horse dealer who is paid in 'ancient coin' by an elderly buyer in old-fashioned dress. At night he is taken inside the hill where he sees a host of armed knights sleeping at the horses' feet. The leader is King Arthur. The horse dealer blows a horn, chaos erupts, a whirlwind ejects him out and he drops dead. The elderly man, Scott tells, is Thomas the Rhymer.

The wizard Michael Scott is said to have cleft the volcanic rock of Eildon into three and this is how the hill became three.

Prehistoric people regarded the Eildon Hills as a holy place for ceremonial gatherings. Several holy wells around the base of the hills were originally sacred to Celtic deities but are now dedicated to Christian saints.

Thomas the Rhymer
The story of Thomas the Rhymer plays a significant part in Scottish legend and lore, particularly in the Scottish Borders. Thomas of Erceldoune was a thirteenth century Scottish laird and reputed prophet from Earlston near Melrose and the Eildons. In literature he takes on the name of *Thomas the Rhymer* or *True Thomas* who is carried off by the Queen of Elfland and returns having gained the gift of prophecy.

The tale survives in medieval verse, in the popular ballad of the same name and in countless folktales and places and virtually all of the arts since medieval times. His is a classic story that comes from fairytales and seems to live in the landscape of the Borders. Thomas has many prophecies attributed to him, and he follows in the tradition of Scottish seers such as the Brahan Seer in the North and those with second sight in the Highlands today who are still revered and consulted.

Arthurian Legends of the Borders
From Arthur's Seat in Edinburgh to the Vanora Stone of Pictish origin in Meigle, Perthshire to the Eildon Hills of the Borders, King Arthur lives in Scotland. The Scots claim him as much as those south of the border, but the Britons of Strathclyde and the Gododdin of Lothian, the early people of Scotland even before the Picts, have a strong claim. Scottish traditions of Arthur are becoming more important every day. Books, conferences, new research are creating a resurgence of

Unknown photographer acknowledged

The Merlin Stone, Stobo Kirk.

interest in a new Arthurian world. Place names and local tales from the Borders to the Moray Firth tell of the power of this enigmatic figure on our ancestors.

One good example lies in the parish of Stobo in upper Tweeddale. The legend of *Kentigern and Myrddin* is told in relation to Stobo Kirk (NT 1827 3765) and a delightful medieval stone there, as well as other Border *Arthurian* sites.

Merlin, the legendary wizard of King Arthur's Court, was said to be living in the wilds of Tweeddale as an old man called *Merlin Sylvestris*, or Merlin of the Woods. He met up with St Mungo, the famous saint of Glasgow, on the Tweed. Mungo baptised Merlin on a large rock, the altarstone, now known as Altarstone Farm, before he died beside a thorn tree at Drumelzier, upstream of Stobo. A stained glass window in the kirk recalls the legend.

A late medieval stone in the kirk at Stobo shows a caricature of a knight incised in stone with sword, hands clasped and knobbly knees. The broadsword dates the stone to the sixteenth century, and although said to be an unknown warrior effigy, it could well be that of Arthur.

Further stories in recent media suggest that Arthur was buried in Scotland, and that the Yarrow Stone, discussed earlier, marks his gravesite with its Latin inscription. The Battle of Camlann could refer to the site in the Yarrow Valley where he met his fate, and the story even says that Excalibur lies beneath a loch near Yarrow. There is a hidden history of the Borders in the time of King Arthur and an Arthur Trail so there is no shortage of lore to follow on the quest for Arthur.

* * *

Scottish
Borders

ST. MARY'S LOCH and GREY MARE'S TAIL

NT 1867 1462 Giant's Grave

At the top of Yarrow Water is the evocative and beautiful St Mary's Loch, one of a twin-loch set together with Loch of the Lowes where both Scott and James Hogg, the Shepherd Poet of Ettrick, met and collaborated on their epic works. On the edge of this borderland with Dumfries and Galloway near Moffat is Grey Mare's Tail, a dramatic waterfall southwest of the Loch of the Lowes, which tumbles down a rocky crevasse into Dumfriesshire of Robbie Burns country. As the fifth highest waterfall in the UK at 197ft/60m, Grey Mare's Tail combines spectacular views with ultimate hillwalking, botanical rarities and wildlife. On offer are rare plants of the Southern Uplands such as Oblong Woodsia, Montane willows, Alpine saw-wort, and wildlife including Peregrine falcon, ring ouzel, wild goats and vendace, a rare freshwater fish in the loch.

Grey Mare's Tail.

The *Giant's Grave* is an Iron Age earthwork situated downstream of Grey Mare's Tail on the edge of a natural terrace overlooking the east bank of the Tail Burn. The earthwork may be either the last vestiges of an eroded settlement or a fragment of a linear earthwork cutting off the head of the valley. This is a defensive and/or ritual pilgrimage site but not a grave, just another good giant story. Remote wild mountainous country goes well with tales of the land in this unique 'hanging valley'. A favourite legend of the Scottish Borders is *The Grey Mare's Tail* in which the Devil extracts the tail of Eros' grey mare as she leaps across the burn above the waterfall in pursuit of Adam and Eve. Robert Burns took this tale and wove it into his famous tales like *Tam o' Shanter*.

* * *

The lines of Sir Walter Scott evoke the spirit of the place:

> Where deep deep down, and far within
> Toils with the rocks the roaring linn;
> Then issuing forth one foamy wave,
> And wheeling round the giant's grave
> White as the snowy charger's tail
> Drives down the pass of Moffatdale.
>
> *Marmion, 1808*

MICHAEL SCOTT
THE WIZARD

The Borders is steeped in folklore and fantastic stories of faeries and magic. The Borders wizard Michael Scott is a real historical person, but the stories about him are incredible and require a pinch or two of salt. Through his studies of arcane books Michael was able to tame demonic forces to his will. His most famous act of wizardry was to split the Eildon Hills into three peaks. He had the gift of prophecy which haunted him throughout his life. In fact he was able to foretell his own death, that he would be killed by a small pebble falling on his head. Thereafter he wore a steel helmet but the prophecy came true after all. Scott was actually one of the most famous monastic intellectuals of the thirteenth century, so skilled at translations that he served the Pope and kings.

2

DUMFRIES
AND
GALLOWAY

DUMFRIES
AND GALLOWAY
PRINCIPAL SITES

Dumfries & Galloway

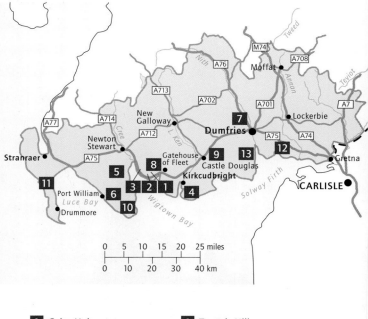

1 Cairn Holy

2 Kirkdale rock art

3 Kirkmabreck rock art

4 High Banks cups and rings

5 Tourhousekie stone circle

6 Drumtroddan cups and rings

7 Twelve Apostles stone circle

8 Trusty's Hill

9 Motte of Urr

10 Whithorn Priory

11 Kirkmadrine cross-slabs

12 Ruthwell cross

13 Sweetheart Abbey

Previous page: Cairn Holy II. Photo: Marianna Lines.

DUMFRIES
AND GALLOWAY

Oh the Gallowa' hills are covered wi' broom
Wi' heather bells in bonnie bloom
Aye wi' heather bells an' rivers a'
An we'll gang oot ower the hills tae Gallowa'.

"*THE GALLOWA' HILLS*" is a popular traditional folk song that sets the stage for Southwest Scotland where the green rolling hills of Dumfries and Galloway are lush and teeming with ancient history and life. The region is made up of the old counties of Dumfriesshire, Kirkcudbrightshire and Wigtonshire, all with quite distinctive qualities. Wild remote hills, forest and farmland, and a rugged, much-indented coast defines this diverse and quiet region far removed from city life yet full of the things that matter like beauty and friendship and a sense of community. Today the region is rich in history and culture and has a thriving arts community. Ruined abbeys, stone circles, rock art and castles adorn a region bordered by the *Scottish Riviera*, the Solway Firth with its long jagged coastline, sheltered coves and the warmth of the Gulf stream.

There are many small towns and villages but it is far removed from city life, and escapes the attention of the mass-tourism market.

Since prehistoric times the communities around the Irish Sea have been linked by their shared seaways. Sea communication remained paramount until the arrival of the railway in the nineteenth century. The first inhabitants recorded in the historic era were the Novantae. Romans, Anglo-Saxons from Northumbria, southern Picts and Celts from Ireland all subsequently left their marks.

Historically part of the Irish Sea province, the Solway was the sea highway between the Irish and Galloway coast. The wide stretch of the southwest is rich in prehistoric monuments and relics, notably the Drumtroddan Standing Stones, Torhouskie Stone Circle and Cairn Holy.

Rock art is a special feature of the prehistoric landscape of Galloway. Cup and ring carvings are found everywhere, quite similar to Argyll's cup-marked landscape. It is said that Galloway has the richest concentration of rock art in the British Isles.

Early Christian sites are strongly represented in Galloway. Around the year AD 400, long before Columba began his famous mission from Iona, a Romano-Briton, Ninian, founded the first church in Scotland, 'Candida Casa', at Whithorn in Wigtownshire. It was an important place of pilgrimage until the Reformation, and is becoming so once again in the modern age. Numerous medieval abbeys, now ruined, remain places of peaceful beauty.

Some of the most interesting and spectacular ancient sites in Scotland are found here and even better, there are plenty of opportunities for the stone hunter to find lost sites. Such is the wildness of the landscape on the southwestern edge of Scotland.

Mythic Galloway is full of legends, stories and cultural quirks, old and new, a cauldron of local folklore. Wildlife is rife. Red kites love Galloway, as do red squirrels, red deer and everything else that flies, swims, runs and crawls in Scotland's open countryside.

PREHISTORIC SITES

CAIRN HOLY

NX 518 540

Cairn Holy is a double site of what can only be called most holy and most spectacular in the realm of the Neolithic. On a hillside above Kirkdale Glen, overlooking Wigtown Bay there are two chambered cairns that lie within 164yds /150m of each other, each so different in style and mood. The skeletal stony remains of these cairns were once covered with smooth layers of stone, perhaps like Newgrange in Ireland, now open to the sky.

Cairn Holy I (NX 5176 5389) is an elaborate tomb, with a curving forecourt of standing stones in front of the tomb. The original chambered cairn behind the façade consisted of an outer and an inner compartment, the inner one closed off from the outer with a great stone slab roof. Excavations show the use of ritual fire at the tomb entrance, and artefacts like decorated pottery and a jadeite ceremonial axe fragment that was imported from the Alps. The owner of such items would have had great wealth and power.

Cairn Holy I.

Cairn Holy II is located higher up the track on the hill and appears to be a dolmen structure with a huge roof capstone over two jagged portal stones with a chamber within. Tradition says this was the tomb of Galdus, a mythical Scottish king. The presence of the past is strong in this 4,000 year-old monument. The tomb builders had widespread contact with the known Neolithic world throughout Europe indicated by the finds.

The choice of this setting for the ancestors is about as good as it gets: the sea, heather-clad hills and a wide view of the world. It is not hard to imagine the ritual ceremonies around these stones.

Cairn Holy II in its magnificent setting overlooking the sea.

Marianna Lines

KIRKDALE ROCK ART

NX 515 533

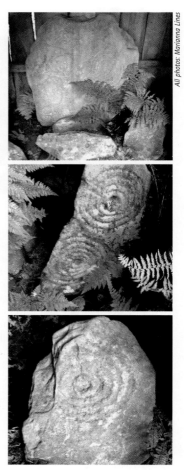

All photos: Marianna Lines

On the road in to Cairn Holy, behind the stately home of Kirkdale House, a collection of fabulous Neolithic rock art is found in a shelter in the garden. These slabs of cup and rings and cup-marked stones have been brought together from the surrounding area and make a strong statement about the ritual site chosen for the Cairn Holy tombs. Three of the rock art slabs were found under the sundial at Kirkdale House. One stone shows a central cup surrounded by five complete rings, a sixth marginally seen, along with a radial groove running from the inner ring to the edge. This design indicates a vessel to hold liquid which has a pouring-out function, surely for ritual purposes. This group is an outstanding example of cup and rings, unusually presented on upright slabs rather than more usually found in rocky horizontal outcrops.

KIRKMABRECK ROCK ART

NX 4839 5629

Sculptured rock art is located on a smooth area of rock outcrop on Kirkmabreck Farm near Newton Stewart in the corner of Wee Eric's Field. The rock bears six cup and ring marks, all in a northeast – southwest alignment, with another few sets further along in the field. Unfortunately a few of the sculptured rocks have been covered over with a cattle-feeder. This is often the case when farmers carry out their work without regard to ancient monuments on their land.

HIGH BANKS CUP AND RINGS

NX 7089 4895

High Banks Farm, SE of Kirkcudbright, has some of Southwest Scotland's most impressive cup and ring carvings. Found on a greywacke rock outcrop at the south end, there are over 350 cup-marks. Greywacke is a hard sandstone rock made up of quartz, feldspar and rock fragments set in a clay matrix, found in Palaeozoic strata. Some of the rock art is grouped to form designs with many cup and rings and multiple rings.

Such a graphic monumental display in stone left in the open air for centuries seems an amorphous mnemonic picture of the Neolithic mind, an ancient code of what they might be portraying or remembering or counting, such as the lunar months.

TORHOUSEKIE STONE CIRCLE

NX 3825 5649

The circle at Torhouse in the Bladnoch Valley near Wigtown has nineteen granite boulders graded in height with the largest boulder weighing some six tons situated in the southeast of the site. In the middle of the oval-shaped circle, with a diameter of 65.5ft/20m, are three roundish boulders aligned southwest-northeast, two large ones with a smaller one between. This setting is reminiscent of the recumbent circles of the northeast in Aberdeenshire, but not strictly a recumbent monument in any sense.

The circle stands on a man-made platform of earth and small stones. An outlier site of three stones stand in a row on a hillside to the east. Torhousekie, also called Torhouse, is clearly aligned to the midwinter sunset as are most of the stone circles in western Scotland. This is one of the best-preserved stone circles in Scotland dated to the Bronze Age *circa* 2500 BC.

Folklore and legend say this is meant to be *King Gauldus's Tomb*, the mythical king of Galloway, but we have heard this before. Cairn Holy also has been dubbed the king's grave. Torhouse is part of a ritual landscape setting of stones like so many found throughout Scotland. There are further settings of stones to the south and east as well as burial cairns. This unusual concentration of ritual sites suggests that Torhouse was a regional centre of some importance in prehistoric times. The archaeo-astronomy of this flattened circle indicates complex geometry to define the rising and setting of the sun and moon. Winter solstice sunset, summer solstice sunrise is the best guess.

Bladnoch also lays claim to being the only distillery in Dumfries and Galloway.

* * *

DRUMTRODDAN CUP AND RINGS

NX 3626 4473

Drumtroddan is a rock art site in fields on a farm near Port
William along the Galloway coast on Luce Bay south of
Wigtown in The Machars area. It is one of several outcrops of
greywacke rock in the area considered suitable over 4,000
years ago for decoration. Ritual cup and ring marks are found in
profusion at Drumtroddan: cups alone, cups with one or more
concentric rings up to 28in/70cm in diameter and radial grooves.

Two standing stones are located nearby to the rock
art site which are 10ft/3m high, once part of a three-stone row
(NX 3645 4430). Set on a southeast facing slope the stone
setting may have been aligned on the southwest midwinter
sunset which is quite standard for this period of monument.

The Drumtroddan standing stones.

TWELVE APOSTLES STONE CIRCLE

NX 947 794

Dumfries & Galloway

The Twelve Apostles is the largest circle in Scotland and one of the largest in Britain measuring 95yds/87m at its widest point. Located a few miles north of Dumfries in a field with hedging that eludes easy discovery, it is a disconcerting place somewhat lacking in atmosphere. Eleven stones survive in a giant ring, four of which are boulders, the rest are quarried; several have deep gouged markings and some are prone. A huge fallen stone, more than 3.5ft/3m in length, suggests by its orientation that the circle was aligned to the midwinter sunset in the southwest. A large number of white quartz pebbles have been found around the stones. Further sites in the area point to yet another ritual landscape here.

Marianna Iines

The name seems odd for a prehistoric site, but there were once twelve stones, and before that there were eighteen originally. These 'apostles in stone' do not make up the most impressive of stone circle sites but with a bit of time the sacred-ness of the place and its stony silence can grow on you.

TRUSTY'S HILLFORT AND PICTISH SYMBOLS

NX 588 560

Trusty's Hill, by Gatehouse of Fleet and near to the village of Anwoth, is defined by a vitrified stone rampart around the summit, an outer bank and a rock-cut ditch on the northern side, with more ramparts to the south. A group of Pictish symbols and perhaps some light-hearted graffiti are carved on an exposed area of bedrock at the entrance to the fort (NX 5889 5601).

Marianna Lines

Trusty's Hill Pictish symbol stones.

Symbols of a double disc and Z-rod and a fish monster are clearly inscribed in a rough but fluid style. Two other questionable carvings, a wee head with a tall dunce hat and a head with spiral antennae have been added later, it would seem. The main Pictish symbol of the double disc has been described locally as being the *De'il's Specs*, or the Devil's spectacles – an interesting take on what is seen as a pagan pre-Christian symbol so common to Pictish art.

Recent survey work has identified an ogham inscription running along the left edge of the slab.

But what were the Picts doing here we ask? It is a long way from the Pictish heartland in Eastern Scotland, and these are the only Pictish symbols in Galloway. Some suggest that when the Iron Age fort was refortified in the sixth to seventh centuries, a raid by Pictish forces took place at Trusty's Hill, which is the relative date when the carvings were made.

However, recent excavation research by the Galloway Picts Project has found evidence to support this being the site of the lost Dark Age Kingdom of Rheged. Based on stunning finds of jewellery and other artefacts, there is a whole new theory for what Trusty's Hill was all about, a royal fort of the kingdom.

This is a superb location with wonderful views out to the Solway Firth, and other ancient sites like Cairn Holy and the stone circle of Cambret Moor are located in the area.

In the same area of Anwoth near Garlieston a recent discovery of rock art has been found at Eggerness Farm (NX 4862 4730). This rock art includes prehistoric zoomorphic images which are very rare. Eight sites have been identified so far, all located on outcrop greywacke rock. The carvings include those of deer and horses, and even a horse hoof, along with a large number of spirals, all created in the 'pecked' style of the oldest stone carving. The panels are covered with turf for protection and preservation, but it is possible to ask to have a look by prior arrangement. This special interest site is most unusual for the British Isles and makes Galloway all the more intriguing in the early history of the region.

Marianna Lines

MOTTE OF URR

NX 815 646

Dumfries and Galloway are particularly rich in mottes, steep-sided mounds on which a timber castle would have stood in the twelfth century. These were feudal settlements based on relatively small baronial fiefs. The Motte of Urr is a magnificent sight on the skyline when approaching from either end of the road north-northwest of Dalbeattie. Even without its timber castle, the scale of the earthwork is impressive, looking somewhat like a Mexican brimmed hat. Located beside the Urr Water, the earthworks are arranged in several tiers with steep angles of mound and ditch. The motte is set at one end of a large outer enclosure known as a bailey where domestic buildings were situated. The bailey ditch is 49ft/15m wide with an outer bank with two entrance causeways on the southeast and northwest. It would have been a great viewing platform for sunrise and sunset in any direction, and ceremonial use may well continue to this day.

Another fine example of a motte is located at Mochrum, which is known as the Motte of Druchtag (NX 3494 4666).

In the same area of the Urr estuary is the Mote of Mark, a seventh century fort that is associated with King Mark of Arthurian times. Legendary this may be, but it reflects in local memory of the fort's history. The main rampart was set on fire in the early part of the seventh century which suggests that this was a stronghold of some warlord of the British Kingdom of Rheged. The circumstances seem similar to those found at Trusty's Hill offering more evidence that the Kingdom of Rheged was involved. The rich birdlife of the Urr estuary and river area may have been a great draw for the establishment of ancient kingdoms.

EARLY CHRISTIAN SITES

WHITHORN PRIORY

NX 4447 4031

According to unbroken tradition dating from the earliest times, and confirmed in the writings of the Venerable Bede in the eighth century, a holy man named *Nynia*, born among the British people, introduced the Christian faith into a significant part of the land now known as Scotland long before the coming of St Columba.

© Crown Copyright reproduced courtesy of Historic Scotland. www.historicscotlandimages.gov.uk

The story begins with the first stone church in Scotland, which was built at Whithorn in AD 397 by St Ninian. Painted white, it became known as *Candida Casa* (Latin), the glittering house, or 'hwit erne' in Early English, hence the name Whithorn. Rebuilt many times, the ruins seen today contain part of the Lord of Galloway's cathedral of the 1100s. The mysterious crypts once housed the tomb of St Ninian visited by many thousands of pilgrims seeking salvation, blessings and cures. The Whithorn Dig on site of the church complex shows an outline of the early wooden Northumbrian monastery, feasting halls and a restored labyrinth cut into the turf. Over 42,000 items were discovered during the excavation and are shown on site in the Whithorn Story. This narrative reflects a vivid picture of everyday life in the sixth to eighth centuries featuring items such as glass beakers imported from France.

The Priory Museum displays the largest, most important collection of Early Christian and Dark Age carved stones in Scotland. This includes the Latinus Stone, a pillar stone with a

Chi-Rho symbol, *IHS*, and the earliest Christian inscription found so far in Scotland. The stone indicates that three generations of Christians lived in the area by the mid fifth century when Ninian arrived to care for an existing community there. The *Whithorn School* of carving produced beautiful ring and wheel-head crosses which once marked the pilgrims' way. These can be seen in the collection which includes the splendid Monreith Cross of the tenth century, illustrated right and below.

Further along the coast through the Physgill Glen to the Solway shore is St Ninian's Cave (NX 4224 3595). This was Ninian's retreat, a cave which was once full of eighth century cross-slabs. The atmosphere is electrifying. Crosses carved on the walls are still visible. Near the cave is a chapel at Kirkmaiden set below the cliffs. The chapel is dedicated to St Medana and dates from the twelfth century but is now restored as a mausoleum. The holy well on the foreshore is reputed to have curative powers. At the end of the peninsula beyond the cave is the Isle of Whithorn, not an island but a sheltered harbour. The walls of St Ninian's Chapel are seen beyond the harbour offering safe crossing for pilgrims visiting the shrine at Whithorn.

Roger Griffith, Wikimedia Commons

Chapel Finian (NX 278 489) is another sacred footstep along the path of Ninian, located above the shingle beach over-looking Luce Bay on the coast road north of Port William. Here in an enclosure are the remains of the foundations of a small chapel built in the Irish style of the eleventh century. The chapel is named after the Irish saint Finnian, the great scholar and monastic founder who taught St Columba.

A new scholarly view holds that Finnian (or Finian), who was educated at nearby Whithorn and died about AD 579, was in fact the real historical figure known as St Ninian, the founder of Whithorn. As every decade comes up with a new twist on the past this is always possible. History changes with the times.

The site houses a well which still survives and is likely to have been ascribed with healing qualities. Naturally for its location the chapel served as a stopping off place for pilgrims.

KIRKMADRINE CROSS-SLABS

NX 0801 4838

Kirkmadrine is located in the far west of Galloway in the area known as the Rhinns of Galloway. A collection of inscribed cross-slabs from the fifth century is a moving memorial to the Christian community in Dark Age Galloway. They are preserved in a glass-fronted porch attached to a nineteenth century burial chapel and were found around the churchyard at Kirkmadrine.

Kirkmadrine. Probably the site of a monastery in the Early Christian period – later a medieval parish church. Right: Carved stone at Kirkmadrine.

© Crown Copyright reproduced courtesy of Historic Scotland
www.historicscotlandimages.gov.uk

Three of the earliest stones each bear an encircled Chi-Rho cross, the crook-like symbol attached to the upper arm of the cross, the sacred monogram of Christ. After the death of Ninian in the late fifth century the seat of the bishopric moved temporarily from Whithorn to Kirkmadrine. It is suggested this was due to the importance of the cross-slabs and their inscriptions. These stones are called *prayer-crosses*, which is a lovely thought. They date from around AD 600.

RUTHWELL CROSS

NY 1005 6821

In the parish church of Ruthwell in Nithsdale, near the Solway Firth, stands one of the greatest wonders of Early Christian art in Scotland.

The Ruthwell Cross is an eighth century runic cross 18ft/5.5m in height sculptured in relief with Biblical imagery and inscriptions in incised Saxon capitals and Anglian runes.

Photos by Doug Sim, Wikimedia Commons

The Ruthwell Cross.
Above: South side showing inscriptions framing the Christ figure.
Right: West face showing runes framing intertwined vines and animals.

The Dream of the Rood is a poem written in Old English that owes its existence to the Ruthwell Cross, its original source. The carvings on this Cross face east and west and are decorated with vine scrolls inhabited by birds and beasts. In this case the cross is the narrator of the story.

The inscriptions and the sculpture mutually supplement each other on this visionary cross which stands in a well in the centre of the church at Ruthwell. This is an Anglian cross of the highest order and a manifestation of Northumbrian Christianity. Its intricate workmanship and iconography reflect the cross fertilisation with eastern Mediterranean models made during the height of post-Columban creative fervour.

Dumfries &
Galloway

SWEETHEART ABBEY

NX 9650 6627

Sweetheart Abbey in New Abbey is the last Cistercian abbey
established on Scottish soil. It was founded by Lady Devorgilla
of Galloway in 1273 in memory of her husband John Balliol.
The abbey church is remarkably complete today with a
precinct wall of such magnitude with massive granite boulders,
that it ranks alongside the wall at St Andrews Cathedral Priory
as the most complete in Scotland.

Marianna Lines

The south transcept of Sweetheart Abbey.

The red sandstone ruins of Sweetheart Abbey have a
romantic beauty that exudes a special atmosphere of calm and
serenity, great trees to overshadow and create a space within
nature that dances around it, the Galloway hills framed
through the transept window arches.

The stone effigy of Lady Dervorgilla can be seen in the
south transept, a replica of the original which was destroyed at
the Reformation. Many other carved stones of the thirteenth
century period grace the ruins. The Cistercian abbey of Dulce
Cor, *Sweet Heart* in Latin, is a shrine to human and divine love.
The monastic ideals live on at Sweetheart Abbey.

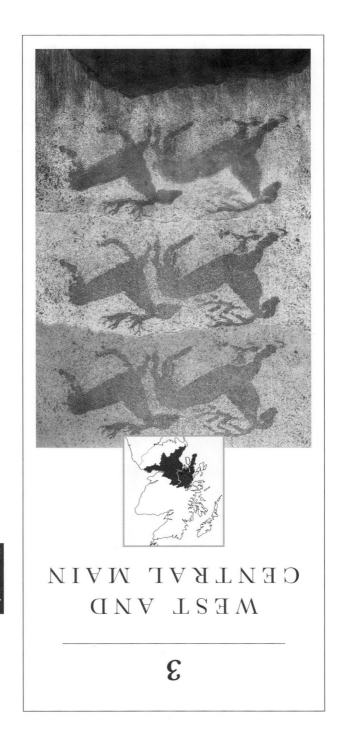

3

WEST AND CENTRAL MAIN

WEST AND CENTRAL MAIN
ARGYLL

PRINCIPAL SITES

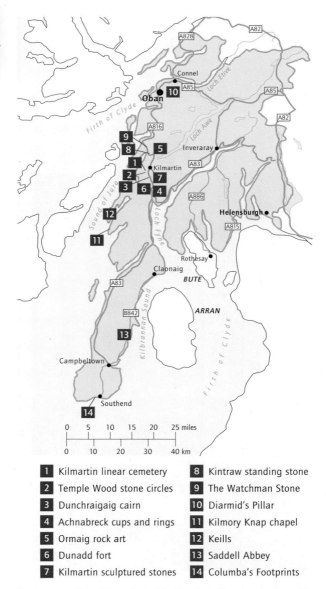

1	Kilmartin linear cemetery	**8**	Kintraw standing stone
2	Temple Wood stone circles	**9**	The Watchman Stone
3	Dunchraigaig cairn	**10**	Diarmid's Pillar
4	Achnabreck cups and rings	**11**	Kilmory Knap chapel
5	Ormaig rock art	**12**	Keills
6	Dunadd fort	**13**	Saddell Abbey
7	Kilmartin sculptured stones	**14**	Columba's Footprints

Previous page: Deer Prints, Craignish Chapel, Ardfern, by Marianna Lines.

WEST AND CENTRAL MAIN
ARGYLL

IN THE LAND OF MOONS and deep blue turquoise seas, there is a place, a sacred place. Ample paps, triple paps soar over the sea, the distancing mystic light creates the Western Way where footprints of the ancient ones trod. Dálriada, Dunadd, the boar of Scythian descent, gold in the land, aurora in the sky. Eden's land, where Picts and Gaels, Cruithne and Celts all met in one great cauldron. This is Argyll, the Heartland of the West.

The kingdom by the sea, a land of blood and beauty in its historical lineage, Argyll is the gateway to the Isles of the West coast of Scotland. This is also the ancient kingdom of Dálriada, *Dál Riata*, which was the power centre of the *Scoti*, the Gaels from Ireland who were later called the Scots. They ruled the West coast of Scotland and Ulster in Ireland during the sixth and seventh centuries. The iconic hillfort of Dunadd was the capital and royal stronghold Dálriada where a footprint *inaugural stone* can be found along with a Pictish carving of a wild boar. The birthplace of the Scottish nation was first established in Argyll at Dunadd in AD 500, and Kenneth MacAlpine was crowned the first king in AD 843.

Historically Argyll included the entire western coast of Scotland between the Mull of Kintyre in the south to Cape Wrath in the far north. Today this glorious world of glittering sea lochs, islands, hills and glens includes eight regions: Oban and Lorn, Inveraray, Kilmartin, Knapdale and Crinan, Kintyre and Gigha, Loch Lomond and the Clyde sea lochs, Cowal and Dunoon, and the islands which are covered elsewhere in the text.

A complex prehistoric landscape is found throughout Argyll. Its terrain of Highland mountainous country laced and graced by the coastal machair of sea and verdant rolling countryside make it arguably the most beautiful of Scotland's coastal areas. A rich cultural heritage threads its way through 3,175 miles of coastline dotted with sixty castles. The highlight of sacred sites and ancient places in Argyll must be Kilmartin – *The Megalithic Paradise* – a Neolithic ritual complex of chambered cairns and standing stones. Argyll is a prominent area for the earliest rock art ever recorded in Scotland, the cup and ring markings which appear like ancient dots in stone, coded messages of 'moon trackings' carved on the bedrock throughout Argyll. The hillside outcrop at Achnabreck is the most important cup and ring site in the West although there are many other locations to choose from.

To delve into Argyll is to dissolve into a land of enchantment riddled with mystery and magic.

KILMARTIN GLEN

NR 835 989 Kilmartin

Lying in Mid Argyll between Inveraray and Oban the landscape of Kilmartin Glen ranges from rugged hills to farmland and flat peat bogs to the waters of the Crinan Canal (NR 79 93) and the River Add Estuary. The last Ice Age formed this land. The steep-sided valleys were gouged out by the ice flowing southwest from the Grampian Mountains, the valley floor affected by receding ice from Loch Awe into Kilmartin Glen. Moine Mhor Moss, or Crinan Moss, one of the few remaining raised peat bogs in Britain today, surrounds the rocky outcrop of Dunadd, once an island on the plain. Eagles soar over moorland and cormorants and sea birds loiter at the waters' edge. Specialist bog plants such as sundew and cotton grass are abundant while many species of dragonflies and rare butterflies such as the Large Heath are found in the area.

The fertile lands and hills that make up Kilmartin Glen bear witness to human occupation since the earliest times when hunter gatherers first changed to a more settled lifestyle. The monuments that survive in this area record the progressive history of these early people: Neolithic and Bronze Age chambered and round cairns, stone circles, rock carvings; Iron Age forts, duns and crannogs. Early Christian sculptured stones and medieval castles herald the modern era.

Within a six-mile radius of Kilmartin there are twenty five sites with standing stones: thirteen are single stones, eleven are arrangements or stone settings, while Temple Wood consists of two stone circles. A monumental alignment of a great earth calendar to chart the movement of sun, moon and stars may well be what these stones have recorded for posterity. The stones bear witness to millennia of sunrises and sunsets and have provided the backdrop to millions of rainbows and earth shadows. These silent beings stand as a testimony of life on earth recorded and remembered in every molecule.

KILMARTIN LINEAR CEMETERY

NR 8286 9793 Nether Largie South

The most dominant feature of Kilmartin Glen is the line of burial cairns that stretch southward from Kilmartin Village. Built over a period of 2,000 years, the first part of the linear cemetery started in the Neolithic with the four-compartment chambered cairn at Nether Largie (South). This large burial chamber pre-dated the individual burial cists of the four other cairns in the group. Included in this group are Nether Largie North, Nether Largie Mid and Ri Cruin cairns. (NR 8256 9711). The cists with-

A cairn at Nether Largie, Kilmartin.

Gordon Thomson

in these sites show great quality of workmanship in the grooved side-slabs, the decoration of the end slabs and the capstones with axe-heads and cup-marks. Glebe Cairn (NR 8330 9894), the most northerly of the group, is an impressive monument 98.5ft/30m in diameter and 10ft/3m high.

TEMPLE WOOD STONE CIRCLES

NR 8263 9782

Gordon Thomson

Temple Wood, located within a grove of young trees and carpeted with bluebells in the spring, is a complicated structure that evolved over a thousand year period dating from 3,000 BC. A stone circle consisting of upright kerb stones, one of which is delightfully carved with a spiral motif around its edge, was once covered entirely by a cairn only partially seen today. An older and smaller circle lies to the northeast. Originally a timber setting, it was replaced at the same time as the main circle with an elliptical ring of stones.

West and
Central

DUNCHRAIGAIG CAIRN and BALLYMEANOCH

NR 8330 9680, NR 8337 9641

Gordon Thomson

Ballymeanoch Standing Stones.

This group of monuments is visible from the main road and includes a cairn, kerb cairn, stone alignments and a henge. Dunchraigaig Cairn is a Bronze Age cairn which contains three burial cists. Beyond the cairn, like sentinels in the field, are the Ballymeanoch Standing Stones. These six stones consist of two sets which are parallel in alignment. The tallest stone is over 13ft/4m high. Two of the stones are decorated with multiple cup-marks, an unusual feature to be found on vertical monuments as they are normally found on horizontal rock faces in situ. In the same field is the henge monument which comprises a round platform with an internal ditch. The henge probably served as a ceremonial and ritual area for these related sites.

ACHNABRECK CUP & RINGS

NR 8555 9067, also NR 8571 9064

Prehistoric rock carvings produced around 3,000 years ago are found at many locations in the Kilmartin area. Small round indentations called cupmarks, they are often surrounded by single or multiple rings and spirals. The site at Achnabreck contains the largest cluster of such carvings anywhere in Britain.

Marianna Lines

Achnabreck rock art.
Impression by
Marianna Lines.

West and
Central

Gordon Thomson

There are 332 individual markings on the three exposed rock surfaces that make up the group.

These enigmatic images are hotly debated and considered to have multiple uses and meanings and endless significance but it is up to the viewer to determine their own answer. As in the question of the Pictish symbols there is no simple answer to their meaning.

Each cup and ring site is different with its own personality of location and style of variations on the theme of cup and rings. The sites often seem to be located on an upland area on a slope with an elevated view facing across a wide landscape. They appear to form a sort of observatory.

ORMAIG

NM 8222 0270

Ormaig is an outstanding rock art site located deep within woodland several miles from Carnasserie Castle. Ormaig presents a magnificent series of over 200 carvings of cup-marks, cup and rings and a unique motif once dubbed the 'telephone dial' – a central deep cup surrounded by a ring of up to eleven small cup-marks reminiscent of the old-fashioned telephone dial.

Gordon Thomson

Other important cup and ring sites in Argyll include Kilmichael Glassary, Cairnbaan and Ballygowan near Poltalloch. An archaeologist once exclaimed: "It's frightening, the whole of Argyll is covered in cup and rings when you lift back the turf." Well, that is almost true, but not quite.

DUNADD FORT

NR 8365 9356

Dunadd is a spectacular hillfort site and the most important of many found scattered throughout Mid Argyll from Lunga by Ardfern to Inveraray and beyond. Situated on top of a rocky outcrop, the fort dominates the surrounding countryside and can be seen from far and wide. It is no surprise that Dunadd became the capital of the ancient kingdom of Dálriada around AD 500. The early fort was besieged in AD 683 and captured by the Picts in 736; its occupation then continued into the ninth century.

The 'footprint' at the summit of Dunadd hillfort.

At the summit of the ridge is a small rock-cut basin on a terrace with adjacent carvings of a shod foot and the pecked outline of another, the famous double footprints once used in inaugural ceremonies. There is a strong tradition of ancient footprint-marked stones that are found throughout Scotland and the islands. These iconic markings are accompanied by an ogham inscription (early Irish/Pictish writing) and a carving of a boar which is comparable to those found on symbol stones

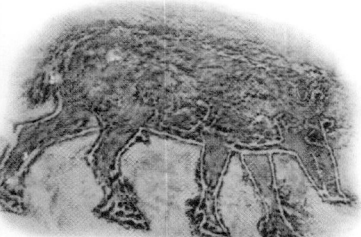

in the prime eastern territory of the Pictish kingdom. It shows the double outline typical of Pictish incised animals. It has been suggested that the ogham reads as the Irish personal name *Finn* which would corroborate the legends told in the area of Fin McCool.

KILMARTIN SCULPTURED STONES

NR 8346 9884

The Church at Kilmartin and the graveyard contain an extensive collection of Early Christian and medieval period monuments. A sculptured cross of the ninth century is preserved inside the church, while a lapidarium of monumental carved slabs from the Lord of the Isles period of Lordship rule in Argyll and the Isles dates from the fourteenth to sixteenth centuries. This represents the largest collection of medieval grave slabs in the West Highlands outside of Iona. The best work of the Loch Awe school of stone carving is found here, and a few from the Iona school. Three full warrior effigies are part of the collection. There are a large

Lord of the Isles, natural dye imression on cloth by Marianna Lines.

number of stones with long incised swords considered to possibly represent the Knights Templar order. Typical Loch Awe slabs display a figure of a warrior in a niche and a pair of dragon heads to crown the niche, an exclusive feature of this style.

The Poltalloch stones are a separate collection from the lapidarium which are gravestones of the Malcolm chiefs from the Poltallach estate nearby.

Kilmartin was a regular stopping-off place for the bodies and accompanying grave slabs of the Lords of the Isles en route to Iona, the sacred isle, for burial and 'eternal life', but often the stone did not make the whole voyage. The view over the linear prehistoric cemetery below the church at Kilmartin is like a window offering a glimpse into the sacred landscape of the past.

At Kilmichael Glassary (NR 8590 9352) in Mid Argyll further West Highland carved stones can be seen in the churchyard , including one depicting an inhabited galley, or *birlinn*, the favoured sailing vessel of the Lords of the Isles.

KINTRAW STANDING STONE

NM 8306 0497

Gordon Thomson

Possibly one of the best vantage points to watch the sunset in Argyll would be from the mighty Kintraw Stone set on a rocky hillside overlooking Loch Craignish above the village of Ardfern. An even better time to visit would be at the midwinter solstice sunset as the sun sets between the Paps of Jura on the Hebridean island of Jura. The Kintraw Stone, standing 13ft/4m tall, has a prominent position on the headland and has been the subject of extensive archaeo-astronomical studies as to its alignment. The stone is located between two large burial cairns. A *Watch Stone* is found further up a steep hillside with a prehistoric viewing platform.

Whether the main stone is aligned to the major lunar standstill every eighteen and a half years, or to the midwinter sun, it is clear that its purpose is to mark the rising and setting of the sun and moon throughout the year. Thus the Kintraw stone could be viewed as a symbol of rebirth.

THE WATCHMAN STONE

NM 8242 0623

Gordon Thomson

On the road to Oban from Kilmartin, a short distance after the left turning for the popular West Highland village of Ardfern, there is a very strange stone that guards a sacred well. This is the Watchman Stone. It requires a scramble down a steep wooded slope to find it near a small burn, not easy. The small inscribed stone has a Celtic head with a halo or wig above it and reads:

"My name is Watchman, heir am I still watching day and night welcoming all persons that comes heir to drink for which end you sie a drinking cupe."

There are further inscriptions on the back and sides of the stone. It is dated 1714. A stone-lined spring flows beneath the stone, and indeed a drinking cup is sitting there (a fine tin one replacing the original). The magical sacred well and its guardian stone are surrounded by the 'tatterdemalion' of rags that signal a Clootie well, a place of Celtic pilgrimage.

Gordon Thomson

The significance of the Watchman site is the Celtic cult of the symbolism of the head and the well. The practice of depositing skulls at sacred wells is an ancient custom. The Well of the Seven Heads at Invergarry in the east of Scotland near Loch Ness is another example.

There is a curious legend associated with this stone at Barbreck, the nearest inhabited property. After the stone had been installed over the spring for a while the owners moved to Campbeltown and took the stone with them but the stone protested and said, "Take me back to Barbreck!" And so it was returned. This is meant to be an oratory stone with oracular qualities and locals swear that the story is true. Many wells are credited with the power of prophecy, and the oracles would be delivered by a head atop a pillar, or a well guardian. All of this fits with the Watchman, possibly a late survival of this belief.

DIARMID'S PILLAR

NM 9076 2895

Diarmid's Pillar is the traditional name given to a tall and impressive standing stone in Glen Lonan on Strontoiller Farm near Taynuilt, Lorn. Both the stone, which is 13ft/4m in height, and the cairn beside it, Diarmid's Grave, are named after the mythical figure of the Irish tales who hunted wild boar in these parts. The Bronze Age cairn is 15ft/4.5m in diameter and ringed with large erratic kerbstones, with white quartz pebbles scattered at the base of the stones. A ritual site such as this one is always marked by quartz stone, the white crystal attributed with significant powers.

Gordon Thomson

Loch Awe, the longest freshwater loch in Scotland.

LOCH AWE

Loch Awe is the longest freshwater loch in Scotland, sister loch to the beautiful Loch Etive located further north. Between the two lochs runs the River Awe which squeezes through the darkly ominous Pass of Brander. Legend tells that an old woman brandishing a scythe was able to hold off an entire army at this point in the steep and narrow pass.

The romantic ruin of Kilchurn Castle (NN 1326 2760) sits on an island at the northern tip of Loch Awe. A walk along the shores of Loch Awe passes through MacKenzie's Grove, a sheltered grove containing some of the largest conifers on the west coast. Remains of a crannog can be seen on the loch, one of over forty Iron Age artificial island fortifications/settlements.

Gordon Thomson

Loch Etive is the longest sea loch or fjord in Argyll running twenty miles from the mountains to the sea. It is intrinsically linked with the legend of Deirdre of the Sorrows and the Irish myth cycle from Ulster. The beautifully haunting Glen Etive, the setting for the stories, sits at the head of the Loch.

On the north shore of the Loch near North Connell is the Priory of Ardchattan or St Modan's (NM 971 349). This Valliscaulian monastic community from Burgundy in France was founded in 1230 by Duncan MacDougall, the Lord of Lorn in Argyll. Ardchattan became a cell of Lismore Cathedral on the Isle of Lismore by the fourteenth century. The Priory building dates from the fifteenth century but when monastic life ended with the Protestant Reformation (1560) the monks' cloister was converted into a private house. Today the Priory offers fine gardens on show and a stunning collection of West Highland carved stones. Among numerous stones of great craftsmanship is the MacDougall Cross, fourteenth century, which was carved by John O'Brolchan, a stone carver from Iona. This is notable in that it is one of the few examples of West Highland carving which records the sculptor's name. Loch Etive is fondly recalled by Mathew Arnold (circa 1830) in his delightful volume on Celtic literature:

West and Central

Of all the sea-lochs or fiords with which the Atlantic cleaves the West Highland coast, none winds so far into the mountains as Loch Etive, or has gathered round itself more interesting human memories. At its outset it sweeps round the promontories on which stand the castles of Dunolly and Dunstaffnage; it leaves the broad bases of the two-peaked Ben Cruachan; it winds its way past Ben Stern, and other mountains of the Black Mount group, till it has receded so far from the sea as to have almost lost its ocean character, and stilled itself to a soft, inland murmur. Well might such a region awake a deep, imaginative interest even in a stranger, much more in one who is native to its borders. But although the shores, headlands and islands of Loch Etive are the main region of the author's research, he wanders from it all down the coast of Argyll, wherever the Dalriadic Scots, who immigrated to those shores from Ireland, have left their traces.

WEST HIGHLAND STONE COLLECTIONS

KILMORY KNAP CHAPEL

NR 7026 7510

Kilmory Knap Chapel is one of many atmospheric chapels or burial aisles in southern Argyll which have outstanding collections of sculptured West Highland grave slabs. The memorial stones date from 1300 to the 1500s and are the most tangible examples of a highly distinctive style of art that flourished in late medieval Scotland. This art also appeared on tapestry, wood and metal. Most striking are the effigies of which there are five at Kilmory

Gordon Thomson

The MacMillan Cross.

Knap. The Kilmory chapel, built around AD 1200, is located in South Knapdale on the shores of Loch Sween. The collection includes forty carved stones of which seven are Early Christian stones and the rest are late medieval grave slabs – memorials to the MacMillan Clan. Two warriors sculptured in stone are clad in armour holding spears and broadswords; other effigies are clerics in their long cassocks. Decorative motifs on the West Highland stones include crosses, galleys or *birlinns*, animals, grotesque monsters, mirror and combs and tools of the trade, such as a hammer and anvil or a chalice.

The finest sculpture at Kilmory is the MacMillan Cross, a disc-headed cross of late 1400 date dedicated to Alexander MacMillan, keeper of Castle Sween. This cross stands 10ft/3m high with a cross and crucifixion scene on one face, a vigorous hunting scene on the other.

KEILLS

NR 6913 8053

Gordon Thomson

A small West Highland chapel in Knapdale near Tayvallich is dedicated to St Cormac and dates from the twelfth century. The chapel houses a large impressive collection of grave slabs that includes examples from all five Schools of sculpture created for West Highland patrons in the Middle Ages from 1300–1500. The sculptors would have come from Ireland to Iona before working throughout Argyll at Loch Awe, Knapdale, Kintyre and Loch Sween where the best collections of West Highland stone art are found. The highlight at Keills is the outstanding eighth century sculptured Keills Cross from the Iona school of craftsmen.

SADDELL ABBEY

NR 7846 3206

Gordon Thomson

The romantic ruins of Saddell Abbey are found on the lower east coast of Kintyre where a large collection of West Highland stones are located. To give a brief historical perspective, the Norse occupied the whole of Kintyre peninsula and much of the West of Scotland in the twelfth century when Somerled the warrior king drove them out and established the clans of MacDonald and MacDougall whose descendants became known as the Lords of the Isles.

Somerled and his son Reginald built the Cistercian abbey at Saddell in 1160 but it was abandoned by the late fifteenth century when the Lordship of the Isles was forfeited to the Crown. At its height of existence Saddell was an important centre for stone carving during the fourteenth to sixteenth centuries. The craftsmen specialised in beautiful life-sized effigies and grave slabs. These stones, numbering a dozen, are the heritage of Saddell, with some belonging to the Iona school of carving but most to the Kintyre school at Saddell. A magnificent carving of a galley, the West Highland *birlinn*, is shown on

A 'birlinn' - the West Highland galley. An impression by Marianna Lines of a fourteenth century stone at Keil Church, Lochaline, Morvern.

several stones there, along with effigies of monks from the Abbey. Just south of the Abbey is an ancient holy well, a spring with a decorated stone basin at its mouth. The Abbey ruins, its stones, and the whole area of Kintyre have a special aura of peace and serenity about it.

Other chapels in the area with special collections of late medieval monumental art are found at Craignish by Ardfern, Kilberry, Kilfinan, Ellary chapel and cave, Kilmodan sculptured stones at Glendaruel on the Cowal Peninsula (NR 9948 8414), and Skipness Chapel in Kintyre (NR 910 575) by the Castle.

Gordon Thomson

The chapel overlooking Loch Craignish.

Gordon Thomson

At Southend, the southernmost village on Kintyre, a footprint stone is found, known as Columba's Footprints. This is said to mark the spot where St Columba first set foot on Scottish soil, along with a ruined thirteenth century chapel below the cliffs. A small Latin cross is incised on the knoll along with the footprints, one of which is thought to be modern.

The original footprint points to the fortress of Dunaverty and may have been associated with inauguration rituals of that period. This is one of many footprint stones found throughout Scotland which are especially numerous in ancient Dàlriada in Argyll. Properly these relics are called *Petrosomatoglyphs*. The Antrim coast of Northern Island is visible from Southend.

Sanda Island, a few miles out to sea from Southend, is a sacred spot of note at the end of Kintyre Peninsula. Sanda contains the remains of an ancient Celtic chapel, two crosses, a holy well, an unusual lighthouse made up of three sandstone towers and seabirds forever. Manx shearwaters, storm petrels and puffins continue to fly on the ancient wings of the Celtic spirit.

West and Cenrtal

West and
Central

CENTRAL, AYRSHIRE, STIRLING AND THE LOTHIANS

PRINCIPAL SITES

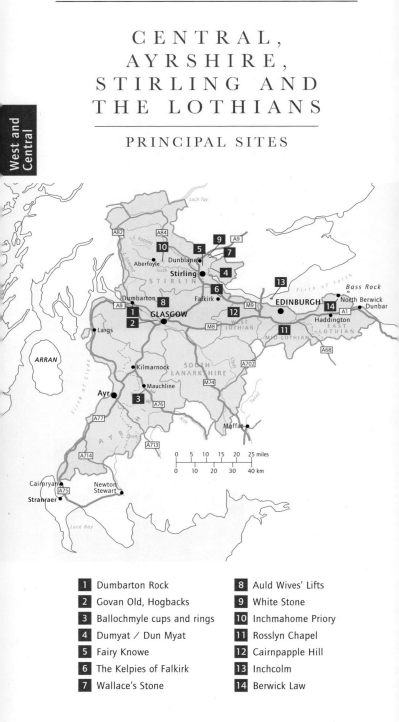

1	Dumbarton Rock	**8**	Auld Wives' Lifts
2	Govan Old, Hogbacks	**9**	White Stone
3	Ballochmyle cups and rings	**10**	Inchmahome Priory
4	Dumyat / Dun Myat	**11**	Rosslyn Chapel
5	Fairy Knowe	**12**	Cairnpapple Hill
6	The Kelpies of Falkirk	**13**	Inchcolm
7	Wallace's Stone	**14**	Berwick Law

WEST AND CENTRAL MAIN

CENTRAL, AYRSHIRE, STIRLING AND THE LOTHIANS

CENTRAL SCOTLAND

TWO GREAT RIVERS, the River Clyde and the River Forth, straddle Britain's narrowest point to create a natural means of communication from sea to sea. This was where the Roman legion built the Antonine Wall in AD 140 to keep the Picts out (of England, as the story goes). Later the chief stronghold of the Kingdom of Strathclyde was Dumbarton Rock in the Clyde estuary. Dumbarton, a massive sheer staggering rock that rises out of the sea, is complemented in eastern Scotland by the capital of Gododdin, the name of the sixth century tribal kingdom during the Dark Ages that spanned the area from Stirling through Lothian and the Borders. This was the land of the Caledonians and the Maeatae tribal groups.

Monuments in the Central region, leading from west to east, include the Clyde Valley to Loch Lomond to the Stirling area of the Trossachs, and Ayrshire to the south opposite Arran. Due to the translation of settlement from farming to industry in this dominant population area of Scotland, there are far less ancient monuments or sacred sites that have survived compared to those on the fringes around the coastline of Scotland and its islands.

However, according to one source, there are eighty-three ancient sites alone listed for Stirlingshire: standing stones, cup-marked stones, holy wells. Highlights are considered below for this area.

* * *

DUMBARTON ROCK

NS 400 744

Dumbarton Rock is a volcanic plug that seems to jump out
of the River Clyde, home to a Dark Age fortress that existed
from the sixth century. It was the major stronghold of the
Kingdom of Strathclyde, captured by the Vikings for a time
in the late ninth century. Two carved stones of tenth century
date are found in the museum there which are similar to
those at Govan.

Dumbarton Rock and Castle, c.1793 [detail]
by Thomas Girtin (1775–1802).

Google Art Project/Wikimedia Commons

GOVAN OLD, HOGBACKS

NS 5534 6591

Govan Old, once the parish church of Govan, the shipbuilding
area by Glasgow, is home to a collection of rare hogback stones
which date from AD 925–1000 when Govan was the capital
of the Kingdom of Strathclyde, the seat of the kings of the
ancient Britons.

These early medieval sculptured 'hogbacks' form a collection that bridges the Celtic and the Viking culture, as they
feature a unique design that represents stylized Viking houses
for the dead. They are decorated with roof-like plates and
animal motifs in a humped shape, and weigh a half-tonne each.

This group is the largest number in one place in the UK and offers a unique window into a little known period of British history as their presence indicates a complex and evolving society that existed at the time. The old Kingdom of Strathclyde was a melting pot of indigenous Celtic and Briton cultural influences with newer Norse culture around the time the Vikings were conquering much of northern Europe. The hogbacks were used as elaborate gravestones to mark the burial of the ancient kings of Strathclyde. Upon entering the sanctuary at Govan these great tombs appear as crouching stone turtle monsters in all their splendour.

Over forty stones, including the hogbacks, survive to form the largest collection of early medieval sculpture in Scotland at Govan Old. This important Early Christian monastic site dating from the sixth century was later dedicated to St Constantine in the ninth century. The stones were found from within the round enclosure of the graveyard and include cross shafts and standing cross-slabs and many recumbent grave slabs all ornately carved with panels of interlace, animals that resemble reindeer in some cases and warriors on horseback.

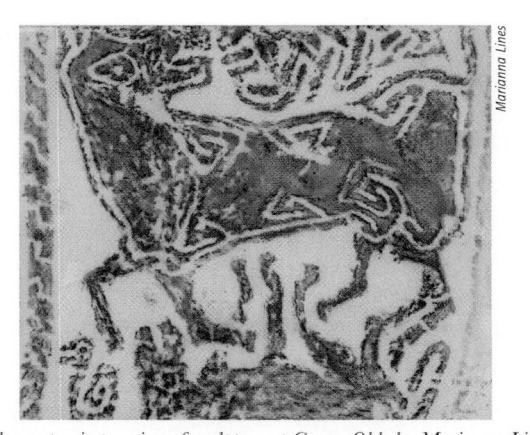

Marianna Lines

Reindeer art – impression of sculpture at Govan Old, by Marianna Lines.

The Constantine Sarcophagus is the finest solid stone coffin in Scotland of the late medieval period and believed to have held the remains of King Constantine. The shrine at St Andrews Cathedral is somewhat similar but decidedly Pictish and of an earlier date.

Other early sculpture around the Glasgow area includes the Barochan Cross, eighth century, now in Paisley Abbey (NS 485 639), and Inchinnan in Renfrewshire (NS 479 689) where three cross-slabs and a fine hogback stone are found which are closely related to Govan. Inchinnan was founded by St Conval in AD 597, later given to the Knights Templar by King David I.

Bob Henery, Pictish Art Society

The Barochan Cross.

The Fairlie Stone in North Ayrshire (NS 2098 5559) is another well-preserved example of the Govan school of sculpture. Similar to both the Inchinnan recumbent cross-slab and Govan stones, it displays the common Govan motif of a beast biting its tail.

AYRSHIRE

BALLOCHMYLE CUP AND RINGS

NS 5110 2548

'Scott', geograph.org.uk

A hidden major display of rock art with extensive cup and rings is found in a wooded glen by Catrine, a few miles from Mauchline in Burns country in Ayrshire. A sheer rock face disguised by trees, it has two large areas of ancient Bronze Age carvings, multiple rings and cups and geometric shapes along this sandstone wall. Mauchline has strong associations with Robert Burns, Scotland's famous bard and national poet who inspired Burns Suppers worldwide. His wife Jean Armour was born in Mauchline and Burns lived for four years up to 1784 in the area near Mossgiel Farm where he wrote many of his famous poems. Near the farm can be seen a remarkable tree with a knot that bears a close resemblance to *Tam O' Shanter* of the famous Burns epic poem.

West and Central

BURNS COUNTRY

Ayrshire is the birthplace of Robert Burns, Scotland's national poet and the most popular literary giant of all time. Burns Cottage in Alloway is a vernacular delight: a low, whitewashed thatched cottage. A true byre in the old sense, both people and animals lived together under one roof. These byres are much like the blackhouses in the Outer Isles of about the same period in the eighteenth century onwards. A Burns National Heritage trail takes the traveller around endless sites associated with Burns throughout the region of Ayrshire.

Ayrshire is also famous for Aisla Craig, a volcanic plug that looks like a giant Christmas pudding in the middle of the Firth of Clyde, a twin to the Bass Rock on the East coast. Aisla Craig, its Gaelic name means 'the Fairy Rock'. With its volcanic columnar cliffs, the island is a bird sanctuary as well as the source for the finest curling stones in the world. Made out of Aisla Craig granite, these exclusive polished stones are used the world over for the indigenous Scottish sport of curling. Gannets go curling from Aisla Rock every day!

Other sites in the region include Crossraguel Abbey near Culzean, a Cluniac monastery from AD 1250. It boasts ornate carving over the piscina and sedilia (monastic stone fittings for communion and meditation) and the vaulted ceiling of the sacristy and chapter house. The grand tower house, added as a luxury feature in 1480, illustrates the corruption of the monastic ideal that spurred the Reformation. Decorative capitals, corbels and bosses display delightful creatures in stone: squirrels, a lion, a triple-faced head and green men who symbolise fertility.

* * *

STIRLINGSHIRE

DUMYAT/DUN MYAT

NS 8324 9736

Near Bridge of Allan in the Valley of the Forth overlooking Stirling Castle are two significant ancient sites, Dumyat and Fairy Knowe.

Dumyat – derived from Dun Myat, 'the fort of the Maeatae' – is an important historic fort and burial cairn with fine views over the surrounding Forth Valley and Ochil Hills. Its location bears witness to its eponymous tribal group whose northern boundary may have been marked by the fort and who lived by the Antonine Wall in the third century. Also known as the 'Miathi' (from Adomnan's *Life of Columba*), they are identified with the southern Picts of the same ethnic group which survived into the sixth century.

Alan Campbell, Wikimedia Commons

Dumyat.

Dio Cassius, Roman chronicler circa AD 197 stated: "There are two principal races of the Britons, the Caledonians and the Maeatae... the Maeatae live next to the cross-wall which cuts the island in half, and the Caledonians are beyond them."

Tacitus stated that the whole of Britain north of the Forth-Clyde isthmus was *Caledonia*.

Local folk memory regards Dun Myat / Dumyat as the legendary outpost of one Pictish tribe. Dumyat is a fine place to ponder the clash of cultures between the Romans and the native peoples. History is told in the place name.

* * *

FAIRY KNOWE
NS 7961 9819

A splendid mound, dubbed the Fairy Knowe, is actually a burial cairn located on the Bridge of Earn Golf Course. Field mounds often were thought to be the abode of faerie folk. A central cist surrounded by a small cairn of stones yielded a fine Beaker vessel upon excavation, dating the site to the Neolithic period circa 3000 BC. Folklore states the obvious while one nineteenth century gentleman thought this place may have been an important site for the Pictish folk.

THE KELPIES OF FALKIRK
NS 906 821

In the shadow of the Antonine Wall a new 'sacred site' is being invented, the folklore of Scotland brought to life in a monumental new sculpture. The Kelpies, those iconic shape-shifting water horse creatures from Celtic folklore that inhabit the rivers of Scotland, have been reborn as a pair of giant horse-head sculptures that stand 98.5ft/30m tall and weigh 300 tonnes. They are located in Falkirk at the Helix Park in the central belt of Scotland for all to see.

Unknown photographer acknowledged

The two kelpies at Felix Park, Falkirk.

This massive art installation is made by Glasgow artist Andy Scott who took inspiration from Scotland's history of working horses which pulled the barges along the Forth and Clyde Canals. The steel structures are named *The kelpies* after the supernatural water horses of Celtic folklore that transformed into beautiful women to lure men into traps. These transformational modern monoliths are illuminated at night and breathe new life into the landscape of the Forth Valley area.

LOCH LOMOND

NS 361 928 Luss Church

The epitome of Scottish scenic splendour can be found on the 'bonnie banks' of Loch Lomond, located so near to Glasgow and on the Highland boundary fault line. Thirty-seven islands are found on the loch, including Inchmurrin with its monastic ruins and Inchcailloch with its oaks planted specially for the tanning industry as well as a fourteenth century nunnery. Inchmurrin is named after the seventh century St Mirin who lived there, while Inchcailloch is the 'isle of the old woman', *cailleach* in the Gaelic. The cailleach has a prominent place in Scottish folklore, as she is the wise woman of the three phases of women – virgin, mother and hag/old woman – and inspires many place names throughout Scotland.

The island of Inchtavannach was the site of St Kessog's first mission from Ireland in the seventh century. The saint was later martyred and a legend told that he was embalmed in sweet herbs which gave the village of Luss its name, *lus* being Gaelic for herb. The medieval church at Luss was dedicated to St Kessog, and the present structure and its graveyard display a medieval effigy of an abbot along with two cross-marked stones, a late medieval stone and a hogback stone carved in the Govan style, but the bronze bell of the saint is lost. The ancient history of Loch Lomond is matched by its tranquil scenery.

ABERFOYLE

The Trossachs in Stirlingshire are the setting for Sir Walter Scott's famous novels circa 1810 *Lady of the Lake* and *Rob Roy*. The legend of Rob Roy Macgregor the outlaw hero is part of the land in the Trossachs. His grave can be seen at Balquhidder (NN 5357 2091), a simple carving of a man with a sword, a cross and a faithful dog.

South of the village of Aberfoyle is the Fairy Knowe by Doon Hill (NN 525 001), where the Rev. Robert Kirk had his tryst with the fairy kingdom. Kirk was the author of *The Secret Commonwealth* (1691), a hefty tome and a treasure for those seeking the truth behind fairy lore. The Rev. Kirk reputedly disappeared into fairyland and was never seen again. Legend tells that he was forcibly removed to this secret *otherworld* as punishment for disclosing supernatural secrets, yet in another version he fell in love with the faery queen and never returned. This is the traditional fairytale of Thomas the Rhymer, told again in a different location. The Fairy Knowe is a most atmospheric place, best seen in the twilight hours, those crepuscular moments between day and night.

WALLACE'S STONE

NN 8307 0215 northeast to NN 8330 0233

It is inevitable that a standing stone would be named after William Wallace, the legendary Scottish independence fighter in the thirteenth century. Located near Dunblane in Stirlingshire, the Wallace Stone was once part of a stone row, a straight line of five upright standing stones. First in the row is the Sheriffmuir carved stone (NN 8307 0215) a cup and ring marked recumbent stone that is 7ft/2.1m in length. Boulder stones along the row lead to the famous Wallace stone, upright and proud on the moorland ridge standing 6ft/1.8m tall. Another large prone stone beyond may be part of the unexplained alignment.

Robert Smallman, geograph.org.uk

Wallace's stone on Sheriffmuir.

Folklore around the stone tells that Wallace and his fighting clans gathered here in 1297 before the Battle of Stirling Bridge, but the stone is more likely to have long been standing and took on the appropriation of history. Blind Harry, the famous Wallace follower and storyteller, first narrated these tales.

AULD WIVES' LIFTS

NS 581 764

A natural outcrop of three great boulders makes up the curiously named site of Auld Wives' Lifts on Craigmaddie Muir north of Milngavie. Two large boulders and a third on top create a sort of cromlech with a space between which has inspired a ritual of use.

Through this opening, so superstition says, "every stranger who visits this place for the first time must creep, otherwise he/she shall die childless". This is a fertility site which has

West and Central

Auld Wives' Lifts.

various carvings, some graffiti, but at least nine carved or incised heads are found on the stones of unknown date along with a circular incised groove of 3ft/90cm in diameter on the uppermost boulder. The Muir is a rolling heather-covered moorland in an area of archaeological richness with two chambered tombs, several cairns and a group of cup and ring markings found in the area.

A favourite legend for the site tells that three old women from Campsie, Strathblane and Baldernock laid a wager as to who could carry the greatest burden, so they brought three stones in their aprons and laid them in position. The name of the site tells it all.

WHITE STONE

NN 8062 0420

The MacGregor Stone, or the White Stone is a 9.8ft/3m tall standing stone located near Dunblane on Upper Whiteston Farm. A further large stone lies flat nearby to the north. The White Stone has a number of cup markings on its eastern face: one large and seven smaller cups. Perhaps some rendition of the solar system may be considered.

Legends attached to the stone associate it with Rob Roy, thus named the MacGregor Stone. It is said that a countryman was sacrificed at the stone by the followers of Rob Roy before a battle on Sheriffmuir in order to satisfy the ancient Highland belief that 'first blood' was an infallible omen of success.

* * *

West and Central

DUNBLANE CATHEDRAL

NN 7815 0138

Located in the market town of Dunblane at the crossroads between east and west Scotland, Dunblane Cathedral is a place of sacred history and artistic innovation. The Cathedral was the seat of the diocese in the twelfth century which stretched from the Forth to Strathearn. A late Pictish stone circa ninth century attests to Pictish settlement and the place name itself, the fort of Blane. St Blane was a Briton of the Kingdom of Strathclyde who lived around 600, founded the monastery of St Blane's on the Isle of Bute, and continued his missionary work to the Picts in the lands of the Forth, following on the work of St Ninian in Galloway. His tomb and effigy are seen in the choir area dating from the thirteenth century.

The Dunblane cross-slab has a large Celtic cross on the main face with a pattern of spirals that make up the ring and spiral terminals above and below. A pair of beasts' heads with long tongues are at the base of the shaft. The reverse side is a Pictish-style medley of beasts and horsemen, all rendered in a rather declining sculptural art form. Green Men sculptured images in wood and stone are found throughout the Cathedral, a symbol of pagan fertility and plenty. This important ecclesiastical centre is a delightful place to find a bit of peace and quiet – and inspiration.

INCHMAHOME PRIORY

NN 5743 0055

Marianna Lines

Set on an island in the Lake of Menteith, Inchmahome is an idyllically situated Augustinian monastery dating from 1238. Much of the thirteenth century church remains; the stone walls of the open nave rise tall and graceful above the trees of this most beautiful island monastery. It sheltered the five year old Mary Queen of Scots in 1547 and her garden, Queen Mary's Bower, remains to this day on the west side of the island. Rich in wildlife, the woodlands are carpeted in wildflowers and the lake, the only 'non loch' in Scotland, is visited by special water-fowl including herons and great crested grebes. Three Spanish chestnuts on the island are listed in Scotland's top one hundred trees. These twisted, gnarled trees are nature's sculpture at its

West and
Central

Some of the marvels of Inchmahome Island: Spanish oak;
Knotwork cross; Effigy of a knight; Warrior – art by Marianna Lines.

best. Many carved stones are found within the Priory including
a caricature-like effigy of a knight of the realm in conversation
with a peacock. To land on the tiny island seems a world away,
another dimension where you can enter into some imaginary
realm all of your own.

THE LOTHIANS

The fertile coastal plain along the south side of the Firth of
Forth offers a few spectacular ancient sites despite intensive
land use over the centuries. Cairnpapple Hill, a henge and
burial cairns at Torphichen, traces a long cycle of prehistoric
ceremonies. History has evolved in the area that lies around the
nation's capital at Edinburgh. The Lothians are rich in Roman
ruins, in forts perched on volcanic hills and in monastic sites.

Top of the sacred sites is Rosslyn Chapel in Midlothian.

ROSSLYN CHAPEL

NT 2748 6307

Rosslyn Chapel is the most celebrated medieval building in Scotland, perhaps due to its media exposure, but it well deserves the claim.

This mysterious richly decorated late Gothic building has a huge history with Templar mystic legends and an architectural splendour of stone mason expertise. It is intrinsically linked with the St Clairs of Rosslyn and the Knights Templar, and of course Hollywood has capitalised on the story with *The Da Vinci Code*.

Wikimedia Commons

'Roslin Chapel' from a tour guide of 1889 - Souvenir of Scotland - Cities, Lakes & Mountains, Published by T. Nelson & Sons.

Located in the heart of Midlothian, Rosslyn Chapel was founded in 1446 by Sir William St Clair, the third Prince of Orkney. It took forty years to build, a testament to a fascinating architectural vision to create 'a building of curiosity and splendour'. However, the original building was never completed, only the choir was constructed along with the retro-chapel, the Lady Chapel, built over an ancient crypt. The decorative carving took the time, all four decades worth, and this abundance of sculptural symbolism both inside and out sets Rosslyn apart from anywhere else in the world.

West and Central

The Chapel stands on fourteen pillars which form an arcade of twelve pointed arches on three sides of the nave. The exterior is exciting enough, with pinnacles, gargoyles, flying buttresses and canopies. Inside is even more intricate, every surface covered in a wealth of sculpture. There are three pillars at the east end of the chapel named the Master Pillar, the Journeyman Pillar and the Apprentice Pillar. The latter is the most famous. The 'Prentice Pillar' takes it name from an eighteenth

by "Guinnog" Wikimedia Commons

The Apprentice Pillar, said to be tied to Freemasonic legend.

century legend: an apprentice mason was inspired by a dream to carve the pillar, the most elaborately carved pillar in the Chapel. On seeing the magnificent achievement the master mason flew into a jealous rage and struck the apprentice killing him outright.

Of the myriad of extraordinary carvings at Rosslyn, a few stand out that tell a story:

1) Farmer's wife rescues a goose from the jaws of a fox, a typical rural scene
2) Knight on horseback, possibly Sir William carrying the Holy Rood, the true cross, back to Scotland
3) Indian corn or maize surrounding a window, a clue to the discovery of America by Prince Henry 'the Navigator' Sinclair, Earl of Orkney, prior to the Christopher Columbus false claim
4) Lucifer the fallen angel, clue to the Templar connection with Rosslyn, as rites of Freemasonry depicted angels in unusual positions such as this
5) Green Man, one of over one hundred green man carvings, a pagan figure with vines sprouting from his mouth to represent growth and fertility
6) Angel playing bagpipes, the earliest representation of bagpipes which first appeared in the mid-1400s
7) Musical Cubes protruding from arches of Lady Chapel with symbols of dots and lines deciphered to be a code of thirteen geometric patterns for musical notes from which a piece of 'music cipher' has been written called *The Rosslyn Motet* by Thomas J. Mitchell.

* * *

Rosslyn Chapel is a symphony of sacred geometry and ancient wisdom encoded in stone, or as some say, 'a tapestry in stone'. There is a great deal for the spiritual traveller to discover within and without. Now after its sixteen-year restoration, the chapel is glowing with new life.

Exterior of the Rosslyn Chapel after conservation work was completed in September 2013.

Roslin Glen is a deep-wooded ravine along the River North Esk below the chapel that holds further treasures. Prehistoric rock art and cliff-side stone faces, Wallace's Cave and Hawthornden Castle are all tucked away in the dramatic gorge. Roslin Castle above the Glen is a picturesque fourteenth century castle with more secrets.

CAIRNPAPPLE HILL

NS 9872 7173

© Crown Copyright reproduced courtesy of Historic Scotland. www.historicscotlandimages.gov.uk

It is said that you can see Goatfell on Arran on a clear day from Cairnpapple Hill, a unique holy place and one of the most important prehistoric sites in mainland Scotland. A Neolithic ceremonial site from 2800 BC, Cairnpapple is located in West Lothian on the Bathgate Hills southwest of Edinburgh near Torphichen.

West and
Central

The Neolithic site has seen traces of human activity from over 5,500 years ago, with six hearths full of potsherds and two Stone Age axes from as far away as Wales and Cumbria. The hearths were covered over by a great oval enclosure with a broad ditch known as a 'henge monument', 65yds/60m across, like that at Ring of Brodgar on Orkney. This ceremonial enclosure had two entrances, and a ring of twenty four standing stones around it.

The site evolved in the Bronze Age circa 2000 BC into a burial chamber with a single monolith 8ft/2.4m tall to mark the important burial. Two Beaker pots were discovered at this point. Burial cists were added, stone-lined pits with a massive capstone on top and three cup-marks on the surface. A much larger burial cairn was finally built over the earlier cairns with upturned cinerary urns inside. A modern dome recreates the effect of this mound on site today with bones and all to view. From a distance, Cairnpapple looks like a great grassy mound of earth as the name aptly describes the place.

IN THE FORTH
ON THE SACRED WATERS

INCHCOLM ISLAND

NT 1897 8267

One of the most magical islands in the Firth of Forth to visit during summer is Inchcolm Island, taking a ferry from South Queensferry. Known as the 'Iona of the East', Inchcolm has no known historical link with St Columba but may have been used

Marianna Lines

as a way-station between the island monasteries of Iona and Lindisfarne. The island is essentially a medieval abbey complex established by King David I in 1235 and dominated by the best-preserved group of monastic buildings in Scotland.

Since the twelfth century the Augustinian canons settled here in splendid isolation in spite of English raids from the fourteenth century, until monastic life ended in 1560. The Augustinian religious community was linked with St Colm from whom its name is derived.

The oldest ruin on the island is the hermit's cell dating back to the ninth century while the oldest relic is the hogback stone, a grave monument of the tenth century decorated in a Norse style.

The architecture of the abbey complex features a complete cloister and an octagonal chapter house and a tower. Fragments of remarkable thirteenth century rare frescos from the abbey are preserved in viewing boxes which retain their beautiful soft natural dye colours.

The *Inchcolm Antiphoner*, probably written on the island, contains priceless surviving examples of Celtic plainchant, some of them hymns in praise of St Columba. Rediscovered and recorded in recent years, the beauty of this music – probably well over a thousand years old – can now be heard again in concerts and recordings. Lyrics from this medieval musical piece read… "*O Columba insignis signifier*".

A medieval inscription carved above the Abbey's entrance reads (in Latin): "May this house stand until an ant drains the flowing sea, and a tortoise walks around the whole world."

While Inchcolm echoes a distant and sacred past, the island is a beacon in the middle of the Firth of Forth that carries a magical atmosphere forth in today's world.

BERWICK LAW and THE BASS ROCK

NT 555 841 and NT 602 873

Berwick Law by North Berwick and the Bass Rock in the Firth of Forth are significant volcanic features in the Lothian landscape. Berwick Law with its distinctive pyramidal shape displays the remnants of an Iron Age hillfort and the famous whalebone landmark.

Bass Rock is home to one of the world's largest colony of gannets: beautiful large white birds with black wing tips and golden heads, the largest seabirds in the North Atlantic. One of the wildlife wonders of the world, it was also the home of St Baldred, a Celtic saint who lived there around AD 600. The ruin of St Baldred's Chapel stands half-way up the island, sited upon a cell or cave where the Scottish saint stayed. A freshwater well is found nearby.

Marianna Lines

Bass Rock viewed from Pittenweem.

Some other important sites in the Lothians

Doon Hill (NT 686 755) an early historic settlement at Dunbar, the hall of a British chieftain in the sixth century.

Hare Law (NT 546 631) a vitrified hillfort at Gifford on a rocky spur of the Lammermuirs.

Traprain Law (NT 581 746) near Haddington, hillfort and the tribal capital of the Votadini during the Roman period. Traprain is the site of a vast hoard of Late Roman silver, which can be seen in Edinburgh at the National Museum (NMS). The Votadini emerged as a kingdom under the name of Gododdin (Brythonic), and Traprain Law was said to be their capital before moving to Dun Eidyn (Edinburgh).

Abercorn (NT 0814 7909) near South Queensferry, is an Early Christian site with a fine collection of carved stones at the church.

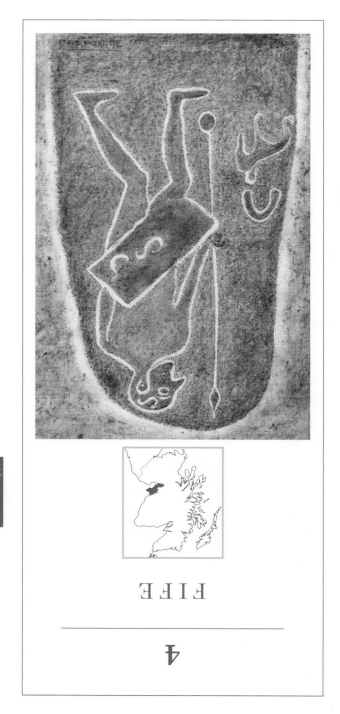

FIFE

4

FIFE

PRINCIPAL SITES

Fife

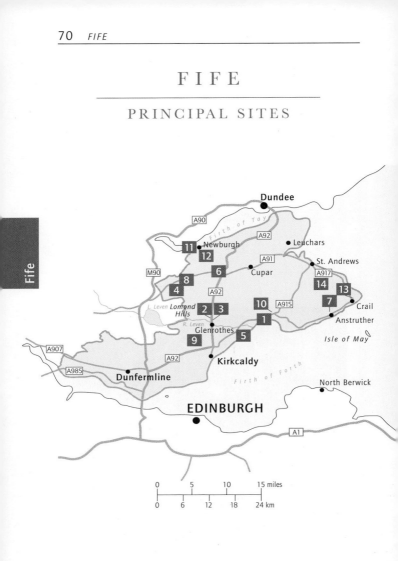

1 Lundin Links stones		**8** Strathmiglo stone
2 Balfarg henge		**9** Dogton stone
3 Balbirnie stone circle		**10** Largo stone
4 The Bonnet Stane		**11** Mugdrum Cross
5 Wemyss caves		**12** Lindores Stone
6 Collessie Stone		**13** Crail stones
7 Skeith stone		**14** Dunino Den

Previous page: Pictish warrior, from the Collessie Stone.
Natural dye painting by Marianna Lines.

FIFE

THE KINGDOM OF FIFE holds many treasures, and as the old saying goes, "It taks a lang spoon tae sup wi' a Fifer". In other words, folk from Fife are said to be somewhat cunning and devious – the original version being 'it takes a long spoon to sup with the Devil!'

Fife is known for its lovely coastline, old fishing villages, castles and ancient stones. Like much of Scotland each area has its own character. Fife folklore tells of the 'pechts' – small people who lived in caves and had such big feet they could use them as umbrellas. This must be a confused memory of the mysterious Pictish people who lived in eastern Scotland during and after the Roman period. As such they may be considered as the natives of Scotland, the aborigines, the First Nation people, the 'people of the designs'. The literal meaning of Picts, from the Latin *Picti*, is 'Painted People'.

These designs adorned their monumental carved stones as well as their bodies so we have a visible remnant of their culture that survives in the great sculptured stones. Yet the Dark Ages remain shrouded in mystery, for no one really knows what these symbols mean. And if they say they do, beware.

The landscape of Fife is dominated by the Lomond Hills, a pair of extinct volcanoes surrounded by a wide swathe of open land for hillwalking with numerous ancient sites dotted around. Rising to a height of 1700ft/522m at the summit of West Lomond, the Lomond Hills form a beautiful distinctive landscape in East Central Scotland. Maiden Castle on West Lomond is an oval-shaped mound, the remains of an Iron Age fort. Although the ditch and bank are visible, the defences were never completed.

'The Fortress of the Picts', East Lomond Hill has the remains of another fort at its summit. Remnants of ancient ramparts are still visible and the discovery of a Pictish symbol stone with the figure of a bull suggests it was in use in Pictish times. This landscape was the home of the Venicones, the native tribal people of Fife, which is documented in Ptolemy's second century AD *Geographica*.

Archaeological remains spanning at least 10,000 years represent a physical and visible record of human activity on the Lomonds. Two carved stones from the Pictish era have been found there, one a single incised figure of a bull, now in Edinburgh NMS, and another Early Christian stone with a cross and fish symbol, a boulder stone in situ on Balharvie Moss.

There are also historical links with Robert the Bruce, Macbeth and Mary Queen of Scots in and around the Hills. The Living Lomonds Project is taking this diverse history in the landscape forward to re-connect people with the hills.

Fife is a peninsula with the Firth of Forth flanking it to the south, from Culross and West Fife round to the East Neuk ('corner') of Fife, an area whose necklace of fishing villages has much appeal for visitors as do the historic islands offshore. The mighty River Tay lies on the north side of Fife, creating another watery border with the counties of Angus and Perthshire.

Folklore frae Fife has its own unique Scots dialect. Carlin Maggie, a stone pillar on Bishop Hill, has a local story about Maggie the witch who challenged the Devil and was turned into stone. This pinnacle style outcrop can be seen high on the western edge of the hill by Loch Leven bordering Perth and Kinross.

Castles of Fife are mostly in a romantic ruin state, such as St Andrews, Aberdour, Ballinbreich and Denmylne, while Kellie Castle and Falkland Palace are bastions of architectural and historical delight. Balgonie Castle (1360) sports the oldest tower intact in the Kingdom.

NEOLITHIC AND BRONZE AGE PERIOD

LUNDIN LINKS STONES

NO 4048 0271

The Standing Stones of Lundin Links are three giant monumental stones now surrounded by the second fairway within the Ladies Golf Course of Lundin Links on the south coast of Fife. There were originally four stones, creating what is known as a 'four poster' or rectangle arrangement, but no trace of the fourth remains visible today (last noted in the 1750s). The tallest stone of 17ft/5.49m stands to the north in the triumvirate, the second stone of 15ft/4.5m tall is in the southwest, and the smallest and broadest in the southeast is 14 feet/4.11m tall.

The great archaeo-astronomer Alexander Thom calculated two possible alignments for this Neolithic or Bronze Age site, one south-southwest to Comrie Hill for minor moonset, the other south-southeast to moonrise behind the Bass Rock which would be a magical moment. As sculptural and graceful as they are powerful and tall, these ancient eroded hoary lichen-whiskered red sandstone monoliths can be visited with permission from the ladies of the course.

Marianna Lines

The Lundin Links stones are aligned to Largo Law, a conical hill, the remains of a volcanic plug which carries legends of buried treasure. Legend tells that the hill was created when the Devil dropped a huge boulder. The top of the Law is known as the 'Devil's Chair': seven steps lead up to it with hidden treasure buried under the hill, allegedly.

A shepherd from Balmain Farm on its slopes once approached the 'resident' guardian ghost of Largo and asked the secret. The phantom said that if he came to a part of the hill at eight o' clock he would learn where treasure was concealed. However there were two conditions which needed to be fulfilled.

"'If Auchendowie cock doesn't crow and the shepherd of Balmain his horn doesn't blow, I'll tell where the gold is in Largo Law'. The rest of the story is lost. Some stories are so absurd they can be disregarded; for example the golden fleece of the sheep on Largo Law is a clue to the 'buried gold' hidden there. In order to clean and protect the animals they are dipped in a solution that often bears a yellowish tint.

A Pictish cairn cemetery dated AD 450–650 was excavated at the beach in Lundin Links in recent years. Many finds were revealed including a jet necklace and the skeleton of a woman. The cemetery of skeletons and long cists were exposed on

Fife

the beach after a severe storm and may have been related to another cemetery associated with an earlier period of the standing stones. This is a possible case of ritual continuity, always a tantalising thought in the investigation of ancient sites.

The local postman who liked to photograph these stones on his rounds termed them 'Whoppers'. That about sums it up.

The Lundin Links Stones.

BALFARG HENGE and BALBIRNIE STONE CIRCLE

NO 2819 0312 henge, NO 2850 0304 circle

This henge and related stone circle comprise a large Neolithic ceremonial site dating from around 3200 BC, a major ceremonial centre of the first farmers of Fife and one of only a few such sites known in eastern Scotland. The Balfarg Henge is now surrounded by a housing estate, while the other surviving part, Balbirnie Stone Circle, is now separated by the A92 and approached by woodland walks.

Balfarg Henge with its two remaining stones.

The Henge was built in two phases : a ditch and bank with wooden posts in six concentric rings.

In the second phase around 2800 BC the posts were replaced by stone megaliths, again in concentric rings. Only two massive stones remain, one part of the circle, while the other was a portal stone marking the entrance to the monument. The site later became a burial place and a recumbent slab in the central area marks the burial of a young male found with a fine handled beaker and a flint knife.

BALBIRNIE is a reconstructed stone circle with eight stones surviving out of ten, located originally 136.6yds/125m to the northwest of the Henge. It lies near Balbirnie House in Markinch on a woodland path by the golf course. There is an inner low rectangular setting of stones and four stone cists for burials where a beaker was found and a cup-marked stone used as an edge stone to the small cremation pit. The multi-cup-marked stone on site is a replica, the original now in the National Museum in Edinburgh. The circle is thought to have had a cairn piled over it in its last period of use from about 3000 BC.

Impression of Balbirnie stone circle – painting by Marianna Lines.

On an autumnal day with the setting sun it has a rather special atmosphere, after rearrangement, and one great grand-father stone dominates the circle that is especially powerful.

THE BONNET STANE

NO 1897 0706

This natural outcrop on the northwest slope of West Lomond is a place of atmosphere and mystery. The Bonnet (or Bunnet) Stane may be one of the strangest places in the Lomonds. You might think you had been transported to the Outback of Australia. The honey-coloured sandstone outcrop, an elevated 'table', has been moulded by wind and rain into a shape that resembles a tammy or bonnet, or perhaps a giant mushroom.

David Cuthbert

The Bonnet or Bunnet Stane.

A hole through the upper stone can just be penetrated and legend calls it a 'birthing stone', a place women would visit for fertility. There are interesting graffiti markings all over the rock outcrop, some which could be quite old. It is also a good place to practise dowsing.

The soft rock has been hollowed out below the Bonnet Stane by people long ago into a cave where a hermit once lived. Known as the Maiden's Bower, the story goes that long ago a young maiden fell in love with the son of a rival family and the stone was their secret meeting place. One day she saw her father's men ambush and kill her lover. She then refused to return home, spending the rest of her life in the cave and becoming known locally as a saint.

FIFE COASTAL CAVES

The south and east coast of Fife has a myriad of caves along its shores from West Fife to Kirkcaldy right round to the East Neuk. In fact they are usually set somewhat back from the present shoreline, reflecting the higher sea levels of prehistoric times. St Margaret's Cave in Dunfermline is a famous pilgrimage site for visitors to the Abbey. Located beneath a car park 87 steps down into the earth, it was used by Queen Margaret for prayer, the wife of King Malcolm of Canmore and mother of three kings of Scotland in the eleventh century.

St Serf's Caves by the Carmelite Nunnery in Dysart are believed to be where the saint once stayed circa AD 540. A Pictish symbol of the arch/gateway is also found in one of the cave recesses there. St Serf's is open to the public once a year in the autumn.

Pittenweem has a famous cave dedicated to St Fillan of the seventh century. Early holy men had an affinity for caves as places of retreat and austerity, and Pittenweem's very name means 'Settlement of the Cave'. This beautiful deep sandstone

St Serf's Cave, Dysart, and [inset] Pictish arch/gateway carving.

recess is where saints would have sheltered and prayed, a sacred place. Ask at the chocolate shop tearoom on the High Street for the key, which is quite a large one.

Further along the East Neuk coast between Anstruther and Crail the Caiplie Caves have many cross markings from the Early Christian period.

But the most famous and accessible are the Wemyss Caves. Weem or Wemyss means 'cave', an anglicisation of Gaelic *uamh*.

WEMYSS CAVES

NT 3456 9723

Along the Fife coast near Kirkcaldy east of the former mining village of East Wemyss are the Wemyss Caves. There are eight caves here along the shore area, most of which have early Pictish symbol carvings. The caves have been used by people over thousands of years – cave-dwellers, Picts, Early Christians, smugglers, hermits, gypsies, all sorts. The caves have suffered in recent times from weathering, coastal erosion, vandalism and destructive mine works causing much damage and loss.

There are arguably more carvings – rock art markings – in the Wemyss Caves than anywhere else in Britain. The Covesea caves of the Moray Firth also have Pictish carvings, but not on this scale. A local action group known as SWAC, (Save the Wemyss Ancient Caves), has worked for years to save these historic caves and raise awareness but perhaps local government has not been as helpful.

The most important surviving caves are called the Court Cave, Jonathan's Cave and the Sloping Cave. The carvings may be quite early in the Pictish repertoire, possibly dating

Both photos: Marianna Lines

Top: Jonathan's Cave, East Wemyss. Above: Ruins of MacDuff Castle.

from the fifth century AD and displaying numerous symbols, especially the double disc and Z-rod, and intriguing animal carvings. There is a certain element of mystery and fun to be had exploring these ancient sites; deciphering the symbols in Jonathan's cave where a nineteenth century nail maker once lived for instance – although one must discount the modern graffiti! Interpretation boards can be found in the parking area, but it is best to decide for yourself what these ancient carvings may have meant.

Medieval MacDuff Castle stands in a romantic ruined state above the caves atop the cliffs. Built originally as a wooden structure for the Wemyss family, it was partially destroyed by Edward I in 1304 because of Robert the Bruce loyalists sheltering there, but it was rebuilt in stone with twin towers and survived in use until 1666. Shades of Macbeth and the Scottish play lurk in this place as it was the home of Clan Macduff, Thane and Mormaer of Fife during the reign of Malcolm Canmore (1058–1093). Inevitably a ghost is said to live here: the 'Grey Lady' who was thought to be one Mary Sibbald.

The story of Mary Sibbald is a sad one, and she is also referred to as the 'White Lady'. Mary was the daughter of the Laird of Balgonie Castle who fell in love with a gypsy living in

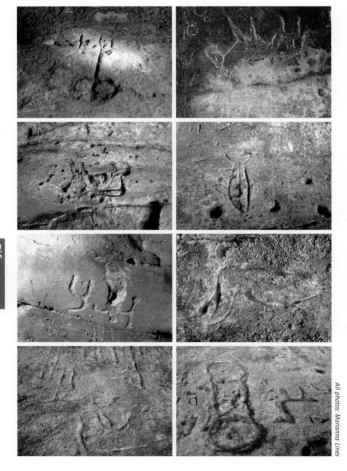

Wemyss Caves Pictish stone carvings.
Bottom left up: Wolf; Fish symbol; Swan; Double disc
Top right down: Pictish Beastie; Warrior; Horse; Trident.

the Court Cave. His former lover Jean Lindsay was so jealous that she planted a brooch under Mary's sleeping mat, then declared her jewellery stolen and Mary as the thief. Being unfairly punished, a lady of gentle manners, she died of a broken heart. The story then brings in King James V who was a frequent visitor to the caves, always disguised as the commoner 'The Gudeman of Ballangeich'. During one of his visits when the wine was flowing and the gypsies revelling, a quarrel broke out, and Jean Lindsay was charged with bearing false witness against Mary. At this point an apparition of a white clad lady with soft blue eyes entered the cave. Jean Lindsay was frightened into confessing.

Fife

The Alexander plant surrounding the ruins of the castle was often used mistakenly as an aphrodisiac in medieval times which may explain Mary's love affair with a gypsy man.

Another story associated with the Wemyss Caves tells that over 150 years ago the youth of Wemyss held a torch lit procession on the first Monday of the year, known as 'Hansel Monday'. The 'Hansel Walk' went along the caves on the shore ending in the Well Cave where there was a healing well. On this night the fairy piper came to collect the dues owed by those who neglected to make a sacrifice to the gods of the dead. A messenger from Tír nan Óg, the piper bewitched his followers with his melodies and led them to the land of eternal youth, Tír nan Óg. Legend tells that one night he played his last pibroch tune as he entered the Court Cave where James V, the last king to rule over an independent Scotland, held his court of gypsies. Like the last of the Stuart kings, the piper never returned. The followers of these torch lit processions are immortalized in the initials carved into the walls of the Well Cave chamber. The curative pure water of the well was used to protect the procession from ill health in the coming year.

PICTISH STONES

Fife was one of seven reputed kingdoms of the Picts known as *Fib*. A name in use from early medieval times, the modern name is derived from *Fib*. There are a great number of early Pictish stones, many of which remain in their original locations.

The Picts were the native people of Scotland – the indigenous race, the ancient nation who ruled the north and east of Scotland from the third to the ninth century AD. They continue to be shrouded in a mysterious aura of tribal lore, gossip and shredded misinformation. They disappeared as a nation when taken over by the Kingdom of the Scots in the mid ninth century when their language, their identity and their artistic culture were lost within about a century. Yet many highly accomplished Pictish sculptured monuments survive, at least 400 of them, even in their weathered and often incomplete state. They still beam their knowledge and energy, a beacon of light from the mostly forgotten history of the so-called Dark Ages. With few written records, these symbol stones are the sagas and chronicles of an artistically gifted, formidable people. Their symbols live on to delight and intrigue, but as yet no 'Rosetta Stone' has come to light to unlock their enigma.

* * *

COLLESSIE STONE

NO 2927 1324

One particularly unusual standing stone in northeast Fife is rather close to the author of this book. The Collessie Stone, 'Collessie Man', or more precisely the Newton of Collessie Stone, stands in a corner of a field between the medieval villages of Collessie and Monimail, three fields in from the farm road.

Marianna Lines

The Collessie Stone, showing the Pictish warrior
featured on the title page of this section.

A Bronze Age standing stone, this monument has the distinction of being re-used for a later Pictish carving of a warrior which was added centuries after it was erected. Sacred stones often get re-appropriated by later cultures, and this warrior figure may represent a god. The Collessie warrior has only one close parallel in the entire corpus of Pictish sculptured stones: the single figure of the Rhynie Man stone in Aberdeen.

The incised, very worn and lichen-obscured carving shows an unclothed Pictish man in profile carrying an oblong shield and a ball-weighted spear. Also on the 9ft/2.7m tall pillar stone are a pair of symbols: the Pictish beast and the 'arch' or 'horse-shoe' which may identify his ancestors' tribal totems. This may be the earliest representation of a human being known in Fife, possibly as early as the fourth century AD. The inclusion of two Pictish symbols together with a characteristic Pictish male figure makes this stone unique in the Pictish repertory of symbol stones with incised figures.

The location on farmland in Collessie parish near Cupar on its original site helps to protect the stone but also means it is not easily accessible. Best to check with Halhill Farm first, located on the back road to Letham.

SKEITH STONE

NO 5708 0464

The Skeith Stone is an incised Early Christian stone which displays the semi-relief carving of a marigold cross, dating from the late seventh century AD. The design is within a circle in which eight lozenge or leaf-shaped depressions form pairs outlining a cross, a type known as a 'marigold' cross. It stands probably on its original site, by a farm track southwest of Rennyhill Farm facing out to the Isle of May on the Firth of Forth near the village of Kilrenny. It is associated with St Adrian or Ethernán in Scots of the medieval monastery on the Isle of May. The monks would have come across to the Mainland from the island and left their mark on this stone as well as in caves along the coast nearby where early crosses are found. Like many of the ancient sculptured stones in Scotland, the Skeith Stone markings are now faint due to the effects of weathering on the stone, not to mention the age.

This parish name of Kilrenny contains the name of an early holy man of Irish origin, Ethernán who died in the early seventh century and was remembered in later tradition as Adrian. He seems to have founded a number of churches or monasteries in Fife. The Skeith Stone may have marked an early boundary round the later parish church and village, while the later medieval priory on the Isle of May also looked back to Adrian as its founder.

Left: Strathmiglo Stone. Right: Impression by Marianna Lines.

STRATHMIGLO STONE

NO 2166 1022

The Deer Stone at Strathmiglo is an early Pictish symbol stone which stands outside the gate of Strathmiglo churchyard beside the kirk [*see bottom left*]. Dating from the seventh century AD, the 7ft/2.1m high pillar stone darkly hints at a pair of incised symbols of a deer head and 'tuning fork', an abstract symbol. Some say these stones were usually set up in pairs within the Pictish Kingdom. The stone was found reused as a gatepost in 1969 west of the village and moved to its current location.

DOGTON STONE

NT 2360 9686

At Dogton Farm by Kinglassie stands the rough trunk of the Dogton Stone, very eroded but once showing pairs of horsemen in a hunting scene. The vagaries of time and stony erosion give the horsemen a Viking look with horns on their helmets but this is more a trick of the eye than what was originally intended. This poor old stone – now protected by circular iron railings – was once a splendid freestanding cross of ninth century origin. A rare survival of a Pictish cross, the Dupplin Cross in Perthshire is the only example to survive in complete condition.

Only the base and lower shaft remain here with ornamentation of interwoven serpents up one side and armed horsemen above two beasts. This stone in its original location is rare and marks the site of some famous battle. Legend tells of the defeat by Constantine of the Danes, but that is a rather outdated antiquarian view, Danes representing any 'foreigner'.

LARGO STONE

NO 4234 0348

Sited on the edge of the East Neuk near Leven is another fine Pictish stone, the Largo Stone. Now 'caged' in an iron grille in the churchyard of Largo Kirk it stands in view of Largo Law and not far from the great Lundin Links Standing Stones. This Class II Pictish cross-slab of ninth century origin, 6ft/1.8m tall, combines an interlaced Celtic cross with Pictish symbols and hunting scenes typical of a tribal people who have been infiltrated with Christian influence and are losing their native 'Earth Mystery' mystical focus. In other words, the Picts were becoming Christianised but retaining respect for their old traditions.

The stone has been badly treated: broken, lost, moved about, mended and now caged but at least it survives. The paired seahorses on one panel surrounding the cross is the most

Fife

Seahorse Love – natural dye impression by Marianna Lines.

delightful image, a playful version of the more formal classic paired seahorses found on the Aberlemno Stone in Angus. A favourite symbol of the *Pictish Beastie* and sometimes called the Kelpie (but never call it an elephant) appears on the reverse side of the stone. Although an elongated eroded version is seen here, the beastie is the most enigmatic of all Pictish symbols.

This once great stone – along with other stones from Fife such as Crail and Scoonie – provide clear evidence of a strong Pictish/ Christian presence in Fife during the eighth and ninth centuries when the Southern Kingdom of Pictland was at the height of its power.

Largo is also well known for its favourite local hero, castaway seaman and buccaneer Alexander Selkirk (1676–1721), immortalised by Daniel Defoe in literary history as Robinson Crusoe. His statue is found in Lower Largo set in the front of a house on the site of his birthplace. His ruined mansion is seen to this day from the main road.

MUGDRUM CROSS

NO 2251 1817

A large eroded sandstone pillar stands on a wooded ridge on the Mugdrum Estate west of Newburgh looking out to Mugdrum Island and the River Tay. Although on private grounds, permission can be asked at the house to visit the stone. Mugdrum, a headless cross, is a late Pictish stone which is contemporary with the Dupplin

Marianna Lines

Detail of the Mugdrum Cross.

Marianna Lines

The Mugdrum Cross – interpretations by Marianna.

Cross and the Dogton Stone.The cross, 12.5ft/3.5m high dates from the ninth century. Ethereally and hauntingly sculptured with tracery and imagery, it is just possible to make out three panels depicting a hunting scene. The quarry is a stag, but could be a boar.

In the place name Mugdrum, *muc* is Gaelic for sow or pig, and drum or druim in Gaelic means ridge. The top of the cross has disappeared but truncated arms suggest its former shape. Both edges of the stone show Celtic style ornamentation of inhabited vine scroll early medieval motifs with winged griffins and other fantastic beasts.

In a fanciful rave, the antiquarian Earl of Southesk suggested that the boar represented the goddess Freia or Freyja in Old Norse of the Scandinavian Triad and was adopted by the Picts into their religion. In his thinking (which archaeologists say is simply not worth quoting) the stone tells the symbolic story of the heathen religion being driven out by Christianity.

The MacDuff Cross is found nearby, supposedly a stone cross base but probably in fact prehistoric in origin.

Finds of interest from the Roman period were found at Carpow just along from Mugdrum where excavations revealed remains of a Roman fort. The finds are now kept in the McManus Galleries/Museum in Dundee.

An exciting recent find was a Bronze Age log boat discovered in the River Tay below Carpow near Newburgh. It was so large that it had to be conserved in two parts, and it is hoped that it can one day be put on permanent display in Perth Museum. It is now on loan to Glasgow Museums in the Nitshill Resource Centre.

* * *

LINDORES STONE

NO 2595 1634

One of Fife's more hidden locations, the Lindores stone lurks
within a stone shelter beside Abdie
Old Kirk near the village of
Lindores. The main face displays
twin Pictish symbols of the crescent
and V-rod below the cauldron
symbol, a Class I stone circa seventh century AD. On one side of
the stone is the Pictish mirror symbol. The stone came from Kaim
Hill above Lindores Loch, later
found in a hedgerow and removed
to the safety of the shed along with
two other later medieval stones
reputedly removed to Abdie from
Lindores Abbey by Newburgh.
These are the Calvary cross stone of

*Lindores Stone. Note the
Ordnance Survey bench mark.*

the fourteenth century and a stone effigy of a cleric from the
abbey precinct which is now a romantic ruin. The roofless Old
Kirk of Abdie dates from the thirteenth century and has a peaceful atmosphere within a churchyard with stones of many periods.

CRAIL STONES

NO 6134 0797,   NO 6103 0788

The quaint fishing village of Crail in
the East Neuk of Fife has relics of
many periods to discover including
three Pictish stones. The Crail Stone
is a late ninth or tenth century cross-
slab now housed in the Parish Kirk of
St Mary, originally from Kilminning
(St Monan) by Fife Ness on the sea. It
is popularly called the *Walking Cross*
or cross with legs. It displays a Celtic
cross in relief and ring of glory decorated with key pattern flanked by
various zoomorphic figures all floating above a torso with legs. In fact
the bottom of the cross shape has legs
attached to it which is rather unique.
This very curious worn stone once
lay on the church floor and so
has suffered much erosion from the
passage of feet. Its images include a

*The Crail Stone –
art by Marianna Lines.*

serpent and beasts, a bird pecking a dog, a swan (also found in the Wemyss Caves), and an enthroned figure: possibly mother and child or harper.

The Sauchope Stone, extremely weathered, stands in Victoria Gardens Park in the village and shows an almost obliterated ghostly image of a pair of horsemen with dogs and a cross on the other side. The Crail Museum in the former Tolbooth displays two fine Pictish cross-slab fragments with interlace and animal figures recently discovered near Kilrenny.

OTHER PICTISH STONES

The Bull Stone from East Lomond Hill now in the National Museum of Scotland / NMS.

Falkland Estate stones (two) from Westfield Farm with Pictish symbols, now in the Laing Museum, Newburgh by appointment via St Andrews Museum.

The Scoonie Stone from Leven now in NMS.

The Walton Stone from Crawford Priory in Springfield, now in private hands near Cults. However, stones move around just like people, so check first before venturing forth.

DUNINO DEN

NO5410 1088

Located near the road from St Andrews to Anstruther, Dunino Den is a mysterious place to visit, a site of great natural beauty with pagan overtones along with a long history. Dunino proba- bly was a pagan cult 'power point' in the ancient world. The Den can be reached from Dunino Kirk down a path which leads first to a rock cut well before descending into a deep narrow glade or den. This is best visited at bluebell time in the late spring when the ground is carpeted in soft blue blossom. The Den is somewhat of a natural amphitheatre, flanked by natural stone 'pulpits' and occasional caves along the river bed of the Kinaldy Burn. A huge rock cut Celtic cross on the cliff face 9 x 6ft/2.7 x 1.8m may not be any earlier than Victorian times as it is not mentioned in early antiquarian accounts despite its size, while other 'Celtic' graffiti are certainly recent. Modern day pagans have started to use the site for 'clootie' and coin offerings.

The two crags jutting out of the cliff-lined Den, which are part of Bell Craig, are called Pulpit Rock and Altar Rock. Steep stone steps lead down into the Den by Pulpit Rock. A rock-cut basin above has a footprint beside it, leading to the belief that this was a site of king-making for the Kingdom of Fife, similar to that of Dunadd hillfort in Argyll, inauguration site of the kings of Dál Riada in the seventh to eighth centuries. Dunino is a tantalising sacred place open to the elements, the seasons and the intrepid pilgrim.

ST ANDREWS CATHEDRAL

NO 514 166

Ruins of St Andrews Cathedral, from the West front.

The medieval town of St Andrews holds many treasures which can be visited in context with this book's theme of sacred sites and ancient places. First recorded in AD 767 as 'Cennrigmonaid', anglicised Kinrimond or Kilrymont, the earliest inhabitants were farmers and fishermen on what was perhaps a royal Pictish hunting estate. Early Christian times brought the arrival of holy men – monks and pilgrims along with some of the bones of St Andrew the Apostle. The legend that bones of St Andrew were brought here from Greece by St Regulus, or Rule, changed the name to St Andrews. St Rule's Tower survives, probably the small eleventh century cathedral, replaced by the great Norman and Gothic Cathedral of St Andrews built from 1160. This established St Andrews as a centre of medieval Scotland's religious, academic and political life. St Andrew became the patron saint of Scotland, and his feast day on the 30th of November is celebrated by Scots the world over as St Andrew's Day.

The magnificent St Andrews Sarcophagus, Pictish, late eighth century.

The best place to visit for stone relics is the Cathedral Museum where the famous St Andrews Sarcophagus is displayed. A late eighth century example of Pictish sculpture at its finest, the magnificently carved stone shrine is thought to be associated with the patronage of King Oengus, son of Fergus (died 761).

Many more carved stones dating from the eighth to seventeenth centuries are found in the Museum along with other treasures. The St Andrews coat of arms carries the motto, "While I breathe, I hope".

ISLE OF MAY

NT 655 996

The Isle of May floats in the Firth of Forth off the coast of the East Neuk like a great whale. High cliffs and low landing harbour make The May a natural nature reserve for seabirds, a conservation island especially attractive to puffins. There were 45,000 pairs of puffin on the island this spring, and these are the most fun of all little birds, with their red saucer-like beaks and black and white costume and sporty red feet.

The monastery on the Isle of May – watercolour by Marianna Lines.

The human history of the island goes back to the time of the Celtic monastic community who settled around the Forth. St Ethernán set up a monastery there in the eighth century, and some fine ruins remain from its last incarnation. During an archaeological excavation of the monastic cemetery a skeleton was found with a scallop shell in his mouth: a sign that he had been a pilgrim to Santiago de Compostela in Spain.

The Isle of May itself became a pilgrimage destination attracting Royalty and the Scottish nobility. Many of today's pilgrims come to see the nesting seabirds – guillemots, razor-bills, kittiwakes, shags which form veritable bird 'favelas' on the steep cliffs. The puffins of course are the stars of the show, along with the terns and the island's grey seals.

The May is a sacred site for monks and puffins, who seem to share a similar ancestry in some circles of Scottish lore.

Marianna Lines

The 'Angel Stacks' on the Isle of May.

Unknown photographer acknowledged

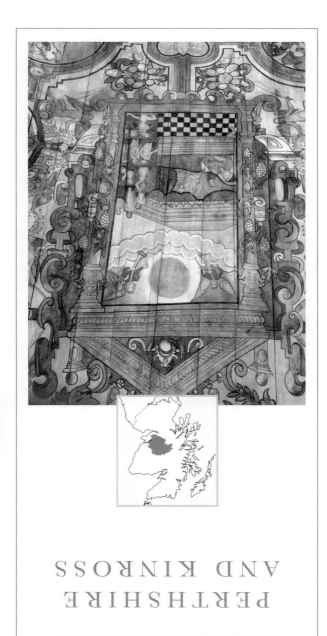

PERTHSHIRE
AND KINROSS

5

PERTHSHIRE AND KINROSS

PRINCIPAL SITES

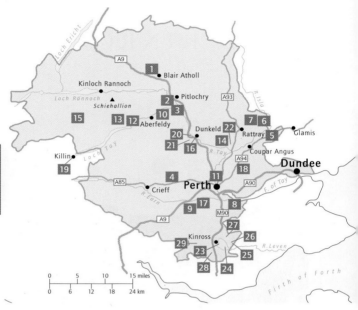

1	Diana's Grove, Blair Castle	**16**	Dunkeld Cathedral
2	Dunfallandy Stone	**17**	Forteviot
3	Logierait	**18**	Dunsinane, hillfort
4	Fowlis Wester	**19**	Killin Healing Stones
5	Meigle Stones	**20**	Niel Gow's Oak
6	Bruceton Stone	**21**	The Hermitage
7	Alyth	**22**	Cleaven Dyke
8	Abernethy Stone		**KINROSS**
9	Dupplin Cross, Dunning	**23**	Lochleven Castle
10	St Mary's, Grandtully	**24**	St Serf's Priory
11	Moot Hill, Scone Palace	**25**	Scotlandwell
12	Croft Moraig, stone circle	**26**	Portmoak Stone
13	Fortingall	**27**	Orwell, standing stones
14	Tower of Lethendy	**28**	Cleish Cross
15	Glen Lyon	**29**	Tullibole, witches' maze

Previous page: The ceiling of St Mary's Chapel, Grandtully. Photo: Marianna Lines.

PERTHSHIRE
AND KINROSS

PERTHSHIRE IS KNOWN AS *THE HEART OF SCOTLAND*, as it lies centrally just north of the twin cities hub, the Gateway to the Highlands.

Perthshire is full of great rivers such as the River Tay, and geologically forms the Highland boundary fault that is midway between Highland and Lowland Scotland. It is also Big Tree country, featuring some of the greatest and tallest trees in Scotland, and indeed some of the oldest. The Fortingall Yew is said to be older than the birth of Christianity.

Perthshire was once the ecclesiastical centre of Scotland with Scottish Kings enthroned at Scone on the Stone of Destiny. Perthshire is an ancient land of stones and stories. Perhaps the most endearing and idiosyncratic of all Pictish stones are found here in the Southern Kingdom of the Picts from the seventh to ninth centuries AD. Myth and legend weave the trees and stones into Perthshire's history. Wizards and fiddlers share the story.

DIANA'S GROVE

NN 8650 6644

Blair Castle and its spacious policies, or grounds, is the setting for a very special sacred site in Highland Perthshire. In autumn one can experience a sunset of colour over the Cairngorms as Blair Atholl is the stepping stone into the Highlands and the big road North. Peacocks often greet the visitor as they follow the path up to the grove of splendid giant trees. An eighteenth century well-aged fine sculpture of Diana the Goddess of the Hunt and her companion deer form the centerpiece of the wood known as Diana's Grove. The atmosphere is powerful; the trees are the crown of Scotland. Renowned for its exotic conifers, some notable trees in the Grove include the tallest Japanese Larch and red fir in Britain, the fifth tallest Douglas Fir in Britain and the tallest in Diana's Grove. The second Duke of Atholl started the project in the 1730s with the first European larches planted in the country.

Nearby can be found St Bride's Chapel, a jewel of medieval Scotland, with a sculptured stone inside the crypt and a large Neolithic period cup-marked stone in the chapel aisle. Cup-marks are round indentions in stone which date from the late Neolithic circa 2000 BC and have a ritual significance.

Diana, Goddess of the Hunt.

Marianna Lines

Unknown photographer acknowledged

St Bride's Chapel, Blair Castle.

PICTISH STONES

The Picts were a confederation of tribes who lived in eastern Scotland until around AD 850. Although converted to Christianity in the late sixth century, their iconography on the sculptured stones presents an earth religion view that leans toward preserving their unique original culture. The Pictish stones in Perthshire display a wide variety of symbolism and high expertise.

DUNFALLANDY STONE

NN 9462 5652

Serpents ring this sculptured stone with mother and father Pict prominently seated in their throne-like chairs holding their symbols like fans. The Dunfallandy Stone, sitting high on a mound with a chapel ruin in gentle Perthshire countryside near Logierait, is a stone of genealogy. This Class II Pictish cross-slab dates from the eighth century and shows a Celtic interlace cross on one face with nine side panels including a figure of Jonah, beasts and angels. The reverse side includes two crescent and V-rod symbols, two Pictish Beastie symbols (dolphin-like fantastic water creatures) two saintly figures and a central warrior on horseback and more related symbols below. Two elongated fish tail beasts holding a human head create the border of the sculptured stone.

Bob Henery, Pictish Arts Society

One of the finest Pictish sculptured stones, Dunfallandy has been recently considered as a Rosetta stone for Pictish symbology as the symbols are clearly associated with the figures and may indicate the tribal totems of the warrior who is commemorated here, and the parents in their chairs with their own clan symbols. Clach an t-Sagairt is its old Gaelic name, meaning *The Priest's Stone*.

LOGIERAIT

NN 9679 5201

The churchyard stone at the atmospheric Logierait stolid white kirk is found in an historic setting by the River Tay near Pitlochry. This eighth century Pictish symbol bearing stone, now broken halfway down, shows a dominant central serpent speared on a rod or lance horizontally in relief below a horse and rider. Not much of the rider survives in this whinstone fragment but a leg and his spear while the horse is a fine Pictish pony with a fringed saddle blanket and an intricate bridle. A simple cross on the reverse with standard knotwork infill has an interesting double spiral base as though it might be modelled from a metal cross worn by St Cedd himself of Logierait.

Perthshire & Kinross

The Logierait stone. Left: Rider spearing a serpent. Right: Reverse, Cross.

Inside the church lies another fine Pictish stone only discovered in 1989 in the company of this author and other members of the Pictish Arts Society one fine autumn day. It has a myriad of puzzling images and symbols, a double-sided stone with a cross on the main face.

Logierait churchyard is considered to be one of the most interesting in Highland Perthshire with the best collection of Adam and Eve eighteenth century gravestones in the country and three iron mortsafes, or 'grave-guards'. The famous Rob Roy MacGregor was imprisoned at Logierait prison in the village in 1717 for a single day when pursued by the Duke of Montrose, a rich catch for the Duke of Atholl but he escaped by getting his guards drunk.

FOWLIS WESTER

NN 9281 2408 (church)

The ceremonial complex of Fowlis Wester is invisible to the passing traveller, but upon turning in to the road leading up the hill to the village, the signs of the ancient world unfold. An earthen knoll surrounded by trees and a fragmented stone circle lie at the bottom of the hill. The thirteenth century parish church of St Bean holds two fine Pictish sculptured stones, while further up the hill beyond the village on open moorland lies a great standing stone, a ring cairn and a scattering of what was once a ceremonial place. It is said that when St Bean came here from Ireland he found standing stones associated with "dark Pagan practices" in the area and thus began preaching the Gospel here.

Fowlis Wester Pictish Stones

A Class II very fine sculptured stone once embedded in the wall of the church can be seen here. Jonah and the whale symbolism and the desert saints, St Anthony and St Paul enthroned in Pictish chairs surround the Celtic style relief cross in its four quarters infill. Two smaller clerical figures are shown beneath the left hand figure. These *Desert Fathers* representing the early monastic Celtic church of the third to fourth centuries, are depicted here with their stylised

All photos: Marianna Lines

Tree of Life symbol, the palm tree. Although damaged on the right side and unfinished, it remains one of the most delicately beautiful of the Pictish sculptured cross-slabs.

The tall Mercat/Market Cross, 10ft/3.15m is now re-housed inside the church with a replica on the original site (NN 9277 2404). Made of very worn old red sandstone, it is so weathered yet still possible to make out a great relief multi-panel hunting scene with a procession of seven monks leading an ox, complete with bell, and the Pictish crescent symbol below. A Celtic style cross on the front with projecting arms beyond the slab, unique of its kind, is a precursor of the full ringed free-standing Celtic cross style found in the Western Isles and on Iona. This is the only known example of its kind in Britain as well as being the tallest stone with Pictish symbolism in Scotland. An iron chain protrudes from the cross side indicating later re-use of the stone in a market square setting.

Both stones date from the late eighth to ninth century.

Ox, from Mercat Cross, Fowlis Wester.
Art by Marianna Lines.

MOOR OF ARDOCH, Neolithic Stones

NN 9242 2492

Half a mile above the village on open moorland can be found a scattered complex of Neolithic period stones considered to be two stone circles. One is collapsed on the eastern side with nine stones remaining, while the western circle retains a robust 6ft/1.8m tall standing stone and a cairn with later confusing additions, as the record tells. These two stone rings are said to be aligned east west on either equinoctial sunrise or winter moonrise with the standing stone as a foresight aligned to the mountain of Creag na Criche nearby.

Marianna Lines

Evening at the stone circle near Fowlis Wester.

* * *

MEIGLE STONES

NO 2872 4459

The village of Meigle, an unassuming wee place on the way to somewhere else, holds quite a few ancient secrets and stone treasures. The Meigle Sculptured Stones Museum in the heart of the village, a Historic Scotland site, is a superb homage to the Pictish culture and their enigmatic carved stones. There was a Pictish church at Meigle, an important centre of power in early medieval Scotland. Many of the stones have been found in the adjacent churchyard and around the village, often under people's steps and in their gardens. The Museum houses an impressive collection of twenty seven pieces of Pictish

sculpture from cross-slabs to recumbent gravestones, a hogback stone and rare architectural fragments, displaying an amazing artistic vigour and skill by these stone carvers. The warrior elite in their hunting life are commemorated in these stones, as kingship and the warrior tribal society was the hallmark of the Pictish kingdoms in the north and the south of the country before it ever became Scotland.

One particular stone known as the *Vanora Stone* dominates the museum collection at Meigle and has an Arthurian romance to it. This is Meigle no.2 which features a relief carved wheel head cross with interlaced beasts on the shaft, and a scene of Daniel in the lions' den on the reverse face.

Both photos: Niall M. Robertson

The Vanora Stone, Meigle.

Local folklore tells this is the gravestone of Vanora, or Guinevere, wife of King Arthur who was abducted by King Mordred and held captive on Berry Hill near Meigle, then later sentenced to death by wild beasts. A tragic event recorded in stone, either a memory of Arthurian Britain or a Biblical story for the Early Christian Picts?

The Meigle stones have a distinct style with an emphasis on aggressive biting beasts, diagonal key patterns on crosses, and a wide range of fantastic beasts from the medieval Bestiary and beyond. One can find a Persian winged deity, a kneeling camel, a centaur wielding axes trailing a Tree of Life, the Celtic God Cernunnos or a mermaid, and a manticore, a legendary creature with the body of a lion and a human head, a *man-eater* also featured in the Harry Potter stories today.

Meigle I: Detail of fantastic sea creature beasties.

Niall M. Robertson

Perthshire & Kinross

BRUCETON STONE

NO 2898 5039

The Bruceton Stone, found near Alyth, is a Class 1 Pictish Symbol Stone with large, clear, incised symbols of a horse-shoe/arch motif above a Pictish beastie. It is located in a field by the River Isla. An area rich in prehistory, there are several standing stones in the vicinity on either side of the Pictish stone site. The same pair of symbols is found on the Angus side of the border less than twenty miles away at Aberlemno on the Flemington Farm Pictish stone. There was a battle in this area associated with Robert the Bruce, hence the possible derivation of the name Bruceton.

ALYTH

NO 2432 4875

The second Pictish stone in Alyth is found in the church porch at the Alyth Parish Church, this being a Class II stone of the early eighth century. The undressed slab has incised carvings, a single double disc and Z-rod symbol on one face, on the other a simple Latin style cross with interlace and coiled rope spiral motifs between the arms. This slab is likely to have been created soon after the conversion of the Picts to Christianity. The spiral or serpentine shapes here are similar to other early carvings in both North Fife and Angus representing a coiled serpent, the ancient fertility symbol of the earth. A link between the old Pagan religion and the newly adopted Christian beliefs is recorded here on this stone. The Alyth stone must have started out as a standing stone, with the symbol added later, then the cross added perhaps another century on to show the development of religious ideas. This is one of the earliest surviving Pictish cross-slabs, and shows its long lineage in this form. The nearby Cistercian Abbey of Coupar Angus was a wealthy landowner in this area in the Middle Ages, adapting the religious traditions begun by the Picts to a more broad European base.

ABERNETHY STONE and Tower

NO 1899 1639

Abernethy, on the eastern fringe of Perthshire by the River Tay, is home to a round tower and a Pictish symbol stone in the churchyard of St Bride's Church there. The dedica-

Bob Heney, Pictish Arts Society

tion to St Bride is enough to entice the traveller as the Irish saint/goddess is also associated with the Nine Maidens, a leg-end that spins around Scotland and has links to the hillfort above the town. The unusual tower here is an Irish import, one of only two in Scotland (the other is in Brechin) which dates from the eleventh century. It is 72ft/22m tall and was used as a bell tower and safeguard refuge. Attached to the tower is a Pictish symbol stone which was found in a garden nearby in School Wynd. It depicts an anvil, a hammer, a decorated tuning fork symbol and the crescent and V-rod. The unusual combination of both Pictish and Irish with the tower, the symbol stone and St Bride/Bridget presents a puzzle for the visitor. There is a local museum beside the kirk to seek more information, where a number of Pictish stone fragments found around the area are displayed.

Such history attests to Abernethy's place as the episcopal centre of the Pictish church from the seventh century until the twelfth century.

DUPPLIN CROSS

NO 0190 1449

The great Dupplin Cross is a highly ornate free-standing Picto-Scottish monument dating from the late ninth century and has more important stories to tell than most other sculptured stones. It is now housed in St Serf's Church in the village of Dunning near Auchterarder, but once lived on the hillside above the village of Forteviot near the River Earn where an important Pictish centre of power was located (NO 0505 1896). A royal palace of the Pictish kings has recently been excavated in Forteviot.

The Cross on its previous site in the Earn Valley.

Warrior, Dupplin Cross.

This masterpiece in stone, 10ft/3m high in local sandstone is richly carved on all four faces depicting rows of warriors with round shields, a harper, manuscript-inspired zoomorphic creatures around the shaft of the cross, a central proud and moustached horseman with sword and an inscription that names the King Constantine (circa 789–820) for whom it was carved. St Serf's Church, one of Scotland's oldest

A side of the Cross showing dragon-like beast and harper. Etching by Marianna Lines.

complete parish churches includes a twelfth century tower where the Dupplin now stands. The legendary founder, St Serf, who was a real saint, slew a dragon on this very spot. Many dragon stories are connected with Pictish stones so this one fits well. This is an extremely rare cross, the only complete example of its kind to survive in Pictish territory.

ST MARY'S CHAPEL, Grandtully

NN 8870 5062

St Mary's Chapel in its landscape.

Marianna Lines

St Mary's is a whitewashed sixteenth century stone church in a lovely setting south of the River Tay on farmland, rather curious in its somewhat hidden location behind a farm. Its outstanding feature is the painted wooden ceiling and walls combining Biblical with heraldic motifs in a folk art style. The chapel was built to serve the hamlet of Pitcairn near the walls of Grandtully Castle northeast of Aberfeldy. It was used as a cattle byre when it fell into disuse. What a view these favoured cattle would have had. Today it is a rare discovery for the passing traveller.

MOOT HILL, Scone Palace

NO 1144 2664

One cannot visit the stunningly picturesque region of Perthshire without visiting Scone, where the Stone of Destiny originated with the famous Stone of Scone inauguration stone. Although the stone itself, which may date back to Pictish times with ancient kingship lineage, now resides under lock and key in the nation's capital at Edinburgh Castle, it carries a history of the nation in stone. It was kept at Westminster Abbey in the Inauguration Chair until recently. The site of the Royal inauguration can still be seen at Moot Hill in the grounds of Scone Palace outside Perth where festive and regal peacocks

parade. Like Tara in Ireland, Scone was a traditional coronation site since the thirteenth century. Coronation sites around
Scotland still exist, from the hillfort of Dunadd in the West
with its footprint stone to Dunino Den in Fife where a similar
king-making footprint stone can be found. Scone is mentioned
in Shakespeare's play *Macbeth*, striking an iconic point in
history as well as the world of theatre. Also known as Boot Hill,
this hill became a symbolic sacred spot by the ninth century as
the ceremonial mount site and a place for royal assembly,
fulfilling the role of a folk-moot or gathering place. The first
king of Scotland Kenneth MacAlpine, son of Alpin, circa 848,
was the first King from the Gaels to assume the Kingdom of
Scone as his dynastic seat. Today a Victorian chapel crowns
the moot hill and a replica of the Stone of Destiny lies within.

CRANNOG, LOCH TAY

NN 7230 4429 crannog site

Val Vannet, geograph.org.uk

The ancient loch dwelling island on Loch Tay known as a *crannog*
is at least 2,500 years old and is one of eighteen crannogs
discovered on this magical Highland loch by Kenmore. The
Scottish Crannog Centre (NN 7703 4486) has made a unique
reconstruction of this Iron Age defensive homestead along with
a fine museum and outdoor craft area to bring the crannog to
life again. The Oakbank Crannog is a peaked thatched round
house using all local and authentic materials.

CROFT MORAIG STONE CIRCLE

NN 7975 4726

On the way to Kenmore and the Crannog on Loch Tay is the
stone circle of Croft Moraig. Developed in three phases, the
site began with fourteen wooden posts in a horseshoe shape
before they were later replaced by eight stones. Finally a circle
of twelve stones with a 39.3ft/12m diameter was set around

the horseshoe. In the southwest area of the banked enclosure lies a 6.5ft/2m long stone with over twenty cup-marks on it said to be aligned with the southern moonset. Cup-marks are unexplained Neolithic cup-shaped indents in stone which have a myriad of hypothetical ritual uses, marking out star alignments or map quests for instance. Two outlying stones form an entrance to the circle with further equinoctial alignments for sunrise.

FORTINGALL

NN 7417 4702 yew tree
NN 7406 4693 Carn na Marbh

The Clachan of Fortingall stands at the head of Glen Lyon in western Perthshire, shrouded in history and famous for its great Yew Tree. Is is reputedly 5,000 years old and the 'most ancient tree in the UK if not the oldest living thing on earth'. History and legends all notch this up as a sacred place not to be missed.

The Yew Tree of Fortingall in its protective enclosure.

Fothergill, its ancient name, has links with Pontius Pilate. According to legend this was the birthplace of Pontius Pilate who was born well before the Roman conquest. Pilate's

Scottish origins may have a basis in fact. After the Romans' first incursion into Britain, Caesar Augustus dispatched envoys to establish diplomatic relations with British chieftains who included Metellanus the Caledonian chieftain whose stronghold was at the head of Glen Lyon. A Roman delegate fathered a child with one of the Caledonian tribe, and when he returned to Rome he brought the child up as Pontius Pilate. The rest of his story can be found in the Bible.

The great Yew can be found in a corner of the churchyard, not the most healthy looking old tree, protected by a walled enclosure. An Iron Age cult centre may have grown up around this tree as their focus.

Carn na Marbh, or Cairn of the Dead is also part of the ancient Fortingall story. This Bronze Age tumulus was re-used as a burial site in the fourteenth century for plague victims. The Plague Stone, originally a Neolithic standing stone, crowns the mound. Local legend tells this site was the focus of ancient Samhain festivals with bonfires built on top and youth competitions held to leap the embers (usually associated with Beltane rituals). These celebrations carried on into the early twentieth century.

The whole area around Fortingall is famed for its monuments of the Neolithic period circa 2000 BC: standing stones, stone circles, a recumbent circle, a cup-marked stone, burial mounds and crop markings of a vallum, an Early Christian monastic enclosure. Fragments of Pictish cross-slabs and an iron Celtic hand bell are also found in the church. Thatched cottages are seen throughout the village.

Legend tells that the Yew marks the actual geographic centre of Scotland, its *axis mundi*, but this is also identified as being at Schiehallion, the holy mountain which is found five miles north of Fortingall. The sacred yew and the mountains are part of the same concept, however, as John Michell writes in his book *At the Centre of the World* (1994).

> "Every Celtic community, tribe and national federation of tribes had its sacred assembly place of law of justice. These were centrally placed at the mid-point of their territories... the first thing that was needed by those who created sacred landscapes was to locate the country's main axis, the preferably north-south line between its two extremities, passing through the centre. It corresponded to the world-tree, the shaman's pole by which he ascends to the world of spirits, and all other symbols of the universal axis... Guarding and overlooking the omphalos, generally to the north of it in the direction from which disruptive forces are traditionally supposed to emanate, is found a lone, conical mountain. Its mythological prototype is the mountain at the centre of the world. The chief god of the pantheon resides there, presiding awesomely over the rituals in his sanctuary below."

SCHIEHALLION

NN 714 548

The Sacred Mountain, visited by 2,000 people a year, is the epicentre of Scotland. Some call it 'Scotland's Holy Land'. The legend tells this is the Fairy Hill of the Caledonians for a secret door leads beneath to fairyland itself. There is also a stone circle on the north side of the east ridge. The pyramidal triangle shape of Shiehallion or *hill of the faeries* can be seen from many distant views around Perthshire and beyond. It could even relate to a theory about Scotland's origin myth link with Egypt.

'Andrew2606', Wikimedia Commons

Schiehallion, the Sacred Mountain, the Mountain of the Fairy Folk, with its characteristic symmetry, viewed across the River Tay.

Schiehallion in its classic pyramid form also provides a handy link to the mythological foundation myth of Scotland. Scota was thought to be the Egyptian 'Queen of the Scots' and daughter of an Egyptian Pharoah to whom the Gaels traced their ancestry, from whence the name 'Scoti' derived and thus the name of Scotland. The legend of Scota first appeared in twelfth century literature as an attempt to create a distinct foundation myth for Scotland: Scota the Egyptian princess married Gaythelos, an expelled Greek prince. The two set off across the sea on a long voyage and found Scotland around 1500 BC. An English creation myth popular in the medieval period suggested they descended from the Trojans, also recorded in the Irish Annals claiming another version of the story.

Scota was also believed to have brought the Stone of Destiny with her, which was in fact Jacob's pillow originally, the stone he rested his head on when he slept at Bethel and saw the angels in his dream. Thus the Stone of Destiny was placed under the throne of Scotland, the legend requiring every new monarch to be crowned while sitting upon it.

Perthshire & Kinross

So to return to Schiehallion, the Sacred Mountain, the sacred geometry of the henge monuments of Britain has influenced the later conical pyramids of Egypt and thus mythically reinforces this foundation myth linking Scota with Egypt. This 'World Tree' or 'omphalos' belief - that this mountain is the centre of the world (omphalos = navel) – can be applied also to Berwick Law, another volcanic plug in the Lothians of Scotland.

TOWER OF LETHENDY

NO 1405 4169

The fairytale Tower of Lethendy near Blairgowrie is a classic stone L-plan tower, three storeys and a garret, of late sixteenth century date with modern alterations. Secreted in the spacious round stair are two carved stones re-used as lintels. One of these, a fine tenth century Picto-Scottish slab, displays the most intriguing relief carved images of a series of musicians, an angel, clerics and a dog. The instruments on this stone depict an early form of Scottish bagpipe, drum and flute. It originally stood in a field nearby, and as is often the case, was simply appropriated for tower repairs to the staircase around 1678. The second re-discovered stone is a fragment of a sixteenth century medieval grave-slab with the effigy of a headless knight. Although the tower is private, permission may be obtained to view the stones.

GLEN LYON

NN58794752 Innerwick church

Glen Lyon is poetically called Scotland's loveliest, loneliest and longest glen. Packed with history from the earliest times, it is a destination for the most intrepid pilgrim traveller. The Glen Lyon 'horseshoe' circuit of four Munro hills of over 3000ft/914m high also includes ancient sites. St Adamnan's Cross (St Adomnan), found near a road embankment near Camusvrachan, is a leaning stone with a cross on both faces. This famous Abbot of Iona (AD 679–704) and the biographer of St Columba is thought to have visited Glen Lyon many times en route from Iona to the Pictish lands of Atholl, so it would be fitting for the cross to be dedicated to him. However, this is more likely to be a Bronze Age standing stone that became Christianised a thousand years later with the coming of the saint.

At Glenlyon Church in Innerwick there is also St Adomnan's Bell, an early Celtic iron hand bell like a number of others revered and preserved in Scotland. Small ring forts and other sites of antiquity can be found throughout this long glen which leads from an adventurous single track road to the west over the flank of Ben Lawers by Loch Tay. A special world is Glen Lyon, carrying both Early Christian and clan history in its aura. This is the home of John Campbell of Glen Lyon who was responsible for the Glen Coe massacre. It is also the legendary home of the Celtic hero Finn McCool, Fionn mac Cumhaill in Gaelic, who lived and died here and spun many a yarn, not just from the local sheep.

TIGH NAM BODACH, Glen Lyon

NN 3805 4271

There is an ancient shrine deep within Glen Cailleach, the Crooked Glen of the Stones, remote and only accessible by hill-walking, known as Tigh nam Bodach. Made up of a collection of bell-shaped river stones in a rough built shelter, thatched in the wider sense of turf covered, this is considered to be the oldest uninterrupted pagan ritual site in Britain, if not Europe. Three principal stones represent the Cailleach, the old woman, the Bodach, the old man, and their daughter, Nighean. For centuries this 'family of stones' have been given ritual care, being taken out to view every spring at Beltane and put away every winter at Samhain. These Celtic fire festivals also link with the annual migrations of Highland cattle to the shielings. This unbroken connection to the Celtic ancestors is a treasured part of Glen Lyon's heritage and fiercely protected. Nearby Loch Tay was formed by the Cailleach when she left the lid off a magical spring well, so local legend says.

Glen Lyon History Society

Tigh nam Bodach, a Pagan shrine. A relic of pre-Christian folk beliefs, high up in the hills north of Loch Lyon.

* * *

DUNKELD

NO 0240 4259

Dunkeld Cathedral houses several fine carved stones dating from the Pictish era circa eighth century. Dunkeld was the ecclesiastical centre of the united Kingdom of the Picts and Scots. As relics of St Columba were brought to Dunkeld by the Scottish King Kenneth

The Apostles Stone.

mac Alpin, so it took on the sacred mantle of Iona. A Celtic hand bell, several carved stones and sacred trees in Birnam wood all link to the past here. The Apostles Stone is a great sculptured slab within the Chapter House of the Cathedral which depicts the Biblical miracle of the loaves and fishes. Heavily dense and eroded images in relief are dated to the late Picto-Scottish period, circa tenth century, with Irish influence. A second simple cross-slab is also there, an Early Christian cross associated with Iona.

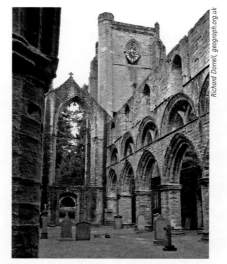

Dunkeld Cathedral – The roofless 15th century nave and later tower.

In the Bell Tower at the west end of the Cathedral there is a fine fragment of a Pictish stone circa seventh century with a horseman and his drinking horn, the earliest carving at Dunkeld. Other stone fragments and beautiful rare wall paintings are seen on the ceiling.

Perthshire & Kinross

Pictish rider with drinking horn.

In the woods of Birnam by the River Tay can be found the great Birnam Oak celebrated in Shakespeare's *Macbeth*. The oak and its neighbour the Birnam Sycamore are believed to be the sole survivors of the great forest on the Tay once known as Birnam Wood, and are at least 300 years old. Both trees are listed in the 100 Scottish Heritage Trees.

FORTEVIOT

NO 052175

The seat of secular power, the Royal centre of the Pictish Kingdom, is found at Forteviot, south of Dunkeld in the Earn Valley. Within the porch of the church lie Pictish stone fragments; nearby on the Earn once stood the great Dupplin Cross now relocated to Dunning and only recently a Bronze Age tomb of great significance has been found. Part of an ongoing excavation programme by the Strathearn Environs and Royal Forteviot project, this burial chamber produced a massive four ton slab capstone over the cist with carvings of axes and weapons on it similar to those found at Kilmartin in Argyll. Grave goods including a bronze and gold dagger and skeletal remains were found on a bed of white quartz pebbles and a woven lattice of birch bark, all high ritual of that early period, circa 2100 BC.

The massive stone carved arch from the ninth century Pictish Palace at Forteviot is now displayed in the Museum of Scotland in Edinburgh.

The fields around the modern village contain one of the largest concentrations of prehistoric ritual monuments identified in Britain. Built of earth and timber, these may be invisible now but they are part of the deeper hidden history of Scotland.

Marianna Lines

Perthshire
& Kinross

DUNSINANE HILLFORT

NO 2139 3167

Dunsinane is the most charismatic hillfort in Perthshire, located near to Kirkton of Collace in wooded countryside. It is featured in Shakespeare's *Macbeth* where he writes, "Macbeth shall never vanquished be, until Great Birnam wood to high Dunsinane hill shall come against him." The woods of Birnam can be seen to the north from the top of the hill. It has been called Macbeth's Castle since the sixteenth century. According to the Royal Commission report of Ancient Monuments (RCAHMS) the fort on Dunsinane Hill is the most spectacular of the fortifications in the area commanding a wide sweep of country across the lower end of Strathmore. The association of its name with Macbeth has led to a series of antiquarian excavations that now disfigure the interior. However, at the core crowning the summit of the hill there is a massively defended citadel which almost certainly occupies the site of an earlier fort. There are also traces of a large outer enclosure.

The remains of two forts occupy the summit and lower slopes of Dunsinane Hill, overlooked on the northeast by Black Hill. This is believed to be the site of a battle where Malcolm Canmore defeated Macbeth in 1054, although history tells a different outcome: Macbeth was finally defeated and killed by Canmore in 1057 at Lumphannan in Aberdeenshire. A slice of personal human history brings the story to life: a small bronze ring with a serpent design was found in 1857 at the gateway to the fort.

The Author at the stone circle by Dunsinane Hill.

A stone circle can be found at the western end of the hill in a somewhat rough state lost in the undergrowth, while two cup-marked boulders are visible on the southwest side of the fort. Macbeth's Well is also located somewhere around the hill and is said to still flow with sweet water from a natural spring. The hill rises steeply and grandly from the flat plain below. Dunsinane, part of the Sidlaw range in Perthshire, means 'hill of ants' in Gaelic.

KILLIN HEALING STONES

NN 5709 3249 Old Mill

St Fillan of Glen Dochart, the seventh century Celtic saint deeply associated with Perthshire, had his own special relics which are known today as the Killin Healing Stones. They are preserved in the Old Mill by the Falls of Dochart in Killin at the Breadalbane Folklore Centre. The ancient ceremony of the bedding of St Fillan's healing stones still takes place every year on Christmas Eve. The ritual, which dates back to the eighth century, consists of renewing and refreshing the

Newly discovered stone at Killin.

bed of river wrack, straw and twigs on which the eight stones rest. The stones are the only relics of St Fillan to be preserved on the site of his ministry and are used to cure various afflictions with each river-washed stone relating to the part of the body it is treating. In fact, the stones resemble the organs they are meant to heal: eyes, kidney, liver, lungs, heart. The stones are still used for healing purposes.

The Falls of Dochart, Killin.

St Fillan, 'little wolf', was a follower of St Columba and came to Killin around the end of the seventh century to preach and heal. The cult of St Fillan served a function far beyond the significance of the saint himself.

Marianna Lines

Niall M. Robertson

A sacred relic of the saint was carried into battle with Robert the Bruce and helped him to win the Battle of Bannockburn. Legend tells that the 'mayne' or arm bone from St Fillan was enclosed in a silver reliquary or casket, and King Robert the Bruce requested it to be brought to the Bannockburn battle site. The Dewar or hereditary keeper of the relic left the bone behind for safekeeping and brought only the reliquary. As they knelt in prayer on the eve of Bannockburn battle a noise came from the reliquary, the door opened and the bone fell to the floor. The Bruce won the battle the next day and he established a monastery to thank St Fillan for the victory. Strangely enough, a medieval carved stone was recently found near Strathfillan with the carving of an arm and a cross on it, which links with the story that St Fillan possessed a luminous glow from his left arm which he used to study and write scriptures in the dark. There are many more sacred relics associated with this mysterious and powerful saint.

Through his association with King Robert the Bruce and the Battle of Bannockburn, Fillan united the two great power centres of Scotland, the Picts and the Scots, thus helping toward the establishment of the nation. There are two different saints named Fillan of two separate periods of Early Christianity and five relics of the Killin Saint Fillan besides the resident healing stones. Two of these take pride of place in the Museum of Scotland in Edinburgh: the bell and the Quigrich, or crosier.

NIEL GOW'S OAK

NO 0123 4243

This ancient oak tree, a sessile oak, is considered to be the most popular tree in Europe and was nominated for an award on that basis. Located near Inver by Dunkeld on the south bank of the River Tay, the beautiful oak takes its name from one of Scotland's most famous fiddlers, Niel Gow (1727–1897) who lived nearby. He played and composed many of Scotland's best loved Strathspeys and reels while sitting under this tree. The Fourth Duke of Atholl who lived across the river at Blair Castle heard the fiddle music of Niel Gow carried by the currents and was a great fan of the musician providing much patronage on his behalf. Pilgrimages are made to visit the 'Fiddle Tree', especially by musicians. Recently a new bench was installed beneath the tree with the inscription, "I'll sit beneath the fiddle tree, with the ghost of Niel Gow next to me", song lines from another famous Scottish musician Michael Marra, singer-songwriter of Dundee who died in 2012. For the weary traveller, the oak is a favourite spot to sit as the great composer did and watch the world go by and the salmon swim.

THE HERMITAGE

NO 0086 4177 Ossian's Hall

Following the path along the River Tay, the longest river in Scotland, away from the Great Oak takes the mystic traveller into another world of trees and Gothic romance. Craigvinean Forest is composed of giant Douglas firs and larches, a fairy castle folly at a stunning viewpoint over the Tay which descends into the Hermitage, an ornamental Victorian woodland garden landscape contemporary with the fiddler himself. There the Hermit's Cave, Ossian's Cave and Ossian's Hall of Mirrors, overlooking the Black Linn Waterfall, brings one face to face with romantic Celtic legend. A classic stone bridge leads over the River Braan to Britain's tallest tree, a whopping 213ft/65m tall Douglas fir planted circa 1860 and growing.

Ossian is a favourite Scottish legend, a blind bard believed to be the narrator/author of a cycle of epic poems not unlike the *Icelandic Sagas* which were published by the Scottish poet James Macpherson circa 1760. This highly romantic Scots Gaelic oral folklore translated from ancient sources about Oisin son of Fionn mac Cumhaill, or Finn McCool in English, the legendary bard of Irish myth was ultimately decried as a fake. Ossian became as un-authentically Scottish in literature as the mythical town of Brigadoon.

Linking diverse literary strands with the Dunkeld area also includes the ever popular and totally authentic Beatrix Potter who lived in the area for some time. Braan, a real river of great beauty, is named after Finn McCool's dog.

CLEAVEN DYKE

NO 155 409 southeast to NO 172 399

This sacred ritual site near Blairgowrie belongs to the Neolithic period and dates from around 3500 BC. Comprising a bank with ditches 1.5 miles/2.4km long, the dyke was probably constructed over a long period as both a burial site and (more prominently) a ceremonial site. Cleaven Dyke was thought to be a Roman defensive structure until excavation revealed that it was actually a Neolithic *cursus*, a ceremonial earthwork, which must have been one of the largest and most labour intensive monuments in Scotland at the time. The dyke runs for 1.5 miles/ 2.4km through an area that is now planted by coniferous forestry, about 6.5ft/2m high and 32.8ft/10m wide in the best-preserved sections. The dyke also incorporates a central mound.

The purpose of cursuses is open to debate: they can be seen as ritual monuments, processional route ways with deep significance to their builders. Cursuses are more associated with Southern England than with Scotland. There is no other earthwork exactly like it but it may be compared with the *vallum* parallel to Hadrian's Wall to the south. The dyke is not too easy to see from the ground today being enveloped in forestry, perhaps better from aerial views, but of great historical significance.

KEILLOR STONE

NO 2733 3976

Marianna Lines

Left: The original stone. Right: Natural dye art by Marianna Lines.

Keillor, a Pictish sculptured Class I stone shows symbols of a wolf, the double-disc & Z-rod and mirror and comb. The symbols are so worn now that some consider the animal figure to be a bear/boar and the comb is not visible. The stone crowns a prehistoric mound in farmland near Newtyle in the Sidlaws.

KETTINS STONE

NO 2378 3903

The Kettins stone has had a rough treatment over the centuries, having been used as a foot-bridge across the burn; its sculptured face is eroded beyond much recognition. This Class III eighth century Pictish stone bears an ornate interlaced cross in relief with panels of intriguing figures, which are shown in the artwork created here by Marianna Lines. To the right of the cross are a winged griffin, a trio of robed bird-headed priest figures, and the ouroboros image of a pair of beasts biting their tails. The stone is in the churchyard at Kettins Kirk near Meigle.

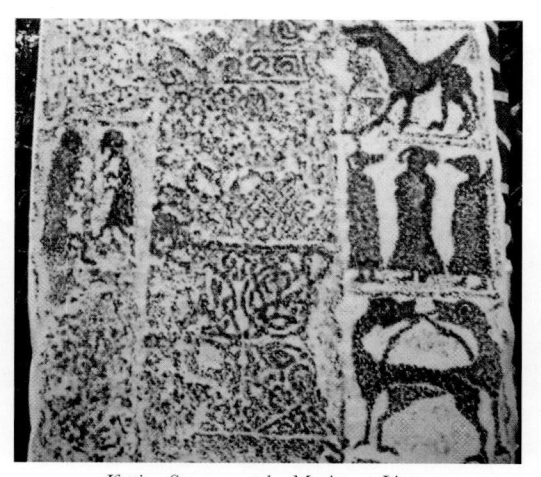

Kettins Stone – art by Marianna Lines.

KINROSS

Kinross-shire is a small county that borders Perthshire to the north, Fife to the east and south and Clackmannanshire to the west. Loch Leven dominates the area, with its famous castle on the loch, the internationally important RSPB nature reserve at Vane Farm, and many sites of antiquity. This wide basin is bounded to the north by the Ochil Hills, with the Lomonds and Bishop Hill to the east and Benarty and the Cleish Hills to the south.

The Loch Leven heritage trail includes Castle Island where Lochleven Castle is located, St Serf's Island with its Priory, the historic well at Scotlandwell and the Orwell Standing Stones near Milnathort. A long history of settlement in the area with a good dose of great people is found here.

Burns enthusiasts may be intrigued to know that the great-nephew of the poet Robert Burns belonged to Kinross. Robert Burns-Begg (1833–1900) was a local historian and sheriff clerk and considered a fine gentleman.

LOCHLEVEN CASTLE

NO 137 017

The island stronghold of Lochleven has a colourful history. Forever associated with Mary Queen of Scots, she was held prisoner here in 1567–8 before her famous escape. Sir William Douglas, the Earl of Morton, was her jailer, and it was here that she was compelled to abdicate in favour of her young son

James VI and before escaping to exile in England. One of the oldest stone castles in Scotland, the curtain wall and tower house date from the early 1300s.

Marianna Lines

The island is a short boat trip from Kinross on the shores of Loch Leven where great crested grebes are plentiful and the wildlife is exceptional. The loch is a haven for thousands of breeding and wintering birds such as pink-footed and greylag geese, and many species of duck.

Marianna Lines

Always a royal stronghold, Castle Island was once said to be the site of a sixth century Pictish fort. The tower-house is the nucleus of the castle and dates from the fourteenth century, one of the earliest and best-preserved in Scotland. King Robert the Bruce first used it as a state prison in 1316 when he confined John of Lorne on the island, only one of the kings of Scotland who used it as a prison. The present tranquil atmosphere on the island is enhanced by pheasants and heron.

ST SERF'S PRIORY

NO 1615 0025

St Serf's Island on Loch Leven serves today as a landing platform for over-wintering geese, but in medieval times it was home to a small priory of Augustinian canons who settled on the site of an earlier Celtic monastery around 1150. Part of the simple early chapel still stands.

St Serf or Servanus (meaning servant) was one of the chief saints of Fife and a popular Scottish saint. The Priory was dedicated to him, who was also called St Moak, the Gaelic version of Serf, which gives its name to the parish of Portmoak. First settled by Culdee monks of this early Celtic community, they established a monastery around the eighth century on the tiny island. Later the Priory became a centre of learning where Andrew Wyntoun, the Prior of St Serf's, wrote his *Orygynale Cronykil*, claimed to be the first book on the history of Scotland. It is one of the only manuscripts composed in Scots verse before the seventeenth century and covers Scottish history from the beginning until the accession of King James I in 1406. Most notably, this history mentions Macbeth and the three witches, a reference later embellished by Shakespeare.

SCOTLANDWELL

NO 1847 0165

Marioma Lines

The healing well of Scotlandwell has been a pilgrimage site since early times. Its Latin name *Fons Scotiae* means the 'well of Scotland'. Pilgrims en route to St Andrews stopped here to drink

Left: Scotlandwell today. Below: Early photo of the well, built in 1858.

the water and take the cures administered by the Red Friars who maintained a hospital close by. The picturesque well seen today is part of a nineteenth century enhancement scheme, with its gabled roof and iron grille. The water runs continuously off the slopes of Bishop Hill above the village and bubbles up through sand, an artesian well which had a great reputation for its healing powers.

King Robert the Bruce is said to have visited this medieval spa for treatment. Legend has it that he was cured of leprosy by drinking the waters. Crystal clear, the water is still collected for drinking and healing by people who come from far and near throughout the year. Another watering hole is the Well Country Inn over the road in the village of Scotlandwell where a key is kept for visiting the Victorian Wash House beside the well.

PORTMOAK STONE

NO 1833 0194 parish church

The Parish church of Portmoak has an elegant Celtic cross-slab dating from the ninth century. This was found on the site of the original parish church which once stood on the shores of the Loch at Portmoak Farm (NO 1735 0087) in 1976. Decorated with a weathered interlaced cross in relief, the stone is preserved in an alcove in the church. The old chapel site is now the local gliding club.

Marianna Lines

ORWELL STANDING STONES

NO 1494 0432

Ewen Rennie, geograph.org.uk

The pair of Orwell Stones looking east.

This pair of prehistoric monoliths on Orwell Farm mark the site of cremation deposits dating back to around 2300 BC. The stones may have been a focus for the burials. They stand in cultivated fields north of the A911 between Kinnesswood and Milnathort. Made of whinstone, the two stones frame the skyline and Bishop Hill behind: the western stone stands 7.5ft/2.3m tall, the eastern stone at 9.6ft/2.9m.

CLEISH CROSS

NT 0945 9809

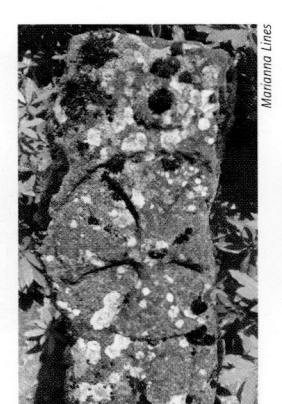

Marianna Lines

A rare fragment of a free-standing cross is mounted in a steel frame in the churchyard at Cleish. The centre boss of a twelfth century cross, it shows the common motif of a cross-of-arcs. A variation on this Celtic design known as the marigold cross appears on the Skeith Stone in Fife and in caves in the Western Isles. The place name of Cleish is derived from the Scots Gaelic *clais* meaning furrow or trench.

The plain medieval stone font is also on display in the churchyard.

TULLIBOLE WITCHES' MAZE

NO 052 005

Marianna Lines

23-4-1662

Robert Wilson

Bessie Neil

Margaret Lister

Agnes Brugh

Janet Paton

A contemporary memorial to the witches of Kinross might be designated as a sacred site in its evolution and installation in the grounds of Tullibole Castle at Crook of Devon. Dedicated to the eleven victims of the Crook of Devon witch trials in 1662, the recently completed memorial is a circle 36yds/33m wide consisting of 2000 beech tree saplings which form a maze of beech hedges. At the centre of the labyrinth is an elaborate sculptured sandstone pillar with the names of the witches etched on it.

Lord Moncrieff who created the memorial and is the laird of the castle said the memorial is intended to remind people to think rationally; to condemn the ignorant and superstitious beliefs of the past as well as those in modern day society. The pentagonal pillar was designed and sculptured by Gillian Forbes of Path of Condie. Its shape represents the five witch trials, displaying 'good' words in the inner ring of the maze to protect the pillar and 'bad' words in the dead ends of the maze.

Perthshire
& Kinross

Marianna Lines

Peacock in the grounds of Tullibole Castle.

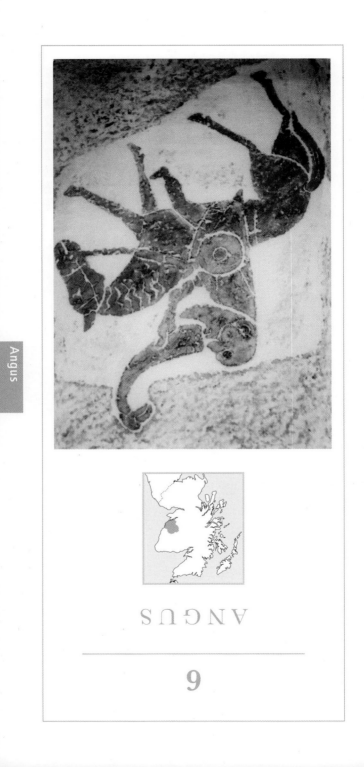

ANGUS

9

ANGUS

PRINCIPAL SITES

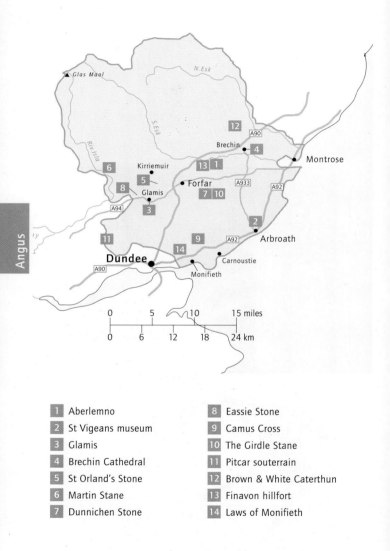

1	Aberlemno	**8**	Eassie Stone
2	St Vigeans museum	**9**	Camus Cross
3	Glamis	**10**	The Girdle Stane
4	Brechin Cathedral	**11**	Pitcar souterrain
5	St Orland's Stone	**12**	Brown & White Caterthun
6	Martin Stane	**13**	Finavon hillfort
7	Dunnichen Stone	**14**	Laws of Monifieth

*Previous page: 'The Drunken Pict', from the Bullion Stone, Invergowrie.
Art by Marianna Lines.*

A N G U S

THE *'HEARTLAND OF THE PICTS'* might be the best epithet for Angus, the area which was the Pictish Kingdom to the south of the Grampians in the first millennium AD. Angus is located in eastern Scotland where intensive agricultural improvement has changed the ancient landscape from the days of the Picts. What remains are hillforts, underground souterrains and many Pictish sculptured stones – testament to the power, strength and importance of the Pictish Nation at this pivotal point in the true beginning of Scotland's history. The Aberlemno stones, north of Dundee, are a trio of perhaps the finest sculpture produced that represent over two centuries of development. Other collections of Pictish monuments are found at St Vigeans by Arbroath, The Meffan in Forfar and Pictavia by Brechin.

Aonghas in Scottish Gaelic was formerly identified as the kingdom of *Circinn*, encompassing Angus and the Mearns. This is one of the seven kingdoms of the Picts, with *Fib* (Fife) to the south and *Fotla* (Atholl/Perthshire) to the west, and *Ce* to the North (Aberdeenshire).

Most significant is that Angus plays a major role in the birthplace of the nation. In 1320 the Declaration of Arbroath was given at Arbroath Abbey to proclaim Scotland's independence from England. A quote from the Declaration reads,

"It is in truth not for glory, nor riches, nor honours that we are fighting but for freedom – for that alone, which no honest man gives up but with life itself."

Kirriemuir in Angus is the birthplace of J.M. Barrie, the creator of *Peter Pan*, that famous children's story that lives forever in nurseries around the world.

* * *

ABERLEMNO

NO 5227 5591 to NO 5224 5587 roadside
NO 5224 5555 churchyard

Aberlemno, a dispersed farming parish north of Forfar, has an important collection of Pictish monuments which range from early Class I through to Class II, both on the roadside and in the churchyard of the parish church. The earliest stone bears three incised Pictish symbols from the seventh century period: serpent, double disc and Z-rod, mirror and comb. The serpent is a powerful work of sculpture as it seems to dance upward on the stone in a vertical position, no Z-rod to hold it down. The double disc operates like a gateway into the two worlds of the Picts, the earth realm and the invisible realm of the otherworld. The back of the stone has a number of Neolithic cup-marks, indicating a re-use of an ancestor stone.

The next stone in line on the roadside is a faintly marked stone with two partial circles, possibly erased symbols. The third stone is a cross-slab of magnificent expertise with a great presence. An imposing ringed cross on the front stands out in true relief sculpture, perhaps once adorned with precious stones in the indented socket shapes of the cross arms. A pair of weeping angels holding books are on either side of the shaft with pairs of animals below the key pattern design.

Both photos: David McGovern, Pictish Arts Society

The reverse is a great statement of Pictish power: large symbols shout from the top of the stone, a crescent and V-rod and a double disc and Z-rod, both beautifully sculptured with much detail of key pattern and spiral infill, *see right*. A lower panel includes a spirited hunting scene with horsemen and trumpeters similar to the great Hilton of Cadboll from the North. The long hunting horns do not seem to be related to the famous Carynx bronze horn but they are evocative of it. The Carynx, a long bronze horn with a boar's head, orchestrated Pictish battles and was common to the Celts all over Iron

Age Europe. The only example in the British Isles was found in Scotland in Deskford, Banffshire, a long horn with a wild boar head, its image depicted on the Gundestrup Cauldron in Copenhagen.

The third panel at the bottom shows a centaur, half-human half-horse figure carrying a tree of life wand next to a scene of David in the Lion's Den rending the jaws of the lion. The range of statements on this stone, from secular to religious, bring an awesome feeling of the sacred to this double-sided stone.

David McGovern, Pictish Arts Society

Aberlemno Churchyard stone is the most famous of all with its fine interlaced cross flanked by imaginary animals, notably the elegant paired 'hippocamp' seahorse motif*. The battle scene recorded on the back of the cross is believed to represent the Battle of Dunnichen in AD 685 won by the victorious Picts over the Angles of Bernicia, the Anglo Saxon kingdom of Northumbria.

Two major symbols appear at the top of the battle scene, the gateway/notched rectangle with Z-rod and the cauldron or triple disc. Much can be told, imagined and remembered from gazing upon this truly magical Pictish sculptured cross-slab, a symphony in stone.

* see box story on the Pictish Seahorse at the end of this chapter.

ST. VIGEANS

NO 6383 4294

A small museum housed in a row of cottages at St Vigeans below the church presents a stunning collection of carved Pictish stones that offers many insights into the religious, secular and mythological life of the Picts. The steep knoll crowned by the church is the site where the stones were found together with an interesting graveyard of later period stones. The Pictish stones date from the eighth to tenth century with cross-slabs and mythical beasts, inscription stones and recumbent carved tombstones, numbering over thirty.

The great number of monuments implies there was a major monastery on the site from the earliest times; the church was dedicated to the seventh century Irish monk St Vigianus or Fechin.

Both images: Wikimedia Commons

© Crown Copyright reproduced courtesy of Historic Scotland.
www.historicscotlandimages.gov.uk

Angus

Above: Drosten Stone, reverse detail
Top left: The Drosten Stone.
Left: Inscription on a side of
the Drosten Stone.

The most important stone at St Vigeans is the Drosten Stone
with a latinised Gaelic inscription which includes the names
Drosten, Voret and Forcus. Drosten was a popular Pictish saint.

Glasgow academic Tom Clancy believes the stone should
be dated to the reign of the
Pictish king Uurad or Uoret,
839–842. This is an unusual
feature in that Pictish stones
can rarely be so precisely
dated. The cross-slab shows
fabulous animals that flank
the cross on one face; the
reverse has a number of
Pictish symbols and a hunting
scene including a hunter with
cross-bow aiming at a boar.
A small side panel bears the
telltale inscription in minus-
cule lettering.

David McGovern, Pictish Arts Society

GLAMIS

NO 3860 4688 Glamis Manse
NO 3937 4654 Hunter's Hill

Two significant Pictish cross-slabs are found in and around the Angus village of Glamis, home of the late Queen Mother at Glamis Castle.

The Glamis Manse stone is a double-sided affair with a Class I type sculpture on one side, and a cross-slab on the other. This impressive massive sculpture is located in the garden of what is now a private house. The Class II side that dates from the eighth century shows a heavily interlaced cross surrounded by dramatic symbols, including a centaur waving axes on the top right, a mythical beast on the top left and a deer head or mask above a cauldron symbol on the lower right. To the left is a scene of two Pictish figures in combat wielding axes overshadowed by a cauldron with pairs of legs protruding. These complex motifs are highly evocative of rebirth, transformation and a Pictish belief system combining Christian with mythological overlays.

David McGovern, Pictish Arts Society

David McGovern, Pictish Arts Society

The reverse side of the stone presents a simple grouping of symbols incised upon an undressed stone surface: the serpent, a large hen salmon swimming toward the right, and the mirror symbol, these being the original earlier Class I side with pre-Christian/pagan symbology. A classic image of the Salmon of Wisdom from Celtic myth and legend, this grouping of feminine symbols represents fertility and earth wisdom with the naturalistic forms of adder and hen salmon and mirror which read as pictograms of this indigenous tribal race.

The second stone at Glamis is found southeast of the village on a hillside known as Hunter's Hill where a stone

David McGovern, Pictish Arts Society

Top: Cross-slab on Hunter's Hill, Glamis.
Below: An impression of the stone by Marianna Lines.

disguised as a larch is almost invisible in the greenish tones of the woodland. This is a smaller version of the great Glamis Manse stone. The cross-slab has varying mythical figures around it which play out another story on the same theme. One corner shows a four-winged angel similar to an Assyrian angel, while the opposite corner motif shows a bird-headed man and a smaller figure. On either side of the cross-shaft is the flower symbol and the same cauldron symbol as Glamis 1, and a hunting scene. The reverse side also bears iconic Pictish symbols, again like the mother stone of Glamis but very worn, of a dog/beast and a wriggling serpent.

The parallels are obvious between the two stones, suggesting that the second smaller stone up the hill was a practice stone for the big one.

BRECHIN CATHEDRAL
Three stones and a Round Tower

NO 5962 6008

Brechin Cathedral is the mother church of Angus with a Celtic Round Tower dating to the eleventh or early twelfth century. This was a *Celi De* or Culdee community in its early ecclesiastical history, recorded as a grant during the reign of Kenneth mac Malcolm AD 971–995 in the Pictish Chronicle. Brechin is located along an ancient pilgrimage way in a triangle that links Iona and Lindisfarne, both linked to the illuminated gospels of the *Book of Kells* and the *Lindisfarne Gospels.*

Brechin Cathedral, from 'The Baronial and Ecclesiastical Antiquities of Scotland' by R.W. Billings, published 15th October 1901.

Brechin's Round Tower is in the Irish style, one of only two round towers in Scotland, the other located in Perthshire at Abernethy. This is a memorial from the Culdee presence of the tenth century when Irish influence dominated the Scots-conquered Pictland. It stands beside the twelfth century Cathedral with its square medieval tower and was originally free-standing, used as a bell tower as well as a watchtower and refuge with seven floors.

A small collection of fine carved stones lies within the

Trish Steel, Wikimedia Commons

'Otter', Wikimedia Commons

*Both sides of the Aldbar Stone. It was found in the graveyard of
Aldbar Chapel near Brechin in 1771, dated c.9th century.*

recesses of the Cathedral. These include the Aldbar Stone,
a late Pictish cross-slab of the ninth century brought from the
old church at Aldbar. A double-sided sculptured stone, the
front bears a Celtic cross, 6ft/1.8m tall along with clerics holding books and various beastie creatures around the cross. The
back shows a crowded scene with a late Pictish menagerie of
zoomorphic creatures with a David theme. King David is shown
rending the jaws of the lion with his symbols of a sheep and a
harp depicted on many Pictish cross-slabs of this period. The
harp is significant in its triangular shape being a true Pictish
harp, and an early example of a *clarsach*, the Highland harp.

Other stones include a fine example of a hogback tomb-
stone of the eleventh century and the St Mary Stone of the
early ninth century carved in Northumbrian style with a rare
depiction of the Virgin and Child within a central medallion.

These stones underline Brechin's role as a major early
ecclesiastical centre in Pictland with links to the great monastic
centres of Iona and Northumbria.

MORE PICTISH STONES

St Orland's Stone at Cossans (NO 4008 5001) stands in the
middle of a field, a damaged cross-slab with double symbols
of a crescent and double disc, the same as on Aberlemno, and
a hunt scene. Most unique is the carving of an inhabited
boat with six people, one of whom appears to be a king.

Standing upon what was probably a small islet surrounded by the marshes of the Dean Water, this is the only Pictish stone with the illustration of a boat.

Martin's Stane, Balluderon (NO 3748 3757) stands in a field north of Dundee, a fragment stump of a cross-slab with two horsemen, the upper one of higher rank and kingship, the lower rider seen with two prime Pictish symbols of the Pictish beast-ie and serpent with Z-rod, and a cup mark or two. The legend of the stone, a popular Dundee tale, tells of a dragon and nine maidens with Martin slaying the dragon represented by the serpent on the stone.

Bob Henery, Pictish Arts Society

    The local rhyme for this famous Strathmartine Dragon goes:

> Tempted at Pitempton
> Draigled at Baldragon
> Stricken at Strathmartine
> And killed at Martin's Stane.

The Bullion Stone, dubbed *The Drunken Pict*, is a non symbol-bearing stone of a late Class III date, circa ninth century. The stone depicts a single figure of an elderly warrior riding a tired old horse while imbibing from a drinking horn decorated with a bird head terminal. It was discovered in Invergowrie near Dundee and now takes pride of place in Edinburgh at the NMS (National Museum of Scotland). This image of inebriation con-

Kim Traynor, Wikimedia Commons

nects with the story of *Heather Ale*, a legend associated with the Picts. It has been said that the Bullion Stone is one of the most extraordinary ancient works of art in its style and a portrayal of this unheroic and individualised subject, a true portrait in stone from a most early period.

Angus

Dunnichen Stone

Seventh century, originated near the site at Nechtansmere (NO 5082 4883) where the famous Battle of Dunnichen may have taken place in AD 685. It displays the flower symbol (or battle helmet with nose guard) and the double disc and Z-rod and mirror and double sided comb, now moved to the Meffan Museum in Forfar.

Right: The Dunnichen Stone. Interpretation on cloth by Marianna Lines.

Eassie Stone

(NO 3526 4745)
A highly decorated Class II cross-slab shows three cloaked figures in procession with a number of Pictish symbols and cattle on the reverse, with the cross side showing a four-winged angel similar to Glamis 2 and another stealthy cloaked warrior figure striding with spear and shield by the shaft. Eassie's fame is also culinary as a major asparagus-producing region.

David McGovern, Pictish Arts Society

The Eassie cross-slab, discovered in 1786; now housed in Eassie Old Parish Kirk. Shown is a cross, a warrior with a spear and shield, a stag and two angels.

Kirriemuir Stones

Now in Forfar at The Meffan. Five Early Christian Stones of Class II and III dating from the ninth century indicate that Kirriemuir, the Gateway to the Angus Glens, was an important ecclesiastical centre in Celtic times.

Kirrie 1 shows an interlace cross with an eagle-headed man above each arm and clerics holding books below. The back shows an enthroned figure beside a loom with mirror and comb symbols, likely to be Mary, mother of Jesus.

Kirrie 2 is even more elaborate, a key pattern-decorated cross flanked by angels and a cloaked figure with staff below, and a medley of animals. The back displays a magnificent hunting scene defined by the double disc and Z-rod symbol above the kingly chief horseman. Hairstyles and costumes are superb on this stone. Other stones in the collection contain sculptured cross-slabs and unusual angels, one with drooping wings. These fine stones display a particular style of carving which is indicative of a Kirriemuir school of sculpture.

Kirriemuir Stone 2.

Camus Cross (NO 5196 3790) is an early medieval Pictish Cross located on the Panmure Estate near Carnoustie by the Barony of Downie. This is a free-standing cross, heavily sculptured with a crucifixion scene, quite rare in the East, dating from the tenth century. Its style is distinctively Hiberno-Scottish in common with other monuments in the area, such as the eleventh century Hogback stone in Brechin Cathedral. Folk tradition tells that the cross marked the burial site of Camus, leader of the Norse army defeated by King Malcolm II at the 'apocryphal' Battle of Barry. Yet no Danish prince of this name has ever existed, and no contemporary account of such a battle exists either.

The Girdle Stane (NO 5279 4985) with its Bronze Age cup and ring markings once lay by the Auldbar Road junction but has now been removed to Letham near Dunnichen. Used as a medieval parish boundary marker, the face of the stone was said to resemble a girdle.

SOUTERRAINS

Underground passages known as Picts' houses, Earth Houses, or fogou, are commonly called souterrains, of which there are many in Angus. These date from the Iron Age, around the first and second century AD. They have their own mystique, often with carved lintel stones or cup-marked stones indicating some form of ritual or sacred use as well as the practical. Often identified as crop markings from aerial surveys, they appear as dark banana shapes in their curving subterranean structures. Best examples in Angus are at
Ardestie (NO 5020 3444), Carlungie (NO 5111 3597), and Tealing (NO41213816).

David McGovern, Pictish Arts Society

Tealing souterrain.

Pitcur (NO 2528 3738) is a stunning souterrain on the border of Angus with Perthshire. It consists of three or more passages, huge roof slabs and two very fine cup-marked stones near the entrance. Reputedly deep in nettles, it is best to choose a visit out of season. This site is said to have an almighty atmosphere and a great place to get a feeling of 'being a Pict' under-ground in their domain. Souterrains are also quite numerous on the Isle of Skye and in Perthshire in Southern Pictland.

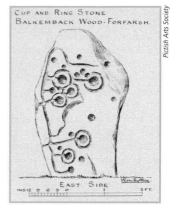

Pictish Arts Society

Cup and Ring marked stone from Balkemback, Tealing, Angus. Drawn by J. Romilly Allen. (Journal of the British Archaeological Association,1881).

HILLFORTS

Brown and White Caterthun (NO 555 668, NO 547 660) – twin forts on adjacent summits in the Sidlaws – are multi-level defensive ramparts with fine views across all of Angus to the North Sea. White Caterthun is crowned by a great stone walled oval fort, said to have been covered in white crystal stones that glowed. A cup-marked boulder on the south west side of the fort bears at least seventy cups. The hilltops of Strathmore were centres of authority over long periods extending into Pictish times.

Finavon (NO 5065 5567) located near Forfar and Aberlemno, is a vitrified fort once totally destroyed by fire. The carved stones at Aberlemno underline the importance of this area to the Picts, although the fort was in use from the first millennium BC.

Laws of Monifieth (NO 491 349) is a fort and broch near Dundee. Only a wall and entrance survives of the broch, but its importance lies in it being one of the few brochs in eastern Scotland and dates from the first century AD. The lookout across the Tay to Fife and the Angus coast is superb.

ARBROATH ABBEY

Arbroath Abbey (NO 643 412), located in the heart of the fishing community of Arbroath on the North Sea, is notable for being the place where Scotland's declaration of independence was issued in 1320 famously known as the Declaration of Arbroath. The Abbey was founded in 1178 by King William I of Scotland 'the Lion' as a memorial to Thomas Becket of Canterbury. The Tironensian monks of Kelso Abbey established the monastery and Abbey Church, which is now an evocative ruin. Its architectural significance displays an expression of European twin-towered church façade design. The most complete part of the building complex is the striking west front with its sunray motif in stone.

Nick Birse, Wikimedia Commons

The most famous document in Scottish history came about when Robert the Bruce defeated Edward II at Bannockburn in 1314, yet the sentence of excommunication was declared by the English. In response a letter was written to Pope John XXII in eloquent style and signed by forty Scottish nobles, barons and freemen to declare Scotland as an independent sovereign nation. This was created in April 1320.

Another rebellious act which the Abbey played a part in was the heist of the Stone of Destiny. In March 1951 the Abbey was in the spotlight again when the Stone of Destiny was found deposited beside the high altar, three months after its removal from Westminster Abbey. The *Lia Fail* of Scotland – the Stone of Destiny and the Stone of Scone – now lives at Edinburgh Castle under lock and key. There is no greater legend in stone than this symbol of the Scottish nation.

WHY IS THE PICTISH SEAHORSE CALLED THE HIPPOCAMP?

The Pictish symbol of the Seahorse, the confronting seahorse image as found on the Aberlemno Stone in Angus, is also called the Hippocampus. Why did the Picts use this symbol? The Hippocampus is an area of the brain that curls through the centre of the brain like a seahorse, so named in Greek for hippos, horse, and is responsible for memory and emotion.

Today the common disease of the brain known as Alzheimer's affects the hippocampus, one of the first regions of the brain to suffer memory loss and disorientation. It is curious that this image appears so often on Pictish symbol stones. The double image of the seahorse is found in various forms on the ancient stones, sometimes singly, more often as a mirror image, and also in the sea serpent form, another part of the 'hippocampus' name – kampos – in the Greek means 'sea monster'. These symbols of emotion and memory must have meant a great deal to this primal race of Picts. The sea monster/sea horse image or glyph is found throughout Pictland but most commonly in Angus on the stones in Aberlemno and St Vigeans, and also in the Meigle Museum in Perthshire.

Dancing Seahorses, design from the Pictish cross-slab in Aberlemno churchyard. Art by Marianna Lines.

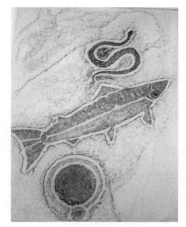

The Salmon of Wisdom, Glamis – art by Marianna Lines.

The Martin Stane, Balluderon – art by Marianna Lines.

Angus

Aberdeen-
shire

ABERDEENSHIRE

7

ABERDEENSHIRE

PRINCIPAL SITES

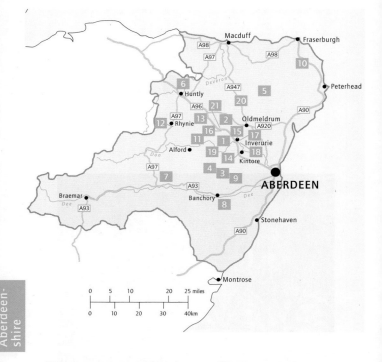

1	Easter Aquhorthies stone circle	12	Rhynie Old Kirk
2	Loanhead of Daviot	13	Picardy Stone
3	Sunhoney	14	Kintore Stone
4	Midmar	15	Brandsbutt Stone
5	Aikey Brae stone circle	16	Maiden Stone
6	The Ringing Stone	17	Inverurie
7	Tomnaverie stone circle	18	Broomend of Crichie
8	Nine Stanes stone circle	19	Monymusk
9	Cullerlie stone circle	20	Fyvie
10	Berrybrae stone circle	21	Logie stone
11	Old Keig, Alford		

*Previous page: 'The Blue Serpent', an interpretation of the
Brandsbutt Stone, Inverurie – art by Marianna Lines.*

ABERDEENSHIRE

ABERDEENSHIRE IS A LAND OF GREAT FERTILITY, the breadbasket of Scotland in many senses. It is also a great field of stones. This region of Scotland is notable in that it boasts such a unique range of prehistoric remains, relics and treasures. The recumbent stone circle is king in Aberdeenshire taking us back at least 5,000 years into Neolithic and early Bronze Age times. A recent book calls them "great crowns of stone". Indeed they are. All seventy one of them to be exact. Recumbent stone circles are delineated by the structure of a large flat 'altar' stone flanked by two stones, one on either side, a bit like dragon teeth with a varying number of stones to make up the circle. Characteristically the recumbent, or ' lying down stone' is placed in the southern quarter of the monument. Folklore referred to these holy places as altar stones.

It is recorded that the densest concentration of stone circles in the entire British Isles can be found in the northeast of Scotland. They are usually found on the crests of hills, ridges or terraces with southerly views.

Aberdeenshire formed the heartland of the Northern Picts from the fourth to the ninth centuries, and of course Pictish symbol stones are numerous throughout. They date from the earlier period of what is known as Class I stones indicating the Northern Pictish Kingdom was stronger in its pre-Christian or pagan period. The use of tribal Pictish symbols rather than the central cross motif is common in this region. Christianity may have come later to this rural area. These symbol stones, in use from the sixth century, are incised on rough boulders with a paired combination of zoomorphic or animal and geometric symbols. The meaning of the symbols remains a mystery.

There are nearly 30,000 sites of archaeological and historical interest in Aberdeenshire. While there are officially seventy one recumbent circles, there are at least 100 more stone circles, mostly ruined.

In the eighteenth through to the mid nineteenth century stone circles were dubbed Druid Temples by the now outdated antiquarian association of stone circles with the Druids. It is not entirely wrong to call them Druidical places of worship as they are believed to be 'ritual sites' as much as burial sites; places for the living perhaps rather than for the dead. Astronomical studies became a more popular explanation for the settings of these great megaliths with Alexander Thom leading the way.

Scottish folklore enters the picture here. Such atmospheric megalithic sites always related to the world of the *sith* (pronounced 'shee'), Scotland's fairy folk, as well as other ghostly carry-ons. While modern Druids persist as well as spiritual gatherings around stone circles, the appreciation and understanding is always in the eye of the beholder. Indeed, geomantic investigations into stone circles, especially in this area, reveal interesting theories about the stones being receivers and transmitters of altered states of consciousness. The modern megalithic revival continues.

Aberdeenshire is also the land of Lewis Grassic Gibbon's famed elegiac work *Sunset Song*, a true literary masterpiece of Scotland. He was based here in the northeast. His work is considered by many to be the most beautiful piece of writing about the rural life of Scotland in the good old days circa 1945.

EASTER AQUHORTHIES stone circle

NJ 7323 2079

Marianna Lines

Located on the higher ridge of farmland set against the magical summit of the Mither Tap o'Bennachie, this recumbent stone circle is one of only a few that now retains its full complement of stones, twelve stones around the recumbent setting. Slightly flattened on the southwest, the stones are clearly graded, reducing in height from the flankers on the south-southwest

LOANHEAD OF DAVIOT

NJ 7476 2885

Aerial view of the ring cairn at Loanhead of Daviot.

Maggie Struckmeier © Aberdeenshire Council Archaeology Service

to the smallest stone in the northeast. Easter Aquhorthies is one of only two recumbent circles with the architectural design of a pair of large slabs set at the rear of the recumbent rather than adjacent to it. An internal cairn is only revealed by the trace of low swelling in the centre of the roundel of the circle. Several of the stones were chosen for their quartz crystal and precious stone inclusions, one being a red jasper stone.

The jasper stone.

Marianna Lines

The Mither Tap o' Bennachie which stands guard over this circle and many others in the area is believed to be of great religious significance to the Neolithic people who built these sites and lived here. The profile of the hill, 1700ft/518m, is shaped like a female breast hence the name *mother tip*. Some believe this is the site of the Battle of Mons Graupius in Roman times. There is an Iron Age fort on the summit but unlike other hillforts there are no vitrification or burned glass-like deposits. Bennachie (*Beinn na Ciche*, hill of the breast in Gaelic) has further legendary associations with Pictish stones in the area and the sacred well of Bennachie. The legendary giant, Jock o' Bennachie ruled the land and other sacred hills like Barra, Dunnydeer, and Tap o' Noth all faced his wrath.

Considered one of the most complete, largest and well preserved of the recumbent circles, Loanhead is located in the rolling hills near Inverurie. Ten monoliths make up the outer circle with a 52.5ft/16m diameter; the giant recumbent has split in two through frost damage. The stones are graded in height, one to the

© Aberdeenshire Council Archaeology Service

View of the ring cairn with recumbent.

east of the flanker stones showing a vertical line of cup-marks on the inner face. Neolithic pottery of Beaker type has been found along with many other finds in the excavation before reconstruction. A central ring cairn with a prominent kerb built over a cremation pyre takes up the interior of the circle. An adjacent late Bronze Age cemetery (1500 BC) is found nearby. Contemporary with other Neolithic sites from the Ring of Brodgar to Calanais on Lewis circa 3000 BC, Loanhead of Daviot and its related recumbent stone circles in the northeast demonstrate the importance of the moonrise and moonset in the southern sky located where the view is open to the south. The recumbent and its pillars appear to frame the moon when standing within the circle.

SUNHONEY

NJ 7159 0570

Marianna Lines

A unique experience is to visit Sunhoney in its most natural state left to the wildness of its ancient past. Located on Sunhoney Farm west of Echt, it is a site that seems to have been left to fend for itself, untamed. A derelict barn bears a handmade sign reading 'Stone Circle' to lead you onward from

Aberdeen-shire

the farm track. It is surrounded by mature trees and fields beyond. On an autumnal evening with setting sun it feels as if one has just discovered it for the first time. The large circle of 83.3ft/25.4m diameter consists of nine standing stones with a broken recumbent in fine grained grey granite which has thirty one cup-marks on it along with two flanking pillars. The cup-marks may indicate a map of the rising and setting moons at the site and lead to the observation that this was primarily a lunar observatory. This is true for other recumbents, especially those with cup-marks. In 1921 the Right Rev. George Browne identified the Pole Star and the constellations of Corona, the Great Bear, Hercules and Cygnus from the Sunhoney display of cup-marks.

Cup-marked recumbent stone.

A low central ring cairn where cremated bone deposits and fire-marked stones have been found lies within the interior. The name Sunhoney may be a corruption of its old name *Seanhinny or Sin Hinnie*, conjecturally meaning 'seats of the firewood', but it rolls off the tongue like honey.

MIDMAR

NJ 6993 0646

The Midmar Recumbent Stone Circle is an odd juxtaposition with the two worlds of Bronze Age and Christianity so far apart, yet it stands within a modern churchyard behind the Kirk only a mile or so from Sunhoney. This stone circle seems all the more massive and incongruous because of its highly manicured state surrounded by Celtic crosses and eighteenth century headstones of angels and skull and crossbones. Its recumbent central stone represents the altar within all altars – an altar to the stars and the moon and the land wherein it lives.

Midmar's circle is 56.8ft/17.3m in diameter with five widely spaced out stones arcing around the recumbent measuring 14.8ft./4.5m in length and weighing twenty tons, with its 'canine teeth' flankers 8ft/2.5m tall. The stone builders went to great trouble to make the recumbent level using chocking stones for the purpose visible here. The circle was tidied up in 1914 when the graveyard was laid out, with the north-northeast stone being re-erected at that time at an inconsistent height compared to the normal grading in such circles. Midmar Kirk was deliberately built beside the circle, as it was believed that the monument was a Druidic religious structure and that Druidism was an offshoot of Christianity in the eighteenth century. The church honours its past which is so well preserved here within its landscaped Christian setting. The potent atmosphere created by the marriage of the two enriches the present.

Marianna Lines

Recumbent stone with Midmar Kirk in the background.

A very fine single standing stone called Balblair, possibly an outlier from the circle, is found in a wood 120yds/110m northwest of the Kirk and circle.

AIKEY BRAE STONE CIRCLE

B9029 Midway between Maud & Old Deer

NJ 9588 4709

The name tells it all. One may get achy bones walking up the brae for it is a long track through a wood to a lovely location for a stone circle overlooking the village of Old Deer in

Buchan. The circle includes five erect stones including the recumbent and the east pillar, and five more prostrate stones within a diameter of 46ft/14 metres. A further upright has disappeared. A broad court in the centre forms a shallow dish.

Aikey Brae.

The ruins of the medieval thirteenth century Cistercian Deer Abbey is located near the village (NJ 9684 4811) where the most beautiful and little known illuminated manuscript, *The Book of Deer* was created. In medieval circles, Deer Abbey is renowned for this pocket gospel book. Now held at Cambridge University, it is thought to have been made in the early 900s on the site of the earlier monastery founded by St Drostan, a follower of St Columba in the sixth century. It is the oldest MS written in Scots Gaelic. Deer Abbey also has the distinction of having had a Pictish symbol stone in its grounds, sculptured on both sides, a cross on one and symbols on the reverse, but this has now vanished. Deer Abbey holds many secrets still.

THE RINGING STONE *Above Rothiemay Station*

NJ 5316 4564

The Ringing Stone refers to a partly demolished ruined yet highly evocative recumbent stone circle remotely located on the hill above Rothiemay Station near Huntly. The great recumbent stone with other toppled stones scattered around it at some distance actually rings when struck with a stone. It is also known as the Iron stone due to its metallic sound. Local folklore says that when struck the stone can be heard ringing through the rocks at Portsoy fishing village seven miles away on the Moray Firth coast. The sound has a hollow bell-like tone; the stone has been the subject of many musical experiments by the Scottish musicologist John Purser. There are other ringing stones around Scotland such as on Iona and the island of Tiree.

Maggie Struckmeier ©Aberdeenshire Council Archaeology Service

Aberdeenshire

TOMNAVERIE STONE CIRCLE

NJ 4865 0348

Marianna Lines

Sitting high above the hills commanding a fine panoramic view of the upper Dee valley, Tomnaverie recumbent circle is on the road from Aboyne to Tarland on the crest of a small hillock like a stage set for a monumental performance of megalithic proportions. This deforested landscape is quite opposite however to what it would have looked like 5,000 years ago when the site was built. It would have been a remote hillock in an extensive wooded and dangerous quagmire full of wild animals. The recumbent (12.5 tons), flankers and five standing stones make up the circle which has been carefully reconstructed after extensive excavation work. At Tomnaverie the orientation of both the circle of orthostats, the standing stones, and the recumbent setting is implicit in the architecture of the cairn in the interior of the circle, for the kerb stones have been graded toward the southwest.

Many detailed observations can be made about this complex site. Cup-marks also adorn the great recumbent here as well as other stones on the site. This great lunar observation platform is orientated to the winter solstice toward the southwest, like most of these northern hemisphere sites. Cup-marks link with the phenomenon of the lunar standstill that occurs every nineteen years and may be tallies to record the moon's behaviour.

The recumbent stone faces toward the distant peak of Lochnagar, known as Dark Lochnagar, a magnificent popular Munro in the Dee Valley on the Balmoral estate. Lord Byron immortalised this mountain in his poem *Lachin y Gair* written in 1807 when he used to visit the Lochnagar area of the northeast in his childhood.

* * *

Away, ye gay landscapes, ye garden of roses!
In you let the minions of luxury rove;
Restore me to the rocks, where the snowflake reposes,
Though still they are sacred to freedom and love:
Yet, Caledonia, beloved are thy mountains,
Round their white summits though elements war;
Though cataracts foam 'stead of smooth-flowing fountains,
I sigh for the valley of dark Loch na Garr.

The first Antiquarian mention of Tomnaverie is found in the Old Statistical Account of 1792 where the Minister of Coull parish describes it thus: "only a few large stones, some upright, some fallen... without any appearance of figures... the remains of a Druidical temple". *Tamnavric*, the old name, means 'the Hill of Worship'.

A most important excavation at Tomnaverie took place at the last millennium which was to change the understanding of recumbent stone circles completely. The new focus is on the relationship of the circle to the internal ring cairn that is common to all these monuments.

On a less formal note in vernacular terms, it is recommended to visit the site at midsummer full moon on the minor lunar standstill when the moon will set over the centre of the great recumbent. Just work that one out.

NINE STANES / Mulloch Wood

NO 7233 9122

Marianna Lines

Located within a mature larch wood on Forestry Commission land known as Garrol Wood, southeast of Banchory, the Nine Stanes of Mulloch Wood has an uncanny Pan-like atmosphere of mystery and beauty, the trees interwoven within the mighty clumps of aged stone to lend a dappled light. There is not a full complement of eleven original stones now, and one of the flankers has fallen. The other upright stones are graded in size on the east side, diminishing to the smallest stone opposite the recumbent which is said to weigh 16 tons. The circle is actually oval, 57.3ft/17.5m long x 47.5/14.5m wide. A ring cairn of 39.3ft/12m diameter can be seen in the interior with a hole in the middle. Charred bone fragments and charcoal mixed with pottery have been found in the cairn.

Recumbent stone, Mulloch Wood.

Marianna Lines

There are two smaller satellite circles in the area suggesting a 'landscape temple' of inter-related sites with ancient rituals of use that we shall never really know. These sites have rather alluring names, Eslie the Greater, a recumbent circle 765.5yds/700m to the northwest, and Eslie the Lesser 984yds/900m to the north.

A way marker sign on the site states clearly that "this site was built 4,500–3,500 years ago to observe the phases of the moon". It is worth noting that there are more than twenty stone circles on both sides of the River Dee in this area.

CULLERLIE STONE CIRCLE

NJ 7851 0427

Rainbow stone and hay bales — watercolour
by Marianna Lines, from a sketchbook.

A regular (non recumbent) stone circle within manicured grounds can be found near to Garlogie by Echt in rolling

Marianna Lines

Cullerlie stone circle.

farmlands. This restored stone circle is easy to access and much smaller overall in girth than the massive recumbent circles. Eight low red granite boulder stones are graded in size to the north surrounding a cluster of eight small exposed burial cairns within the circle. The cairns were erected later, circa 1800–1200 BC on consecrated ground which was burnt over by setting fire to a pile of willow twigs. These yielded burnt human bones, charcoal, pottery sherds and worked flints as well as oak charcoal and hazel of a later date indicating a long period of use. It is recorded that there were nine other smaller similar circles to the southwest of Cullerlie, but no trace remains. Cup-marks can be found on four of the stones on both inner and outer rings, one quite large.

An outlier stone is seen nearby in a field, shining white in the sun.

BERRYBRAE STONE CIRCLE Minor road S off A90 W of Crimond

NK 0275 5715

Maggie Struckmeier ©Aberdeenshire Council Archaeology Service

Way far up in the northeast seven miles south of Fraserburgh, Berrybrae is a complex recumbent site consisting of several distinct phases. As is fairly normal for a recumbent site, it is located in a clump of trees by fields. Originally the oval-shaped ring consisted of a recumbent and nine standing stones around

Aberdeen-shire

an earthen bank with a varying diameter of 42ft/12.8m to 6ft/1.8m. A ring cairn was found within the circle with three burials. Today only five stones remain including two massive stone blocks in situ and many broken ones. Excavations tell us that the site was partially destroyed by intrusive Beaker people circa 1900–1550 BC, and a beaker burial found. The stones were toppled and smashed to create an enclosed cremation cemetery.

There is scattered rose quartz found over the site and the recumbent is shaped somewhat like a boat. Within six miles of Berrybrae many more sites can be found: White Cow Wood Cairn, Strichen Stone Circle, Loudon Wood Stone Circle, and Memsie Round Cairn. Here the ancient peoples' landscape of stony bones reveals more than we might perceive; visiting such ruined, transformed and densely clustered sites in a region like Aberdeenshire is part of the megalithic experience.

OLD KEIG by Alford   NJ 5965 1939

Bg92 (Insch to Whitehaus Rd) Crossroads, go W on minor Rd
2 km – visible on L

This is a recumbent circle not to forget or miss, as Old Keig, east of Alford in the heart of Deeside, Aberdeenshire, has the greatest size recumbent ever recorded: 53 tons! Although little remains of the circle itself, a visit to the king of all stones is worth it. Recorded in the books as the largest surviving recumbent ever, it sounds like the largest whale ever seen – the great blue in the greatest ocean to survive. The two flankers are still in position and one other standing stone in a 65.5ft/20m diameter circle. The recumbent was quarried from the Don Valley over 6.2miles/10km away and is composed of gneiss, the same stone as Calanais stones on the Isle of Lewis. It is perfectly level on its setting as one could rest an egg there without it rolling.

Marianna Lines

The Author atop Old Keig, celebrating the Summer Solstice.

Aberdeen-shire

The midwinter sun sets over this stone and the eastern flanker is aligned to the major southern moonset. The hillfort, *The Barmkyn* sits above Old Keig overlooking and guarding the site.

The historic record tells us that: "...at once communal and anonymous, the essentially Neolithic nature of the recumbent stone circle is perhaps nowhere better seen than at Old Keig, the circle located on a slight crest on rising ground with distant, magical views over the Howe of Alford. When created, the site was first levelled before the giant recumbent was dragged uphill at the last stretch at a gradient of 1:14 (7%), requiring over 100 people." It is with awe that we are able to witness a setting that still exists today after 5000 years or more.

PICTISH STONES

There is such a large corpus of Pictish symbol stones in Aberdeenshire alone, not to mention the rest of Scotland, that it is not possible to discuss them all in detail. Pictish aficionados may take it further but for the sacred site traveller a select list is given with discussion to follow on the highlight stones.

It is worth pointing out that the ancient peoples must have loved Aberdeenshire above all else as it is home to so many of their incredible monuments.

RHYNIE

NJ 49942650

Rhynie Old Kirk has a small collection of stones that now lie in shelter outside Rhynie Old Kirk-yard. Two Class I symbol stones dating from the fifth century era, the first shows a beast's head above a mirror and comb. The second shows a Z-rod with crescent and V-rod.

The Rhynie Man, a famous single figure stone, depicts a man wearing a knee length belted tunic, pointed shoes and carrying a battle axe/poleaxe over his shoulder. Found at Barflat Farm in the 1980s during spring ploughing, this unique carving of a Pict has been re-housed in the Council HQ in Aberdeen (NJ 9118 0693). A second fragment was also turned up with

Maggie Struckmeier ©Aberdeenshire Council Archaeology Service

Aberdeen-shire

the single incised carving of a Pictish beastie, the kelpie image. This coupling of male figure striding in profile together with a beastie symbol, his totem symbol, matches the same combination on the Bronze Age pillar stone in Fife. A Pictish figure in profile along with the paired symbols of an arch and a beastie are found on the stone by Collessie on Halhill Farm.

The Craw Stane (NJ 4974 2634) stands on a hill in fields above Rhynie with a pair of symbols, the salmon and the beastie, a unique pairing of these two arcane symbols which both repre-sent the element of water.

Impression of the Craw Stane, by Marianna Lines.

PICARDY STONE

NJ 6099 3025

The splendid Picardy Stone is a Pictish Class I symbol stone circa fifth century AD set in the middle of a field overlooked and framed by Dunnideer hillfort by Insch. No better way to present a piece of sculpture can there be. The approach,

Marianna Lines

along an avenue of lime trees, helps the visitor to appreciate the beauty of this quartz veined 'mar-bled' stone decorated with a double-disc and Z-rod, serpent and mirror. The stone is in such good condition that it could have been carved yesterday, as they say.

Dunnideer (NJ 6123 2814), set on a perfect pyramid-shaped hill, is a vitrified fort with outer defensive works and tri-vallate sys-tem of defences.

Aberdeen-shire

To crown the summit there are the remains of a medieval stone castle, a singular rectangular tower of the thirteenth century mostly built of material from the prehistoric vitrified fort, which is a glassy stone created by a great fire within the area. This structure represents the earliest authenticated example of a tower house in Scotland. The combination of three periods of history in such iconic architecture and landscape is unparalleled.

KINTORE STONE

NJ 7930 1627

In the centre of the village of Kintore en route to Aberdeen at the gates of the churchyard of Kintore Kirk stands a double-sided Pictish symbol stone, a granite block with a characterful cartoon style Pictish beastie and the crescent and V-rod. The reverse presents a salmon above a cauldron. These are simple stylish carvings with economy of line and powerful symbolism,

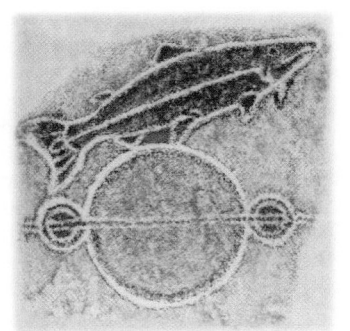

'Salmon Moon', hen salmon with cauldron – art by Marianna Lines.

both very clear to read. Kintore is a Class I stone of seventh century origin. Its symbols evoke the great Celtic tales of old with the Cauldron of Plenty, the Celtic grail, and the salmon as the source of ancient wisdom that swims in the pools of knowledge. Three other symbol stones also came from Kintore but are now housed elsewhere. The nearest is in Inverurie Museum which shows a beastie symbol, a rectangle and a mirror fragment.

BRANDSBUTT STONE

NJ 7599 2240

A poor old stone shot to hell by pagan-fearing Calvinists long ago is found in the middle of a housing estate in Inverurie along with a few rough stones and a cobbled outline indicating the presence of a stone circle there long ago. The Brandsbutt, or Serpent Stone, is carved with a crescent and V-rod above a serpent and Z-rod. Ogham writing vertically down the left side presents a new perspective on the early Pictish symbol stone as this may indicate who the stone is dedicated to. A transliteration reads *IRATADDOARENS*, meaning 'Ethernán' (Adrian) a Scottish saint. More than thirty ogham inscriptions have been found in Pictish territories from the sixth to tenth century. It is an alphabet imported by the Picts from Ireland using slash marks across a bar. Never a verbal language, it was only used for inscriptions, much like the Norse runes.

These Brandsbutt symbols, in common use throughout Pictland, suggest they are symbols of fertility for the earth.

MAIDEN STONE ½m S A96 NW of Inverurie
minor rd 1 mi W Chapel of Garioch

NJ 7037 2471   (Balquhain)

Marianna Lines

The Maiden Stone may be Aberdeenshire's favourite Pictish symbol stone. The pink granite stone stands 10.2ft/3.1m tall beside the road near Inverurie on the way to the Chapel of Garioch, a cross-slab of the eighth century with intricate carvings on both sides and a great legend to further enhance it. The east side bears a centaur, a gateway/notched rectangle with Z-rod, a leaping Pictish beastie, and a mirror and comb while the west side shows a long Celtic style cross topped by a pair of fish monsters and a triple spiral mandala below. An angled corner is also carved with the Celtic *triskele*, symbol of eternity.

The legend of the Maiden Stone links with the shape of the stone itself, the story of a maiden tricked by the Deil'. The maiden of Drumdurno, the daughter of the local laird, made a wager with a stranger that she could bake a bannock before he could build a road to the top of Bennachie, 1600ft/487.5m up and two miles away, by sundown. The stranger was none other than the Devil and he won the bet and came back to claim his prize but the maiden tried to escape, was caught and instantly turned to stone. Thus the place where

The Maiden Stone — top: hand-tinted aquatint etching by Marianna Lines; right: lower section of stone.

his hand touched her shoulder is marked by the notch in the stone. This is a reversal of the Celtic shape-shifting stories in folklore such as in the Mabinogian or Taliesin tales.

Over the road is a private sculpture park within extensive grounds with a gigantic modern stone sculpture of the Maiden herself or the Goddess Demeter as she is called. She is an interpretation of the Pictish stone, holding a mirror in her hand, a beautiful symbol of fertility.

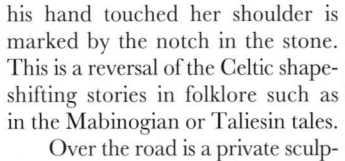

Marianna Lines

INVERURIE STONES

NJ 7800 2062

Within the beautiful <u>Inverurie churchyard</u> with the winding River Urie running through it can be found four Pictish symbol stones and multiple layers of history. In fact this area is a landscape temple of sites with a prehistoric henge and stone circle not far away at Broomend of Crichie. The stones were discovered built into the walls of the old medieval church, now replaced in a row beneath the sycamore trees by the river. All are Class I, from the fifth to seventh century. One is a tall pillar stone with two sets of incised symbols: the crescent and V-rod and mirror-case above a serpent and straight rod with double disc and Z-rod; the second shows a mirror-case and an elaborate arch/horseshoe symbol (now broken), and the third an incised double disc and Z-rod.

A Pictish pony, festively decorated. Interpretation by Marianna Lines.

The fourth stone is the real treasure here as it sports a unique incised figure of a Pictish pony, this being the only occurrence of a single horse on a Pictish stone. This pony is called a *cuddie* in Scots, a favoured term for a horse. He appears to be decorated for a festive occasion with a headdress as often used for workhorses at country fairs. Epona was the Celtic horse goddess revered in the Dark Ages, a link with the horse cult that became associated with Pictish tribal symbols.

There are two outstanding motte-and-bailey earthworks within the churchyard as well, serpentine in their design with swirling paths to the top overlooking the sacred river confluence of the Don and the Urie. Known as the Bass of Inverurie (39.3ft/ 12m high) and Little Bass (16.3ft/5m high), these natural mounds were converted to a motte-and-bailey castle for the earldom of Garioch in the late twelfth to thirteenth centuries. These mounds which are seen all over Scotland in rural areas are also known as hollow or faerie hills in folklore. As there is a large one adjacent to a smaller hill, they could be seen as an Adam and Eve pair.

BROOMEND OF CRICHIE   S of Inverurie

NJ 7792 1967 henge and symbol stone

©Aberdeenshire Council Archaeology Service

On the outskirts of Inverurie to the south lies a prehistoric henge or earthwork and a stone circle within which can be found a fine Pictish symbol stone. Incised with a Pictish beastie and the crescent and V-rod paired symbols, of Class I seventh century period, the stone was moved into the Neolithic henge monument in the nineteenth century. The henge and circle have been recently excavated to reveal a ceremonial site of great significance. Only two standing stones remain of the original six of the stone circle with a stone avenue that led up to the henge from the circle. There were seventy two stones in this processional avenue, a double avenue of thirty six stones on each row leading on to the River Don, which was sadly broken up with gunpowder in the nineteenth century. Only one outlier monolith remains in view and a few more on private land. The importance of Broomend of Crichie cannot be understated. A henge, an earthen bank surrounded by a ditch, is a rarity in Scotland. This henge is enormous and well defined. A truly exciting site to behold.

MONYMUSK

NJ 6850 1524

The granite pillar of Monymusk is said to have lain from time immemorial in a field by the River Don until it was removed to the parish church at Monymusk in the nineteenth century. A beautiful highly grained stone, it bears an equal armed interlaced cross in low relief, the stepped rectangle symbol with curvilinear terminals, and the cauldron or triple disc symbol. Like other sculptured stones of the eighth century era, an Ordnance Survey benchmark was added in the nineteenth century, an act of wanton Victorian vandalism. The stone defines a transitional period between incised symbol stones and the cross-slabs as it contains both elements of symbolic design.

Monymusk is highly important to Scotland's history as it is the place of origin of the famous Monymusk Reliquary of St Columba. The *Breachbeannach* as the sacred relic is known, meaning 'speckled or multi-coloured, peaked one', is a small silver casket with inlaid bejewelled panels in the roof and sides and was believed to contain a bone of St Columba. This reliquary was carried before the Scottish host at Bannockburn to bestow victory in battle. Considered to be of Pictish metalwork design of the eighth century, the Monymusk Reliquary, the most sacred relic of the Celtic Church in Scotland, now takes pride of place in the National Museum of Edinburgh.

FYVIE

NJ 7684 3777

Three symbol stones of early Pictish Class I date are built into the east gable of the parish church of St Peter's in Fyvie, a fine northeast farming area with the great Fyvie Castle nearby. The first whinstone slab titled the *Baldyquash* Stone shows a crescent and V-rod above a Pictish beast and a mirror, the carving done in rather folksy childlike style perhaps by a local apprentice mason. The second stone, a fragment, shows only half of a double disc and Z-rod above a headless eagle, the characteristic Pictish sea eagle as seen on other stones in the northeast. The third stone, originally from Rothiebrisbane, shows an unusual Class I early symbol stone with rather wonky relief carvings of a skewed horseshoe symbol above a sun disc with three inner circles. The Kirk commands a fine view of the Ythan River valley, typical of sites chosen by early Celtic missionaries for their churches and chapels. Holy wells are popular in the area with at least five having been recorded. And in a more contemporary vein, the protagonist of the bothy ballad in folk tradition, *Tifty's Annie*, is buried in the seventeenth century churchyard. *The Mill o' Tifty's Annie* is still sung at folk clubs throughout the country and beyond.

Ye parents grave, who children have
In guidin' them be canny
Tak' kindly tent, lest ye repent
Remember Tilly's Annie.

LOGIE STONE

NJ 7032 2589

The Logie stone, set in the tranquil leafy grounds of Logie Elphinstone House, is an unusual and beautiful early Class I symbol stone. The symbols of a crescent and V-rod and double disc and Z-rod are carved below a sunwheel circular ogham inscription. The message may read 'stone of entrance', letters reading *QFTQU*. Pictish ogham writing is still being studied but not always translated. A palimpsest can be seen on this stone where two carved symbols, both being the double disc, are overlaid and partially erased, possibly a sculptor's error in the carving process. Yet the mystery carries on as there are three stones on site with a fourth disappeared, one having a variation on the same combination of symbols without the ogham, the other bearing the same symbols as found at Broomend of Crichie (beastie + crescent and V-rod). It is likely there was a lapidary here in Pictish times with such duplication of symbol stones. These three blocks of whinstone which remain on the site are recorded as having lain on the Moor of Carden until the area was planted in the early nineteenth century and moved to the house.

Marianna Lines

The Logie Stone, art by Marianna Lines, presented on site.

Aberdeen-shire

8

MORAYSHIRE

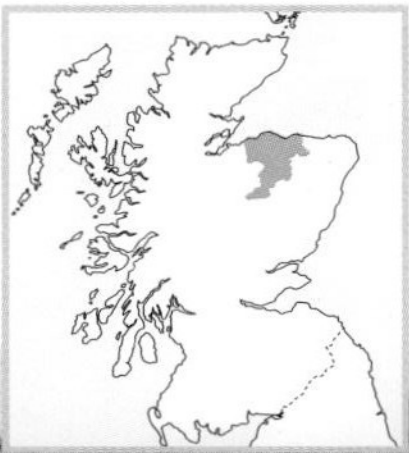

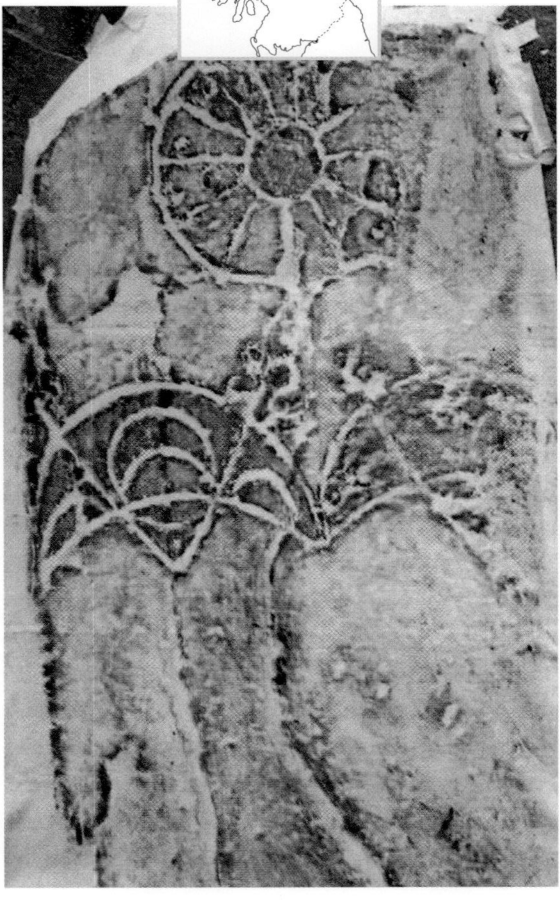

MORAYSHIRE

PRINCIPAL SITES

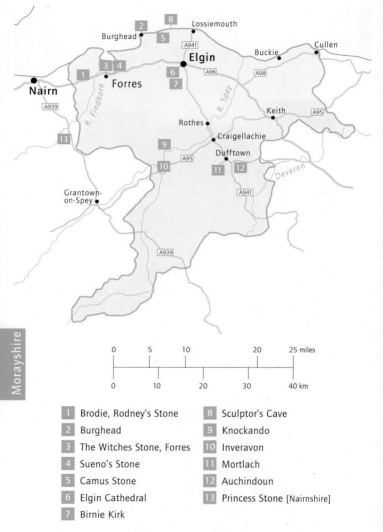

Morayshire

1	Brodie, Rodney's Stone	8	Sculptor's Cave
2	Burghead	9	Knockando
3	The Witches Stone, Forres	10	Inveravon
4	Sueno's Stone	11	Mortlach
5	Camus Stone	12	Auchindoun
6	Elgin Cathedral	13	Princess Stone [Nairnshire]
7	Birnie Kirk		

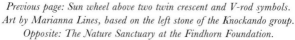

Previous page: Sun wheel above two twin crescent and V-rod symbols.
Art by Marianna Lines, based on the left stone of the Knockando group.
Opposite: The Nature Sanctuary at the Findhorn Foundation.

MORAYSHIRE

MORAYSHIRE IS A REGION of Scotland open to the sea, the mountains and two of the great rivers of Scotland. It borders on the beautiful Moray Firth to the north, Aberdeenshire on the south and east, and Inverness-shire in the west. Each area of Scotland is a gateway to the ancient sites and each has its own distinct flavour and style.

Morayshire is rich in natural landforms created by the sea: caves, sea stacks, and a wide array of early settlement and stone carvings from Pictish times yet wholly lacking in the great stone circles of Aberdeenshire.

Marion Leigh

It is also the location for a more contemporary 'sacred place', the *Findhorn Foundation*, a community that started in the Sixties and has become a beacon for enlightenment in the modern world. This is eco-consciousness on a higher level. Yet where Findhorn has lain down its roots is also where other civilisations have been lost; villages are buried under the sands and under the sea at Findhorn village on the Moray Firth. We sense rather than see the vibes of the past. Holy wells, sacred waters, fairy castles and ancient stones are part of the enchantment of Morayshire.

Consider the Moray Firth in ancient times. The importance of this area with its fine harbours and rich hinterland is reflected in the Pictish culture that survives: the great number of symbol stones and cross-slabs as well as the great fort at Burghead. With its vast sandy beaches and intricate rock formations, cliffs and coves, the southern coast of the Moray Firth gives way to a land-scape that extends inland towards the fringes of the Cairngorms. Here are the moors and glens, habitat of golden eagles and red deer and the heartland of malt whisky, Speyside.

Morayshire

SCOTLAND'S
FIRE FESTIVALS

ANCIENT RITUALS PERSIST into the modern world no matter what. Whether they are pagan hangovers or recent revised Victorian inventions, the tradition of a ceremonial collective happening is as passionate and infectious as a football game to the sporting world today. The use of fire was a primal element of the megalithic world as the fire of the sun was the centre of life in the circles of our ancestors. The Celtic Fire Festivals are still practised in Scotland, the more north the better and whether they are authentic really matters not. It is all part of the inventive spirit of life.

Combining the primitive impulse to light up the long nights with the ancient concept that fire purifies and chases away evil spirits, and the Scottish impulse to party all nicht', midwinter becomes a festival all of its own that carries on till spring and long after the snowdrops drop their blossoms.

Mike Pennington, geograph.org.uk

In the far north in Shetland is the annual *Up Helly Aa* Fire Festival, held on the last Tuesday of the first month of the year or so it links to Hogmanay and the turning of the year, the changeover from winter solstice to welcome the return of the sun. This is also a boat festival as a Viking replica boat is paraded through the town and toasted in fiery revels before being burned in a great conflagration with tossing torches from the mighty squad of Shetlanders in Viking horned helmets and costumes.

It's all a cheery mixture of cultures and something that the entire community takes part in throughout the many Shetland Islands.

Anne Burgess, Wikimedia Commons

Further south on the mainland on the Moray Firth coast is the annual *Burning of the Clavie* in Burghead held on the 11th of January on

Auld New Year, the date on the old Julian calendar of New Year's Eve. This fire festival is about purification and augury for good luck for the village and for the fishing, a blessing of fire. A tar barrel is stoked with tar and staves and carried like a fire bomb on a ritual procession around the old town boundaries by a select group of male-only Burghers. Then the Clavie is hoisted on top of Doorie Hill beside the ramparts of the Pictish fort as a giant beacon of a bonfire. Everyone takes a bit of the 'faggot of good luck' for the year, to be kept on the hearth for the coming year. Further down the coast on the North Sea beyond Aberdeen lies Stonehaven where the Fireball Festival is held on Hogmanay. A team of sixty odd locals swing caged balls of fire through the streets, finishing with a 'Viking funeral' throwing the flaming balls into the sea. These daredevils have to keep the sixteen pound balls of fire lit and swinging over their own heads in this spectacle of madness. The Perthshire village of Comrie has a variation on the fire festival on New Year's Eve.

Gonzalo Mazzei

The Comrie Flambeaux procession takes a virtual forest of birch trees, paraffin soaked, set aflame and processed as eight great torches around the town and then thrown into the river along with the whole cargo of local evil spirits. This is purification on a community scale.

Further down into the central heartland on the River Tay there is a more curious twist on the fire tradition where the Oddfellow Torchlight procession takes place in Newburgh on Hogmanay. The youngest member of the Oddfellows Order wears a white robe and mask and rides backwards on a horse, led through the streets with guisers carrying torches behind him. This is a symbolic ritual about the initiation rites of youth and the Janus theme of looking backward into the old year while riding forward into the new.

Bigger in South Lanarkshire has its own 'Biggar Bonfire' at Hogmanay that has gone on for centuries with a torchlight procession, pipe and drums and the ritual of the oldest resident lighting the fire. Ancestor worship and respect for the elders is remembered here.

Morayshire

Bonfires are always part of the Scottish tradition on Guy Fawkes Night to celebrate the attempt to burn down Parliament. On the theme of independence, this follows on the tail of Samhain at Hallowe'en time. Appropriately, Scotland has a popular folk band called *Blazing Fiddles*, so the 'fire wall' runs on into popular culture on all levels.

Beltane has its own rituals with the 'Need Fire' and the clootie (offering of rags) dressing of the holy wells such as the Clootie Well on the Black Isle. The Lammas Fair in St Andrews in August at Lammas harvest time is a local ritual, more commercial funfair style these days, while another surreal ritual takes place in South Queensferry on the Firth of Forth at this time with the Burry Man. This is about the sin-eater, a scapegoat to banish all evil. A man is dressed in sticky burrs and paraded around the town, witnessed by all before being cast away. It is said by some-one who has seen this event that "There is no one else like the Burry Man! He is encased completely in a costume of thousands of burdock heads, wearing a flowery bowler hat. Two attendants help him as he walks seven miles on his rounds for over seven hours through the day, using staves to support his arms and stop the burrs from sticking to his body. He can only drink whisky through a straw. This is a luck-bringing custom that is followed by the Ferry Fair and the crowning of the Ferry Queen."

Ferries and faeries, fire and fury, hell hath none in these here *pairts* with all these safeguard rituals.

* * *

BRODIE, RODNEY'S STONE

NH 9842 5766

The great Pictish cross-slab known as Rodney's Stone stands in an artistic setting of a modern willow sculptured backdrop on the entranceway to Brodie Castle between Forres and Nairn. The main face displays a highly decorative combination of Pictish symbols in relief dating from the eighth century. A pair of confronting fish monsters with tongues of flame frames a cluster of symbolic geometric shapes. Below is a dominant hor-izontally placed Pictish beastie with Celtic interlace, and a double disc and Z-rod. The cross face bears an interlace cross with a medley of designs and animals within the four quarters, far more weathered than the reverse. A distinctive feature of this stone is the ogham writing with inscriptions running along three corners, the longest known ogham on a Pictish stone. Note the high relief of the carving and the careful way the grey sandstone has been dressed.

Rodney's Stone showing the cross and the two 'fish monsters'.

The stone had been discovered in nearby Dyke church-yard in 1781 and re-erected in Dyke village to commemorate Rodney's victory over the Count de Grasse in the Battle of the Saints, 1782. It was removed to the parkland of Brodie Castle which is famous for its many varieties of daffodils and majestic copper beech avenue in the early nineteenth century. A later version of the origin of its namesake was said to be the gravedigger who dug up the stone, named Rodney.

A metaphysical interpretation of the Brodie stone saw this monument as a record of the great deluge, astronomical portents in the sky, a recording of the seven known planets in the solar system at the time, and all manner of esoteric symbolic arcane explanations.

BURGHEAD

NJ 109 691

Beneath the early nineteenth century fishing village of Burghead lies one of the power centres of the kingdom of the Picts. Burghead is the largest known Pictish fort in Scotland. Two other features underline its importance: a huge well and a series of bull carvings. This was surely a royal fortress strate-gically located on a promontory jutting out into the Moray Firth. Originally the promontory was cut off from the mainland by three great ramparts and ditches. An upper citadel and a lower ward, surrounded by a rampart, still survive. A massive timber-laced stone wall, believed to have been decorated with a frieze of carved bulls, is now a grassy rampart round the citadel, the bulls being a symbol of power. Only six bulls survive out of thirty, two locally in the Headland Trust Visitor Centre and two in Elgin Museum, the others in Edinburgh and London. The great fort is dated to the fourth to sixth centuries AD and was destroyed by fire by the tenth century. The radiocarbon dates for Burghead fort range from the third to the eleventh century AD.

The entrance to Burghead Well.

On the east side of the fort is a great well chamber cut out of solid rock with a water-filled cistern surrounded by a platform. At one time called a Roman well, Burghead Well is now firmly in Pictish domain and was originally part of the fort. Whether it was a ritual baptismal well is one theory, but situated deep in the earth it exudes a great atmosphere of ancient use, even when it is flooded, as is often the case. Wells and springs were often places for worship while pagan rituals may have practised drowning as a method of execution.

A Pictish cult centre is the best possible description of Burghead in the early decades of the first millennium AD with its ritual bull carvings of fertility, the well within the earth, the horned ramparts and the fire ceremonies that continue to this day.

The Doorie Hill, just within the fort area at the headland has further pagan significance, being the site of the annual fire festival known as the *Burning of the Clavie* on Auld New Year, the 11th of January. It was also where the last witch was burned in Morayshire around the seventeenth century.

The Clavie stone on Doorie Hill.

THE WITCHES STONE Forres

NJ 0435 5929

> "We went forwards the same day to Fores, (Forres) the town to which Macbeth was travelling, when he met the weird sisters in his way. This to an Englishman is classic ground"
> Samuel Johnson,
> *A Journey to the Western Isles of Scotland*

The story of the Witches Stone in Forres takes us back to Shakespeare's famous play *Macbeth* and the real story of Macbeth with some hard evidence. One granite stone, 3ft/0.9m high, remains of three stones said to mark the graves of the three witches who bewitched King Duncan in 960. It is clasped by an iron band with a plaque that reads: "From Cluny Hill witches were rolled in stout barrels through which spikes were driven. Where the barrels stopped they were burned with their mangled contents. This stone marks the site of one such burning." It is located on the main road from Forres to Elgin in front of the Police Station. Yet the Witches Stone is one of only a few remains of the witch mania that swept Scotland in the sixteenth to seventeenth centuries. The Scottish composer James MacMillan has written a piece, *The Confession of Isobel Gowdie*, about this most famous real woman in the witchcraft stories of the time. He writes:

> It is an extraordinary fact that in the centuries before the Reformation the number of known executions for witchcraft in Scotland was in single figures; but in the years between 1560 and 1707 as many as 4,500 Scots perished because their contemporaries thought they were witches. The persecution of witches was a phenomenon known to Catholic and Protestant Europe at this time but the Reformation in Scotland gave an impetus to the attack on 'witches' which became a popular and powerful crusade. Medieval notions of good and evil spirits had been repressed by the Reformers – to seek the intercession of saints was no longer a virtue but a superstition, to leave out milk for the fairies or to give oatmeal to a witch was seen as a Satanic act. And so Scotland's experiences with witch-hunting can be seen as defensive responses to the fear of alien traditions and cultures, and to the more basic fear of those who were different from the majority.
>
> Many of the victims were women whose sex alone seems to have been the inspiration for their persecutors' zeal. Mass hysteria surrounded the suspicion of these women from whom confessions were extorted through torture of the severest kind. In 1662 Isobel Gowdie from Nairn confessed to having been baptised by the devil and joining a coven of 13 who met at night; she had journeyed to the centre of the

earth to feast with the King and Queen of the fairies; she could fly, or become a hare, a cat or a crow; she used waxen images and bags of boiled toads to cause inflictions…

(from Composer's notes)

Isobel Gowdie was one of the coven of thirteen witches of Auldearn, a town near Nairn where she was born. Much of what is known about witches in Scotland came from Isobel's confessions in the seventeenth century. She tells of travelling to Elfland, being a guest at a ball held by the King and Queen of Fairyland. Her story is full of remarkable accounts of transforming corn stalks into horses and taking part in wild hunts, shape-shifting or transmogrifying into various animals along with the correct incantations. Isobel preferred being a hare above all else, enabling her to come and go undetected. The hare is a sacred animal, especially in Scotland where they are abundant. She was a friend of Jean Gordon, niece of the Wizard of Gordonstoun in Moray, Robert Gordon. Isobel met her death, so legend tells, by being 'worrit', or strangled and burned on Gallows Hill outside Auldearn.

The Wizard of Gordonstoun

Sir Robert Gordon (1647–1704) was the Laird of the barony of Gordonstoun, an estate in Duffus near Elgin with a once marshy Bog o' Plewlands, now a small loch and home of the smart Gordonstoun School. Robert was a student of alchemy, earning the title of 'Wizard of Gordonstoun' – 'the wisest of warlocks'. It is told that he made a pact with the devil. To ward off this fate he built the Round Square at Gordonstoun, a place with no corners for the deil' to hide in. He escaped to Birnie Kirk, pursued by the dark horseman and hounds, but he died before the devil took his soul as he had sanctuary there.

Recently a foul smell at the school was the cause of the discovery of Sir Robert's long lost dungeon found beneath a hidden trap door. The dungeon was 14 feet deep and only 2 feet wide and there was water in the bottom of the pit. Sir Robert was known to have imprisoned estate workers and locals with whom he was displeased.

Truth is, the Gordon family were not too popular in the Laich of Moray, having come from the east of Scotland. He was always practising the Black arts and thought to be in communion with the devil.

A rhyme of the time tells…

"The gowd*, the Gordon, and the hoodie craw
are the three worst ills that Moray e'er saw…"
* *gowd* = weeds

Gordonstoun today is a possible model for Harry Potter's

Hogwarts that boasts such alumni as Philip Mountbatten, the Duke of Edinburgh, and Prince Charles. The school is divided into 'houses' which compete fiercely against each other in sports, just as at Hogwarts.

SUENO'S STONE

NJ 0465 5953

Considered to be the greatest sculptured stone in Scotland if not 'the most remarkable sculptured monument in Britain' according to Historic Scotland, this elegant obelisk is located on the northeast outskirts of Forres and now housed in a purpose-built glass protective pavilion. Late ninth to early tenth century, Sueno's Stone records some great battle although the Danish King Sueno – who belongs to a later period of the eleventh century – had no connection to the monument. Thus it is a misnomer to call it Sueno's Stone.

The weathered sandstone sculpture stands at the great height of 21.3ft/6.5m bearing a complicated medley of battle scenes on the main face and a cross on the west face. Over 100 figures are involved in the battle story: massed foot soldiers and cavalry, decapitated heads and scenes of war and destruction. The present consensus is that this stone is about a battle between Picts and Scots in the ninth century. Won by the Scots and their ruler inaugurated king of Scotland, this monument becomes propaganda for the victorious Scots enabled by a Pictish master craftsman. The edges of the stone bear interlace decoration and inhabited vine scroll, a motif borrowed from Northumbrian art.

Marianna Lines

Marianna Lines

Morayshire

CAMUS STONE

NJ 1529 6838

The Camus stone is a solitary standing stone located on a farm track near Inverugie by Duffus, not far from Sueno's Stone but totally different.

This is a small blocky prehistoric stone, 5.7ft/1.75m high composed of quartzose micaceous schist rock. Two sets of carvings are found on the north face of the stone, each comprising a cup within five concentric rings along with a group of cup-marks between the two ring areas. Spiral designs could appear to be what is carved there but such a worn old vintage stone can reveal little now. The name of the stone comes from a legendary commemoration of the victory of Malcolm II over the Danes whose leader was Camus, a similar misnomer to its taller cousin Sueno's Stone. It may be a boundary stone, perhaps even part of a long lost stone circle on the hill.

Nearby is the village of Duffus which has a four-teenth century ruined kirk and Duffus Castle (NJ 189 672), a romantic ruin that seems to be toppling down the hillside as it follows the contours of the hill. A dragon carving has been seen on a lintel inside the castle. It is also a popular local place for egg rolling at Easter time. Ancient customs never die.

Duffus is also the location for Gordonstoun School where the Wizard of Gordonstoun once held court.

* * *

Photos: Marion Leigh

ELGIN CATHEDRAL and Stone

NJ 2219 6305

All photos this page © Aberdeenshire Council Archaeology Service

'The Lantern of the North' is the affectionate name given to Elgin Cathedral, now a magnificent ruin, which dates back to the thirteenth century. The Cathedral was the spiritual heart of Moray until the Protestant Reformation when it was burnt down by the infamous Wolf of Badenoch in 1390.

Within the Cathedral can be found a fine granite cross-slab of Pictish origin, Class II, eighth century. Heavily weathered, a cross appears on the front face flanked by four figures of the Evangelists and a panel of interlaced animals beneath. The reverse shows Pictish symbols of the double disc and Z-rod and crescent and V-rod above a classic hunting scene complete with falcon, dogs and stags.

GODDESS STONE, BLACKHILLS

NJ 2704 5867

On the revered garden estate of Blackhills east of Elgin where rhododendrons are famed for their glorious colours, there is a curious stone known as the Goddess Stone. Housed in a pagoda

Marion Leigh

shelter by the main house, the pillar stone is sculptured with a double spiral motif on one face and a Pictish style cres- cent and multiple cup- marks on the other side. This stone has never had the fortune to be taken seriously into the corpus of Pictish sculp- tured stones, yet it bears both Neolithic and Pictish markings. It was said to have come from the nearby village of Llanbryde (re: St Bride) as the market cross, but this is not recorded.

There is also a modern built stone circle at Blackhills created by Sylvester Christie the great Laird back in the 1980s. He always maintained he was only the guardian of these ancient monuments, not the owner. His wife Georgie was proud to be descended from Lewis Carroll (Charles L. Dodgson) of *Alice in Wonderland* fame, and Blackhills could well have been the inspiration for the story. Blackhills has always been a favoured spot for the Findhorn Community to visit at the height of spring flowering when the nature spirits are at their happiest.

The garden at Blackhills was started at the beginning of the twentieth century by Thomas North Christie, a retired tea planter who eagerly took advantage of the many new species of rhododendron that were being discovered in remote mountainous regions of Tibet and China. There are Scots Pines which are 250 years old and 360 species of Rhodo- dendrons in this sixty acre sheltered valley with a micro climate that is auspicious for these rare species.

BIRNIE

NJ 2065 5871

Birnie Kirk with its oval-shaped Celtic churchyard is only a few miles south of Elgin near Fogwatt. A Norman church on the go for 800 years, Birnie was an ancient seat of the Bishops of

Moray. Its dedication was to St Brendan the Navigator similar to other early church sites in the Spey valley. A Pictish sculptured stone of the Class I period, circa seventh century, stands at the west gate marking time and showing an incised carving of an eagle twinned with a gate-way/notched rectangle and Z-rod symbol. A granite slab, this type of stone is very hard to carve but being so weathered it is difficult to make out. Inside the chancel under the Norman arch can be found a Celtic hand bell made of iron. These Celtic hand bells are rare and wonderful. Others are found in special Early Christian sites around Scotland. A number of excavations have taken place at Birnie in recent years so there is more to discover.

Stone at Birnie Kirkyard.

Aberdeenshire Council Archaeology Service © ACAS

SCULPTOR'S CAVE

NJ 1750 7072

Along the coast of the Moray Firth from Burghead toward Lossiemouth is the area known as Covesea, marked by great sea stacks. The Sculptor's Cave at Covesea is located near the base of impressive cliffs where the Moray Firth meets the sea, only accessible at low tide from the coast level. The cave interior 44.3ft/13.5m long is reached via twin passages which are 36ft/11m long leading from the large entrance canopy.

There is a somewhat macabre history to these caves for when they were excavated there were skulls found of children along with a range of objects of Late Bronze Age date: bronze arm rings, ring money, a swan's neck pin, pottery, and a very large quantity of human remains. Today what can be seen are Pictish symbols on the cave walls of the salmon, the crescent and V-rod, triple oval, mirror case, pentacle/pentagrams, flower symbol, and rectangular symbols. Like the Pictish sculptured caves at East Wemyss in Fife, the carvings are near the double entranceway.

The very nature of this site – so sacred in its time – of a cave difficult and dangerous to access, a dark and frightening place, is likely to have made this a highly appropriate location for the undertaking of ritual practices. Situated between land and sea, the symbolic upper world and underworld, this was a liminal location for rites of passage that may have taken place,

Morayshire

an access point to the underworld – somewhat like the *sipapu* of the Native American kiva.

In the same area of Covesea, close to Hopeman, are more ancient remains: dinosaur footprints of a much much earlier age, fossilised prints on rock slabs beside Clashach Quarry. And even a Pictish imprint at Clashach Cove, a crescent and V-rod symbol carved on the east side of a natural arch eroded into the sea cliffs is found here.

The Braemou Well, a holy well that has been somewhat revived on the coastal walk below Hopeman House, was described in antiquarian writings as a specific to cure the evil eye, some say to heal eyesight. Waters of this well have been used in modern times for the preparation of flower essences in homeopathic healing with Findhorn Flower Essences.

KNOCKANDO

NJ 1863 4287

Up in the remote hinterlands of Morayshire stands a beautiful white church with a round tower on a high knoll, a round Culdee rath above the River Spey. Antiquities are all around in this rather fey otherworldly location beset with the mists of whisky aroma from Knockando Distillery nearby and a wauk mill, one of the last original working wool mills in Scotland down the road. Set into the surrounding wall of the churchyard at the entrance gates are three rough sculptured stones, two of which are early and very eroded Pictish symbol stones, while the third is said to bear Scandinavian runes of the ninth to tenth century.

Reproduced from 'Sacred Stones, Sacred Places' by Marianna Lines

The first stone bears a sun wheel above two twin crescent and V-rod symbols, the right side being almost indistinct now looking somewhat like floating umbrellas below a twelve-spoked incised sun symbol (calendar clock?), a 5ft/1.5m tall gneiss slab. The taller slab to the right shows very faintly a serpent, a flower symbol, and a large mirror and partial comb. This stone is broken in the centre, set into a concrete plinth. The stones were brought to Knockando in the 1820s from the old burial ground and church site at Pulvrenan dedicated to St Brendan the Navigator. A local story tells that the stones came from the Spey, brought up river by St Brendan in his coracle. Such a romantic notion seems to fit, but who knows. It is part of the mystery of this rather strange place.

INVERAVON

NJ 1828 3759

The Spey River, source of salmon and legend, winds in serpentine fashion around the wooded haugh of St Peter's Church at Inveravon where four Pictish symbol stones can be found in a most beautiful setting. At the confluence of the River Avon and Spey is a fertile plain, sustenance for *Druicial temples and sepulchres* (as these sites were once known) from time immemorial, ancient civilisations that lead from stone circles to artistic stone carvings.

Walter Baxter, Wikimedia Commons

Now located in a porch shelter on the north side of the church, the Pictish stone gallery unfolds. The largest, Peter's Stone, 5ft/1.5m tall in blue slate, shows a dominant finely incised eagle below a decorated mirror case along with the mirror and comb double symbol [*see photo above*]. This bird is none other than a sea eagle, once common in Scotland, with its long short-legged body, long curved beak and large talons. The second stone, also of Class I, from the sixth to seventh century, has geometric symbols of the crescent and V-rod, triple disc or cauldron and mirror and comb which appear on the stone as though they were lanterns floating in a stony sky.

A delicate fragment of a Pictish beastie head is the third small stone which features the graceful curve of the beak of this water-horse/kelpie symbol, so appropriate to be found here by the Spey where legends of kelpies and the *White Horse of the Spey* are told. This mystical water horse takes an unsuspecting victim in the dark of night as its yearly sacrifice. The fourth stone has carvings of a much-weathered crescent and V-rod symbol paired with the full image of the Pictish beastie.

Spey Eagle Stone, Inveravon. Hand-coloured natural dye fabric painting by Marianna Lines.

In the Speyside area of Inveravon and Knockando there are a number of stone circles at Ballindalloch along with the sixteenth century romantic fortified tower house of Ballindalloch Castle. Marionburgh stone circle (NJ 1830 3640) is a 'Clava type' with central cairn ringed by standing stones, while the upper Ballindalloch circle, although ruined, powerfully crowns the hill above the valley, a lower circle seen below by the road. These paired Clava type chambered cairn/ruined stone circles are defined in the Council records as Lagmore West or Upper (NJ 1765 3583) and Lagmore East or Lower (NJ 1796 3595). The Moray Council Sites and Monuments Record for the Marionburgh site describes this as a Clava type cairn standing on a terrace above the River Avon. The circular cairn measures 46ft/14m in diameter, a bank of small stones around a central space. The cairn would have been revetted on both sides by kerbs or boulders. Now only one remains. Originally a circle of standing stones surrounded the cairn, now only five are standing, two fallen, one leaning, one now embedded in the wall. This description is quite similar to those for the Lagmore circles with the addition of a cup-marked stone at Lower Lagmore. A number of cup-marks are found there on the northeast stone. The Ballindalloch Golf course now includes the Lower Lagmore site.

St Peter's Well can also be found in the area, known for its curative powers, its waters still used for christening by the family in the castle.

MORTLACH

NJ 3241 3924

Located deep in Spey whisky country near Dufftown, Kirkton of Mortlach, Mortlach churchyard has a fine Pictish stone tucked in amongst late Victorian headstones. Carved out of green slate in relief, the cross face shows a pair of fish monsters above a simple Latin cross with spiral infill, and a guardian lion-like beast. The reverse has incised carving of a fine Spey eagle (very eroded), serpent, bull's head and a horseman and hound. The Class II stone dating from the ninth century is called the Battle Stone, depicting the story of the famous Battle of Mortlach won by Malcolm II over the Danes in 1010. Folk memory or fact, it is common to associate a monumental stone with an historical event.

Within the porch of the church hides another smaller symbol stone known as the 'Elephant stone', an early Pictish stone circa seventh century carved with a Pictish beast and the curvilinear wave symbol, as well as an eleventh century Calvary cross stone.

AUCHINDOUN

NJ 3488 3745

Aberdeenshire Council Archaeology Service © ACAS

Auchindoun Castle is a romantic ruin of the first degree in a lonely and commanding setting, gaunt and imperious on the crest of a high bank overlooking the River Fiddich in the Cabrach of Strathdon. Upon setting eyes on this startling ruin it seems to evoke memories of a turbulent past and intense feuding between warring clans. It stands within Iron Age earth-works where there was a hillfort. Auchindoun Castle dates to the fifteenth century, built by James or Thomas Cochrane. It is first recorded in 1509 as a medieval fortress which changed hands from the Ogilvys to the Gordons and back, clan warfare causing fires and destruction.

In its heyday Auchindoun became the stronghold of the Gordons. A supporter of Mary Queen of Scots, Sir Adam Gordon in his evil deeds became known as the Edom o' Gordon. The bloody history of Auchindoun tells that in November 1571 Adam Gordon of Auchindoun, who was still supporting the deposed Queen Mary, attacked and burned

Morayshire

Corgarff Castle killing 24 people including the wife and family of the laird John Forbes and servants. Many murders and behead- ings later, the Mackintoshes sought revenge and burnt down Auchindoun itself. As a result he was beheaded by the Countess of Huntly's cook! And so it goes on. Soon after, Patrick Gordon was killed in 1594 in the Battle of Glenlivet. The castle later returned to the Ogilvys, but by 1725 it was derelict.

The traditional Scottish Child ballad no.178 printed in 1755, *Edom o' Gordon* recounts the gruesome events of Gordon's burn- ing down of his enemy's castle. In the ensuing story of the fire, the lady throws sheets down to catch her baby, but instead she is thrown from the blaze and Gordon impales her on the end of his spear. The story documents the real historical event, and Edom o' Gordon is usually identified as Adam Gordon of Auchindoun.

A sophisticated L-plan four story tower house built with fine stone vaults, Auchindoun was said to be a favourite picnic spot of Queen Victoria and her consort Albert when she visited her beloved Highlands. A famous folk ballad immortalises the story of Auchindoun:

> *As A cam in bi Fiddichside on a may mornin*
> *Auchindoun was in a bleeze, an hour before the dawnin*
> *Crawing, crawing, for a' your crouse crawin'*
> *Ye burnt yer crop an tint your wings an oor before the dawnin*

PRINCESS STONE, GLENFERNESS

NH 9365 4260

The Findhorn River takes in a 63 mile journey into some of the most magical awe-inspiring and historical countryside in all of Scotland. With its dark rich tannin waters, it makes a rapid whirling descent from the Monadhliath Mountains to Findhorn Bay and out into the Moray Firth passing through the deep gorge of Randolph's Leap with its foaming whirlpools. Along its way there is a rich and diverse brew of history and drama. The Princess Stone is the only carved stone monolith along the Findhorn, standing proud in the grounds of Glenferness Estate beside a path leading to the Princess Pool.

A Pictish symbol stone with a sad heart, this stone tells the tragic love story of a captive Danish prince who fell in love with the daughter of the local Pictish warlord or mormaer. As the two escaped on horseback they were swept into the swollen waters of the river to their death, a twist on the classic Tristan and Iseult Celtic legend. The sculptured stone, Class II circa eighth century, shows a relief cross with interlacing spirals above a pair of figures who may be embracing in their deteriorated weathered state, a story captured in stone that bewitches any clear interpretation.

On the front is a complex array of Pictish symbols including from the top a hooded kneeling archer with cross-bow, a small Pictish beastie, crescent and V-rod, a hound, a large double disc and Z-rod, and a large beastie with interlace scrolling partially buried in the earth. This beastie is very similar to that on the Brodie stone a few miles away east of Nairn. The stone is broken and propped up with concrete pillars in a poor state of antiquated romantic disrepair, lichen enveloping what images remain. The veins of quartz in the soft sandstone sit proud to almost skeletonise the stone. Such a setting 'in the wild' is so very appropriate for a Pictish sculptured stone as you would never get such atmosphere in a museum.

FINDHORN RIVER LORE

A grove of ancient beech trees line the bank as it falls away to the River Findhorn, meaning 'white horn'. This 'nature power point' looks on to Randolph's Leap where yet another clan warfare saga brought tragedy as one warlord (not named Randolph) leapt the divide on horseback. At the confluence of the River Divie with the Findhorn is a small hill known as Thomas the Rhymer's Hill linking another folk legend of the den of the last wolves of Moray with a place of otherworldliness and raw natural beauty. The Findhorn River valley may well be one of the most naturally undisturbed and mystical wild places in all of Britain. Its peat-stained waters are a reflection of river gold, salmon run and wild places.

THE LAST WOLF

'Last wolf' legends are found in many parts of Scotland, although the very last was allegedly killed in 1743 near the River Findhorn by a stalker named MacQueen. The River Divie is a tributary to the Findhorn at its confluence at Randolph's Leap and holds the story of the wolves. The den of the last wolves of Moray was said to be located at the deep ravine at the wee stone bridge at Glenerney. Two brothers from Feakirk went to kill the cubs, but one brother encountered the mother wolf and the other fled, resulting in the murder of the adult wolves. The unfortunate brothers were hung on the small hill known as Thomas the Rhymer's Hill near the Findhorn. There is no real connection with Thomas the Rhymer other than the hill may be perceived to be a faerie or 'hollow hill'. Many landscape anomalies along the river exist such as ancient sand dunes and overgrown hillforts.

Note: by historic fact, the date of 1743 is too late for the last wolf in Britain, even in the Highlands. This story may be symbolic, according to Highland storyteller/author Bob Pegg. He suggests that the date is so close to Culloden, time of the death of the clans, and the ending of an old way of life. The wolves are that death.

Bow Fiddle Rock at Portknockie, a natural sea arch resembling the bow of a fiddle, rising about 50 feet high off the coast on the Moray Firth, silhouetted by the night sky Aurora on the 27th of February 2014.

Morayshire

Opposite page: Rosemarkie Stone – art by Marianna Lines.

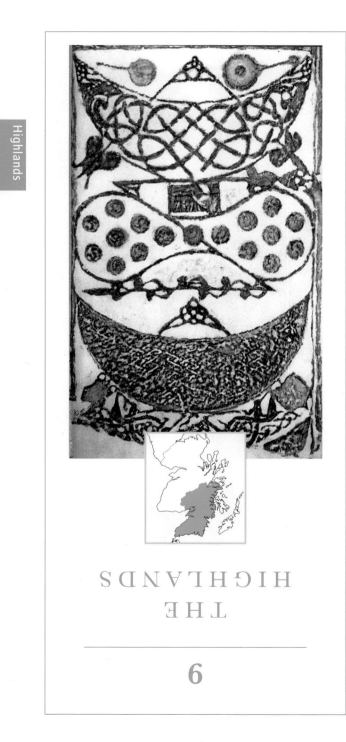

6

THE HIGHLANDS

PRINCIPAL SITES

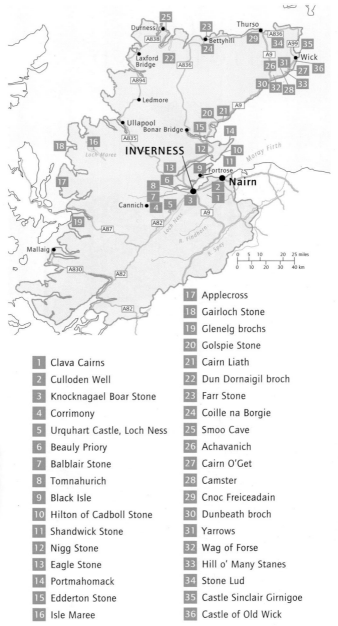

1 Clava Cairns
2 Culloden Well
3 Knocknagael Boar Stone
4 Corrimony
5 Urquhart Castle, Loch Ness
6 Beauly Priory
7 Balblair Stone
8 Tomnahurich
9 Black Isle
10 Hilton of Cadboll Stone
11 Shandwick Stone
12 Nigg Stone
13 Eagle Stone
14 Portmahomack
15 Edderton Stone
16 Isle Maree
17 Applecross
18 Gairloch Stone
19 Glenelg brochs
20 Golspie Stone
21 Cairn Liath
22 Dun Dornaigil broch
23 Farr Stone
24 Coille na Borgie
25 Smoo Cave
26 Achavanich
27 Cairn O'Get
28 Camster
29 Cnoc Freiceadain
30 Dunbeath broch
31 Yarrows
32 Wag of Forse
33 Hill o' Many Stanes
34 Stone Lud
35 Castle Sinclair Girnigoe
36 Castle of Old Wick

Highlands

THE HIGHLANDS

ONCE THE TRAVELLER ASCENDS to the north – the Highlands of Scotland – they have arrived at the top of the world. Sacred sites in the north include some of the greatest ancient sites on the planet, a hyberbole that is not unfounded. Inverness-shire lays claim to the great stone temple network of the Clava Cairns, a breakthrough in Neolithic stone building. Stone rows in Caithness are twins to those of the great Carnac in France. Brochs in Sutherland are awe-inspiring feats of architecture and beauty. There are fairy glens and clootie wells, Pictish stones and the kingdom of the Northern Picts. The land of the ancestors is alive in this place, a sacred place to explore in its quiet and peaceful beauty.

The Scottish Highlands is the region of the north main-land of Scotland, an area north and west of the Highland Boundary Fault. The Great Glen divides the Grampian Mountains to the southeast from the Northwest Highlands. Culturally it is the language of the Gaels, Scottish Gaelic, that defines the region as distinguished from the Lowlands where Lowland Scots is (or was) spoken. In a sparsely populated area, mountain ranges dominate the Highlands, including Ben Nevis the highest mountain in the British Isles at 4,408ft/1344m above sea level.

Before the nineteenth century the Highlands was home to a much larger population, but due to the infamous Highland Clearances following the Jacobite Rising of 1745, life changed forever. Mass migration to urban areas, the introduction of sheep to replace people, and the outlawing of the traditional Highland way of life all contributed to what is now seen virtu-ally as a ghost land in the far north. However, once you find yourself there, it is well worth the journey.

* * *

According to a well known Highland storyteller/musician Bob Pegg,

> "In the Highlands and Islands every river, loch, bay, cave, mountain, burn, castle, croft, hillock, has its own story to tell. Wolves, selkies, kelpies, ghosts, Picts, Vikings, Neolithic tomb builders, and the good people, have been a constant source of inspiration since I came to live in the far north."

To know the Highlands is to truly live there.

CLAVA CAIRNS

NH 757 444

The evocative Clava Cairns are one of Scotland's most sacred prime prehistoric sites. Three burial cairns in a clear alignment with ley lines running northeast to southwest indicate a mid-winter sunset setting for which this site was clearly built. Totally unique in all of Britain, the Clava Cairns date from the Bronze Age, about 4,000 years old. The cairns, two with entrance passages and the central one a ring cairn, are each encircled by massive standing stones as a separate element from the tombs themselves. The central chamber is large enough for a small group to gather providing a perfect echo sounding chamber for chanting.

HER-Historic Environment Team, Highland Council

Marion Leigh

Highlands

The site is located at Balnauran of Clava near the River Nairn in a small enchanted wood with outlier stones and cairns dotted around the area and Culloden battlefield, another sacred site of Scotland's bloody history, a mile north. The Culloden Moor viaduct, all twenty eight spans of Scotland's longest masonry viaduct, overshadows the site in a dramatic extended historical landscape.

It is believed that these tombs were built to house the privileged elite among the farming community as few burials have been found.

Cup-marks are found within the passages of the chambers as well as on a kerbstone on the north cairn which looks like a stargazer's map with its multiple cup and ring marks. Recent excavations by the archaeologist Richard Bradley has revealed that the stones of the circles are graded in height, with the tallest facing the setting sun in the southwest in order to highlight the veneration ceremony at midwinter solstice. His report reads:

> "In addition to the finds underground, a thorough survey of the upstanding remains revealed hitherto unnoticed connections between the colour and texture of the building materials, the architecture of the monuments and their known relationship with the rising and setting sun."

For maximum atmospheric effect to appreciate this site, it is best to visit around sunrise or sunset or at midwinter's close of the day around the winter solstice. This Bronze Age cemetery complex thus comprises passage graves, ring cairns, kerb stones, a smaller kerb cairn, standing stones, prehistoric rock art and the remains of a chapel within a magical setting. When the haar rolls in, the spirits arise.

CULLODEN WELL

NH 7235 4523

The Culloden Well has worn many names over its long history of ritual healing use. *Tobar na Coille* is the Gaelic, then Well of the Wood, Well of the Lady, Rag Well, and St Mary's Well as it is sometimes known today in association with the church site nearby of that name. This is a clootie well located in the heart of Culloden woods. To reach the well you need to trek through the forest to a damp dark clearing where an eerie enchanting spot reveals trees festooned with coloured rags or cloots and a stone-built wall around the natural spring.

Clootie wells date back to pre-Christian times when people would take a 'cloot' or cloth and soak it in the well water, rub this on the ailment and hang on a nearby tree as an offering to the local spirit or saint. The idea traditionally was that the local 'genie'/ spirit of the well would cure the ill as the cloot disintegrated. It was always bad luck to take any cloots away from the site as it would cause a transfer of the malady.

As the well is associated with Culloden, it has been told that originally the women of the soldiers who fell in battle would tear strips off their petticoats or tartan to offer to the well for their dead. The historic battlefield of Culloden nearby was the site of the last pitched battle in Britain. On the 16th of April 1746 an army led by Bonnie Prince Charlie was vanquished by government forces in less than an hour, ending Jacobite hopes of restoring the exiled Stuart dynasty to the throne. The haunting plain of Culloden and the whole area of the well and the Clava Cairns down the road are all part of the powerful electric atmosphere of this area. Clootie wells are a Celtic phenomenon that can be found through the Celtic world of Scotland, England, Wales, Ireland, Brittany, and beyond.

KNOCKNAGAEL BOAR STONE

NH 6567 4134 original site [Knocknagael Farm]

The Boar Stone. Inset: Wild Boar – art by Marianna Lines.

A splendid carving of a wild boar dominates this massive slate boulder, one of the most iconic symbols of the Pictish tribal people. The boar is shown with curvilinear spiral infill indicating muscular prowess, the boar being a symbol of strength and power. His high ridge of spiky bristles is raised for a fight. Directly above the boar is the mirror case symbol. Dating from the seventh century, this pre-Christian early Class I Pictish stone may relate to the tribal clan lineage of a warrior, as the boar symbol also appears in the west at Dunadd hillfort. The stone was originally found on Knocknagael Farm on the southern outskirts of Inverness but has been moved for safety to Highland Council HQ in the town, so can only be observed through a glass, darkly.

CORRIMONY

NH 3831 3030

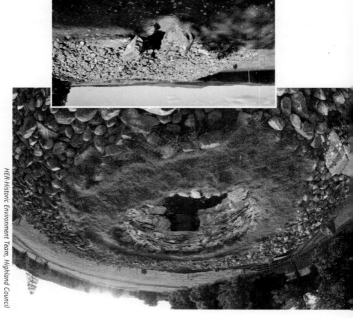

HER-Historic Environment Team, Highland Council

Highlands

The remarkable well-preserved Corrimony Chambered Cairn is a Clava type cairn near Cannich in Glen Urquhart, Strathglass, inland from Urquhart Castle. Dating from the third millennium BC, Corrimony is a passage grave with an open chamber in the centre and defined by kerb stones, those of great size at the entranceway. The original massive capstone decorated with a multitude of cup-marks has been moved to the side of the cairn. A circle of eleven standing stones surround the cairn which may have been a later addition. Built by Neolithic farmers skilled in working stone, this was a co-operative society that continued into the Bronze Age, working the land and domesticating animals.

The cairn was built for collective burials although only one crouched burial has been excavated. As with other passage graves, the alignment is oriented towards the southwest for the winter solstice time of ceremony to welcome the return of the sun to the north. Nearby to Corrimony's ancient site lies a remnant of the great Caledonian forest, as ancient a woodland as the stones and where an excellent RSPB Nature Reserve has black grouse courtship displays in the spring along with other rare Scottish birds.

LOCH NESS/URQUHART CASTLE

NH 5309 2864

The Loch Ness monster is much more than a tourist myth or a folk legend. This is the subterranean water horse, a formidable senior to the kelpie, the *each-uisge* that appears on the mystical Pictish symbol stones. It has been recorded that St Columba met 'Nessie' and befriended or tamed it. Many people have witnessed this supernaturally real dinosaur-age creature of the deepest waters of Loch Ness. One elderly lady who lived on the Loch kept a map and used a needle and thread to dowse for the monster in its lair, and claimed to always be correct. She was what is called a white witch in the Highlands. The best viewing spot is on the far side of the Loch at Foyers where it is quieter. The over-run tourist attraction at Urquhart Castle is a magnificent romantic ruin but not where a sensitive ancient water horse would venture except under cover of darkness.

Each Uisge (Scots Gaelic for water spirit) is the name given for the Highland supernatural water horse, the most dangerous of Scottish water-dwelling creatures which inhabits sea lochs and fresh water lochs. This creature has the ability to shapeshift in order to lure people into the water to an unkindly fate. Loch Ness is the perfect place for such a creature to exist, located on the Great Glen fault line and being the deepest and largest freshwater loch in Scotland, all 23miles/37km long and 754.5ft/230m deep at its lowest point.

It has been suggested that the folklore of the water horse stems from real encounters with such water dwelling creatures in deep lochs. Indeed Loch Ness and Loch Morar in the western Highlands are famous for these 'cryptozoological' sightings. Loch Ness is also known for its deep peaty colour of gold, similar to whisky, arising from the surrounding high peat content of the soil and its extensive underwater passageways. There is also an Iron Age crannog in Loch Ness known as Cherry Island.

With Urquhart Castle on the eastern end of the Loch, there is ample space and scope for anything mysterious to dwell in these waters.

There has been a fortification on this promontory ever since Pictish times. St Columba is said to have visited the area of this stronghold in the sixth century to meet the great Pictish King Brude or Bridei, where he converted the Pictish chieftain to Christianity and indeed introduced the legendary Nessie-lassie to history around AD 554 according to the saint's biographer Adamnan. Once one of Scotland's largest castles, Urquhart today displays marvellous ruins including a tower house with splendid views down the Loch to the Great Glen. It witnessed considerable conflict throughout its 500 years as a medieval fortress since the thirteenth century and was a prominent site in the Scots struggle for independence in the fourteenth century when Robert the Bruce took control of the castle as King of the Scots. It is not the last time there was a pitch for independence in this fiercely independent country.

BEAULY PRIORY

NH 5275 4648

HER-Historic Environment Team, Highland Council

The legend of the Brahan Seer figures prominently in the landscape around Inverness where other seers such as Thomas the Rhymer (thirteenth century) also held forth. Beauly Priory is the resting place for many nobles of the Mackenzie Clan to which Kenneth Mackenzie, or Coinneach Odhar belongs. Located at the end of the Beauly Firth on the Black Isle, Beauly was said to be named by Mary Queen of Scots on a visit when she exclaimed: "Quel c'est beau lieu". The Priory, founded in 1230 by the Valliscaulian order of monks from France, lasted for 300 years until the Reformation of 1560. Within the roofless ruins in a beautiful setting of tree canopy, the red sandstone buildings contain the vault dedicated to Kenneth Mackenzie of Kintail, d.1492, with an effigy of a knight.

The Scottish clairvoyant of the same name, Kenneth Mackenzie, however belongs to the seventeenth century. Legend has it that he was born in Uig on the island of Lewis in the Outer Hebrides, and while sleeping on a fairy hill he found a small stone which provided his oracle to the future. Among many prophecies come true, like the coming of the oil, he foretold the downfall of the Mackenzie family for whom he worked. He was burnt to death in a barrel of burning tar, the punishment for a witch at that time. Chanonry Point at Fortrose has a memorial cairn to the Seer beside the shore where the popular Moray Firth bottle-nosed dolphins frolic. Like many popular legends, none of the story of the Brahan Seer can be proven but the story of a man of humble birth who gains magical powers and foretells the demise of nobility is akin to a Scottish hero, remembered as the 'Scottish Nostradamus'. Second Sight is a virtue prized by the Highlanders above all others.

BALBLAIR STONE

NH 5518 4357

Moniack Castle, a lovely wooded property at Balblair, Kilmorack, has a very special rockery by its front door. A strange Pictish stone is found there, perhaps invisible to most but it shows, in its eroded state, the figure of a Pictish man in his traditional habit of the tunic, walking in profile wearing a mask/helmet and carrying a staff. Some might even call it a cricket bat. There are cup-marks on this stone, indicating it has been re-used since earlier Neolithic times. As Moniack Castle operates the Moniack Winery, perhaps more inspiration will come as to the true meaning of this rather odd Pictish stone. A second Pictish stone also came from the rockery, this being a symbol stone of seventh century date with the triple oval symbol and the crescent and V-rod, which is now in Inverness Museum. The triple oval symbol only seems to occur in the north, with two further examples known in Caithness.

TOMNAHURICH

NH 6558 4415

Tomnahurich is the fairy hill of Inverness, a mound covered in trees on the west side by the River Ness and visible from all around the city. The hill is a natural rarity, an esker, which is a ridge of murrain left over from a glacier.

This *hill of the yews* has an enduring tradition of fairyland associated with it. The famed Thomas the Rhymer is buried beneath it. Amongst the modern cemetery the paths wind up to the top where a clearing in the wood is found, this being the invisible opening into the underworld. The legend of one or two fiddlers who were lured into playing in a great hall beneath the hill tells of their return after one night, which was in fact a hundred years. They turned to dust once they came back into the real world, walking down the streets of Inverness.

The difference in time between this world and the world of faerie is an important folklore motif in tales about the otherworld.

"Normality is nothing but an illusion."

* * *

BLACK ISLE

ROSEMARKIE

NH 735 576 museum

Rosemarkie, a tiny village with a big history, lies northeast of Fortrose on the Black Isle, nestled in a hollow in the hills with a beautiful sandy beach on the Firth and backed by red sandstone cliffs. In Gaelic Rosemarkie means the *headland of the horse stream*. An early monastic centre, this was known as the shrine of St Boniface or Curitan, a place of pilgrimage.

In a simple building along the High Street can be found the Groam House Museum which houses some of the great wonders of the Pictish nation in sculpture, a fine collection of stones.

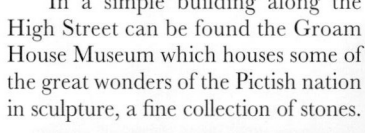

David McGovern, Pictish Arts Society

Susan Seright, University Museums In Scotland

Rosemarkie Stone.
Crescent and mirrors detail.

The stunning Rosemarkie Stone takes pride of place, a work of both Pictish and Northumbrian inspired designs, 9ft/2.7m tall and sculptured on both faces with a decorative repertoire from Insular art of Pictish and Anglo- Saxon cultures, as well as a strong reflection of the *Book of Kells* illuminated manuscript. Art historians declare this cross-slab an astounding work of art. Every surface of the stone is carved with intricate ornament. Only the very top is missing, the third of three crescent and V-rod symbols, along with a large double disc and Z-rod symbol between the two crescents. Two mirror symbols appear beneath the lower crescent. The dominant symbols central to the stone are a strong statement on the power of the Pictish nation. A cross is found on both sides of the stone, equal armed crosses. The rest of the stone is covered with panels of exquisite interlace.

A number of other decorative cross-slab fragments and Pictish figurative stones are displayed in the museum along

Highlands

with an integrated interpretive display of all the great Pictish stones of Easter Ross in natural dye wall hangings by Marianna Lines to further illuminate the colourful and powerful nature of Pictish art. All of these stones in Groam House were found in the vicinity of Rosemarkie, which attests to this being a major monastic centre from the eighth to ninth century.

FAIRY GLEN

NH 735 578 Entrance

Marion Leigh

Just on the outskirts of Rosemarkie is a natural woodland known as the Fairy Glen, not far beyond the sandy cliffs on the shore. A beautiful magical glen deeply incised in the landscape with the Markie Burn running through it, geans, birches and rowans are part of the deciduous tree mix, two waterfalls, deep pools and fossilized trees with bits of old coin offerings. The Glen is a haven for wildlife of all types including the faeries, who must be greeted when visiting at any time of year. Sand pillars of great geological interest can be found there, being eroded soft sandy rock, extremely rare in Britain. Any sacred site pilgrimage is not complete without a visit to this nature power point.

CLOOTIE WELL

NH 639 536

The Clootie Well by Munlochy on the Black Isle is a healing well dedicated to St Boniface. Conveniently located on the roadside, it has now become a highly popular shrine festooned with old rags and modern bits of odd clothing that stretch from the road where the basin offers a continual drink on up through the woods where the spring originates.

The Clootie, or cloot, is a strip of cloth or rag, and the well-head area surrounded by trees offers a convenient hanging place for the offering, much like the tradition of prayer flags in Tibet. The prescribed ritual is to visit the well at

Beltane, preferably dawn, dowse the cloot with the sacred water making a wish and then make a sunwise circle three times with the cloot before offering it to a perch among the trees, but never take anything away. The water is pure for drinking and healing and can be used in various preparations. Clootie wells are found throughout the Celtic nations, including Scotland, Ireland and Cornwall. It was believed that a goddess or nature spirit inhabited the well with special healing powers until Christianity replaced this guardian with a saint.

St Boniface or Curitan is the Black Isle saint who is also associated with Rosemarkie and its monastic origins. There is another less well-known clootie well around the bay at Munlochy that the locals use at Beltane, but it is a well-kept secret.

ROSS-SHIRE

Ross-shire, Ross and Cromarty, includes both Easter Ross and Wester Ross, two very distinctive areas of the Northern Highlands, the eastern half a rural farming land, the west a wild mountainous terrain of more sheep than people with the most dramatic mountain scenery in Western Europe.

HILTON OF CADBOLL

NH 8731 7686

Three great Pictish sculptured stones, all cross-slabs, are found within a few miles of each other on the Tarbat peninsula all within sight of the North Sea. They represent a triumvirate of power and purpose of Northern Pictland, reflecting a constellation of related sites and associated hermitages or cells, a liturgical landscape temple somewhat like Iona, perhaps.

They also share a format, a decorative repertoire that is similar but individual to their position in the landscape.

Hilton of Cadboll site on the Tarbat peninsula once had the magnificent monolith of the Hilton of Cadboll stone, but this has been hijacked to the Museum of Scotland in Edinburgh. Today St Mary's Chapel, now a mossy mound in a rectangular enclosure, remains along with a fascinating piece of modern art, the complete life size reconstruction of the Hilton stone by a single sculptor.

The original Hilton of Cadboll stone, which is dated AD 800 standing 7.5ft/2.3m high in local sandstone, displays classic Pictish Royal hunt iconography along with strong symbols framed by elegant vine scrolls. A weighty cross on its front is surrounded by writhing beasts. The aristocratic hunt scene is unique in its presentation of a woman riding side saddle wearing a fashionable penannular brooch and holding a falcon, a mirror and comb symbol shown next to her. This great cross-slab was re-used later as a family gravestone with its carvings hacked off on the cross side. Excavations at the chapel site have now revealed thousands of fragments from the original piece.

Wikimedia Commons

Modern sculpture interpretation of Hilton of Cadboll Stone by sculptor Barry Grove.

The reconstruction on site by Barry Grove reveals a modern eye yet true to the original in spirit. It is a wonder to behold in its own right. The New Hilton of Cadboll stone is the largest single relief reconstruction of a Pictish stone in over 1200 years.

The sculptured recovered base of the original sculpture can be seen in the Seaboard Memorial Hall in nearby Ballintore. The local community is keen to keep this fragment.

Highlands

SHANDWICK STONE

NH 8554 7471

Impression of the Shandwick Stone by Marianna Lines, with its panel of triple-spirals and below, the reverse side of the actual stone.

In its original position and standing in relation to a burial ground, the great slab at Shandwick faces east with the rising sun playing on its spiral-encrusted cross set high on the slab, the bold Pictish iconography facing inland. Crowning a rise in a field on Shandwick Bay beside the seaboard village of Shandwick, the stone was a useful sea marker for the once important harbour. It is thought by some to have functioned as a prayer stone. The cross is outlined with raised serpentine bosses. A perfect metre square spiral mandala panel on the symbol side offers a meditation platform with its symbolic number 8 sacred geometry design. On the back of the stone is a series of panels showing from the top large symbols of the double disc and Pictish beastie, a delightful scene of animals and figures representative of life at the time such as a crouched archer with a falcon, dancing men, deer and birds of prey. Below this is the spiral panel, fifty two symmetrically arranged spirals in concentric circles and more interlace decoration at the base. All of this fantastic sculpture is encased in a glass box for protection.

* * *

NIGG STONE

NH 8043 7170

HER-Historic Environment Team, Highland Council

The Nigg Stone, the third great cross-slab of the Moray Firth, now stands in shelter adjacent to the church at Nigg, reassembled from various breakages and standing 7.2ft/2.2m high, a Class II Pictish sculptured stone of similar dating, circa AD 800. Carved in high and low relief, the cross side combines panels of geometric key pattern and interlace with elongated animals woven in intricate patterns, a master sculptor's work with background panels of bosses encircled by serpents. The triangular pediment shows the biblical story of Paul and Anthony in the desert: a raven has brought them a loaf of bread. The back of the stone depicts an exciting hunt scene, deer pursued by hounds and horsemen and foot soldiers, along with the Biblical David symbology with his slaying of a lion; there is also a sheep, a harp, the musician and the warrior. Two Pictish symbols of the Pictish beastie and the eagle frame the top, with integrated interlace. Such a mighty complex stone takes a long viewing, not to be rushed.

The Sutors of Cromarty on the headland provide an exhilarating walk to digest the Pictishness of the moment. The entrance to the Cromarty Firth is guarded by these two precipitous headlands. Called the *Sutors* from their shape resembling a couple of shoemakers (*souter* in Scots) bent over their benches, the Firth extends for nineteen miles beyond Nigg Bay.

EAGLE STONE, Strathpeffer

NH 4849 5850

Strathpeffer, the Spa town of the north, is famous for healing waters and also for its historic wealth. The Eagle Stone is a Class I Pictish symbol stone circa seventh century AD located on the outskirts of Strathpeffer. A Pictish sea eagle and the arch or horseshoe symbol adorn this rough boulder formed of blue gneiss, which carries many legends. Its Gaelic name

Clach an Tiompain means 'sounding stone' indicating this stone may have a ringing quality when struck. Its broken right top is another clue.

There is a legend that the seventeenth century Brahan Seer predicted about the Eagle Stone, that if the stone fell three times, the surrounding valley would be flooded and the stone used as an anchor. The stone has in fact fallen twice and is now cemented into the ground on a hill overlooking the valley. On a ridge above the spa

The Eagle Stone, Strathpeffer.

town is a fine prehistoric fort known as Knockfarrel, 'the cat's back'. The fort was defended by a timber-laced stone wall, set on fire to create a vitrified fort, possibly destroyed as early as 1100 BC but in use for much longer.

PORTMAHOMACK, Tarbat

NH 9147 8402

The Tarbat Discovery Centre by Portmahomack, a seaside village named after the Port of Colman, the Celtic Saint who may have founded it, has been a hive of Pictish activity since the seventh century.

Recent excavations have confirmed that Portmahomack is the site of the first confirmed Pictish monastery. One of the largest and longest archaeological investigations in Scotland directed by Martin Carver has produced over 200 pieces of sculpture including the exquisite Calf

The 'Dragon' Stone.

stone, a cow and bull licking their calf. Dating from AD 550 and destroyed by fire circa AD 800 in a Viking raid, it had a burial ground with cist burials, a stone church, at least four monumental stone crosses and workshops making church plate and Early Christian books, including the making of

Example of a key pattern.

Highlands

vellum. The discoveries are displayed in the restored Tarbat Old Church museum.

Great sandbanks, or *gizzen brigs* are seen from the coast here looking north towards Sutherland and the Dornach Firth.

EDDERTON STONE

NH 7083 8507

The great standing stone monolith of Edderton near Tain is actually a signal Pictish symbol stone displaying a leaping salmon above the double disc and Z-rod. Also known as Clach Biorach, the pointed stone, or Clach Chairidh, the 'Weir' Stone, this red sandstone pillar is surely a re-used standing stone. It has also been identified as part of a fascinating archaeo-astronomy study of the landscape by Doug Scott of Tain who has found this stone to be the centre of a great lunar observatory landscape.

WESTER ROSS

LOCH MAREE: Isle Maree

NG 9310 7236

Marianna Lines

In a remote corner of northwest Scotland there lies the most beautiful loch in the Highlands, Loch Maree, surrounded by remnants of the old Caledonian pine forest. Similar to Loch Ness, it is the fourth largest freshwater loch in Scotland and even has its own secretive monster. It is also a loch studded with islands. Among the five large wooded islands and twenty five smaller ones, there is a special one known as the *Queen of the Faeries Island*. It is told that on that island there is a small hidden loch on which there is yet another island where on certain nights of the year the queen of the faeries holds court. This is called Eilean Subhain. It is the only island in Britain to contain a loch within an island within a loch!

And then there is the famous island with a magical history that is only accessible by boat from a nearby hotel. This is Isle Maree, or Innis Maree, which has an ancient burial ground, a wishing tree, a holy well, and a Druid story or two. The now lost remains of a small chapel were believed to be the eighth century hermitage of St Maelrubha (d. AD 722) after whom Loch Maree is named and who founded the monastery of Applecross in 672. Ancient oak and holly on the loch, found nowhere else, have been linked to the ancient Scottish Druids. The waters of Loch Maree are said to have curative effects, one remedy being immersion in the loch as a cure for lunacy. Another healing cure for insanity was offered from the small covered well, consecrated by St Maelrubha.

Incised stone cross.
Below: The money tree.

Photos: Marianna Lines

The broken remains of the holy oak tree on Isle Maree which stands near the shore is riddled or 'jeweled' with ancient coins and nails stuck in the tree like a clootie well for offerings or healing wishes. Now copper green, these coins may be what killed off the old clootie tree. Two carved stones marked with incised crosses in the old graveyard are possibly of the eleventh century and lie end to end. They are said to cover the graves of a Norwegian princess and her lover – the Tristan and Iseult of Isle Maree. Further stories tell of bull sacrifice on the island suggesting a place of pre-Christian pagan worship. The well is dried up these days but the 'clootie tree' and the old stones remain. The atmosphere on the island sanctuary is soft, dense as porridge and potent.

APPLECROSS

NG 7135 4583

Applecross, which means *The Sanctuary* in Gaelic, was originally Pictish territory until the ninth century, the name *Aporcrosan* being a Pictish name, meaning 'confluence of the Cossan'. St Maelrubha the 'red priest' of Ulster founded the monastery there in AD 673 and became its first Abbot for the next fifty years until his death.

Highlands

A large unfinished ringed cross-slab in the churchyard, site of the early monastery, and three highly skilled carved fragments preserved in the church are evidence of the high status of the early monastery.

The boundaries of the sanctuary were once marked by crosses. A holy well is found near the shore. The Early Christian sculpture in the churchyard is Pictish in style and tradition with close links to St Vigeans Pictish monastery in Angus as well as to Rosemarkie's high cross of Pictish provenance. Bird head zoomorphic terminals appear along with superb triple spiral work on these intricate stones.

Extremely isolated, Applecross peninsula was only accessible by boat until early in the twentieth century after which the only road was over the Bealach na Ba, the 'Pass of the Cattle', rising up to 2054ft/626m in height. As it lies on the mountainous edge of Wester Ross looking

Cross-slab photo by Bob Heney

HFR-Historic Environment Team, Highland Council

Top: Cross-slab at Applecross.
Above: St Maelrubha's monastery.

across the Inner Sound to Raasay and Skye, this was a perfect outpost for Northern Pictland with its fertile valley and broad sheltered bay. The Picts found their way to Skye as well, leaving several important carved stones as their calling cards.

GAIRLOCH STONE

NG 8074 7565

A rare thing to find on the west coast of Scotland in the Torridon area of Gairloch is a Pictish Stone, now housed in the Gairloch Heritage Museum. Discovered in 1880 in Achtercairn, the field of the cairn, this Class I, seventh century stone of Torridon sandstone shows the salmon in Pictish style, this being the cock or male fish, incised below the eagle symbol. Only the claws and tail of the characteristic Pictish sea eagle remain on the broken slab.

GLENELG BROCHS, Kyle of Lochalsh

NG 8290 1725 Dun Telve
NG 8340 1724 Dun Troddan

Twin broch towers of monumental proportions are found in Glenelg above the Kyle of Lochalsh in Glen Beag. These are two of the best preserved brochs in Scotland set in utterly beautiful surroundings looking over to Skye. Dun Telve is the second tallest broch at 32.8ft/10m tall while Dun Troddan is set on a terrace above the valley in a non-defensive prestige setting. At Dun Telve a long passage leads to a side guard cell and stair with five galleries within the wall still standing.

David McGovern

Dun Telve Broch.

Pictish stones are quite rare in the west and its existence here on the most fertile track of land in the area testifies to the likelihood of a Pictish settlement here between AD 400–600.

Another Pictish stone has been discovered recently in Poolewe old burial ground (NG 8602 8095), a few miles northeast of Gairloch. A long regular hewn slab, the familiar Pictish crescent symbol with V-rod is faintly inscribed at the upper end of the stone. The crescent contains two spirals which join to form a pelta or small shield as well as an arc of small pearl-like hollows around the outer edge of the crescent. This delicately inscribed ornamented crescent is another anomaly for the northwest Highlands.

Top: Poolewe inscribed Pictish stone: Above: Art by Marianna Lines.

Dun Troddan Broch.
Inset: Stairway within the walls.

The two concentric drystone walls are tied together by large horizontal slabs which also form the floors of the narrow galleries between. The second broch is 546.7yds/500m east along the glen with a corbelled entranceway and stands 25ft/7.6m tall with a stair leading to upper galleries although now ruined. Dun Troddan still shows evidence of occupation, with a broken quern stone for grinding corn set into the hearth and possibly quarters for animals on the ground floor similar to Viking longhouses or the familiar Scottish 'butt-and-ben'.

Brochs are circular fortified towers or forts (*dun* in Gaelic) dating from the Iron Age 2,000 years ago. Classified as 'complex Atlantic roundhouses', the brochs are unique to Scotland, and are the most impressive of Iron Age buildings to survive. The twin setting of these brochs at Glenelg is unusual as the famous ones in Shetland and the Isle of Lewis are both found in isolation.

Glenelg is also the location where the iconic *Ring of Bright Water* otter novel by Gavin Maxwell was written.

SUTHERLAND

A contemporary Scottish artist who has memories of his childhood spent in Sutherland, like so many Scots, sees Sutherland as a vital influence on his life. "Sutherland has it all", George Macpherson says. "Mountains, rivers, bagpipe and fiddle, and mist." Something that dims our vision but awakens our imagination. Probably one of the least inhabited of all the regions of Scotland, Sutherland still suffers from the problem of the

Clearances. Sutherland is a land of brochs, a unique Iron Age architecture of the north, and a wealth of Pictish sculptured stones. Stark elemental beauty in eerie isolation, the peaks of Sutherland are sculptures in the wilderness.

GOLSPIE STONE, Dunrobin Museum

NC 8504 0080 castle
NC 8522 0088 museum

Dunrobin Castle, the home of the Earl of Sutherland, is a white fairytale castle not far beyond Disney, located on the Moray Firth at Golspie, its grounds lapped by the sea and its turrets reaching to the clouds.

A tremendous lapidary collection of Pictish stones can be found in the castle's eclectic Victorian Museum in the grounds of the formal gardens along with stuffed elephant feet, giraffe heads and numerous rare birds in cases as well as a plethora of intriguing ethnographic collectables. It was once described as "a fascinating distraction".

The sacred sites traveller may find it more than a distraction – more like a revelation for the Pict in you. Over twenty Pictish stones have been gathered here from around the Golspie and Sutherland area featuring some of the most sensitive and delicate carvings of symbol stones in the entire corpus of Pictish Stones. The greatest stone at Dunrobin is the Golspie Stone, a Class II Pictish purple sandstone cross-slab of the eighth to ninth century. A virtual cavalcade of Pictish symbols is found on the reverse side to

*Impression of the Golspie Stone.
Art by Marianna Lines.*

*The Princess Stone.
Etching by Marianna Lines.*

the interlaced cross face, an epic story carved in stone. These range from the notched rectangle at the top, the Pictish beastie in swimming rather than leaping mode, a Pict in full tunic wear wielding a double axe and a knife beside the lion of St Mark, the salmon, flower symbol, crescent, and double disc with a pair of intertwined fish-tailed serpents below. An ogham inscription runs around the upper edge and side of the stone. This iconic stone has been described as the story of the evolution of man but many other interpretations are possible. The rest of the Pictish stone collection in the Museum is breathtaking and exciting and requires a full book to describe them all.

CAIRN LIATH

NC 8703 0137

Iain Maclean, Caithness Broch Project

One of Sutherland's prime brochs, known as Cairn Liath, stands by the Moray Firth between Golspie and Brora. The walls of this Iron Age tower have been restored to a height of some 11.5ft/3.5m with a fine thick lintel over the entranceway. Made super defensive with an added strong outer wall and a secondary stone lining, later domestic buildings outside indicate re-use of the old tower. Stone-lined pits are found in the floor for storage of food and water. A doorway opposite the entrance leads to a stair within the wall. A mysterious adventure awaits any traveller to this ancient site.

DUN DORNAIGIL Broch

NC 4571 4501

On the northwest coast of Sutherland far beyond any sensible reality for most cosy travellers lies another broch in a most stunning setting. Dun Dornaigil broch is located in Strathmore between Cape Wrath and Tongue. The wall of the broch rises almost 23ft/7m high over the entrance, collapsed to nearly 7.8ft/2.4m elsewhere in the round stone edifice, an

Photos: Iain Maclean, Caithness Broch Project

extraordinary sight to come upon in its ruined arc of ancient sculpture. It is said that the broch was built too close to the edge of a terrace above the river causing the extreme collapsed variation in height. A massive triangular lintel is set over the very low entrance with an interior of 47.5ft/14.5m in diameter. The broch was also known as Dun Dornadilla, named after 'Dornadille' in the early king lists.

FARR STONE

NC 7141 6224

A fine Pictish cross-slab can be found in Bettyhill on the far north coast of Sutherland in the churchyard beside the Strathnaver Museum. The Farr stone dates from the late ninth century and bears a ringed cross with a rounded base against a background of interlace pattern and panels of key pattern. The cross head has a central boss carved in high relief with a triple spiral. A pair of intertwined swans occupy the panel arch at the base of the cross. Further detailed carving reveals links

Impression on site of the Farr Stone by Marianna Lines.

with other foreign cultures in that the curvilinear pair of rams horn motif on either side of the central cross-shaft are comparable to the same designs seen in Anatolian Turkish killims. This is a symbol of fertility. Although very worn, the Farr Stone is one of the most intricately carved of any Pictish cross-slabs and all the more astonishing in its location so far north. The stone is blue slate with quartz veins and over 6.9ft/2.1m tall.

COILLE NA BORGIE

NC 7150 5903

The archaeological landscape of Strathnavar traces a long history of settlement. Mesolithic flintwork some 12,000 years old has been found in the estuary at Bettyhill and the township of Rosal some 12miles/20km south dates from the eighteenth century. Chambered cairns, hut circles and brochs are found on both sides of the valley. Of special interest are the Chambered cairns of Coille na Borgie south of Bettyhill. These are the iconic horned cairns found only in the Sutherland and Caithness areas of Scotland. Along the contours of the hillside are two impressive long cairns set in a line. The southern cairn, best preserved and 78.5yds/72m long, has projecting horns at either end and a burial chamber at the northern end. Only one upright tall slab survives from a long row of stones on the façade.

A further long cairn (NC 7224 5674) is found just over 2miles/3.3km south at Skelpick. This is 63.3yds/58m long with projecting horns and a well preserved chamber. Several more chambered cairns continue along the River Naver valley which imply extensive and intensive Neolithic settlement.

SMOO CAVE

NC 4188 6714

The largest coastline cave in all of the UK is set into the limestone cliffs of Sutherland, as dramatic and spectacular as any man-made sacred site and with a deep historic past. Only a few miles from Durness on Scotland's most northerly coast, Smoo Cave – from the Norse word *smjugg* or *smuga* (hiding place/hole) – is formed by both sea water and freshwater, passages formed from rainwater dissolving the limestone. A path leads from the headland over a waterfall down to the cave which stretches back to Neolithic if not Mesolithic times and onward to the Iron Age and Norse period of use. Inside the cavern the high arched mouth opens into three great chambers with watery pools, Gothic stalactites and stalagmites. Smoo Cave, at 200 ft/61m long, is a key site in terms of both archaeology and geology.

CAITHNESS

North and east of all the great mountains of Sutherland and Wester Ross, Caithness is just plain flat. It is known as the flow country, a land of peat and a vital environmental wilderness in the north. Mysterious, deceiving, inspirational, this is a land absent of trees. Only stone and sea, cliffs and castles, chambered cairns with long horned chambers reside here – a place apart, unlike the rest of the country. Bordered by the Pentland Firth (=Pictland Fjord) and the North Sea on two sides, it is the jumping off point for Orkney and the mythical Isle of Thule, the Scotland that faces north to the Arctic Circle.

Caithness is the land of the cat clan, the Northern Picts. The Kingdom of *Cait* was one of the seven Pictish kingdoms in Alba, said to be the area now defined as Caithness and Sutherland. Although the modern Pict may be thin on the ground, the land is rich with the relics of prehistoric occupation.

There are around 4000 sites in Caithness from prehistoric times. Most of the sites have not been excavated and others may have been tackled in days before the knowledge of how to go about it was better understood. However, Caithness has been settled for thousands of years and each new period has left distinctive traces. Mysterious and haunting places chosen with care by their builders leave us with few clues as to their true nature. With over 100 Broch sites and many other sites from a variety of periods, Caithness has a rich history. What is known provides a fascinating glimpse of long disappeared tribes and people who may or may not be connected to people in the area now. Reading about these sites cannot compare to seeing them and standing next to these ancient places. Whether beside a loch, on a hill or by the cliff tops, it is an unforgettable experience.

ACHAVANICH

ND 1878 4176

Ewen Rennie, geograph.org.uk

Highlands

A unique megalithic horseshoe can be found near Loch Stemster at Achavanich, 'field of the monks'. In this Bronze Age site, a fanned out arrangement of small standing stones, no more than 6.5ft/2m high, faces south-southwest in this horseshoe U–setting, looking west towards the midwinter solstice sunset perhaps. Out of the original fifty four stones, only thirty six remain. Unusually the Achavanich stone slabs are set side on rather than face on, and follow a low cairn of earth and stone. With further stone remains dotted around the area, this is clearly a region of ritual significance over centuries.

Visually impressive to see this stone setting against bare moorland, this is Caithness in a nutshell.

CAIRN O' GET

ND 3132 4112

The chambered cairn known as Cairn o' Get is part of a remarkable concentration of prehistoric monuments in the area between the Lochs of Yarrows and Watenan near Ulbster. These range from chambered cairns and standing stones to forts, hut circles and brochs. A path leads from Get, or Garrywhin to other features in this ancient landscape. This now roofless cairn provides entry via a passage through two pairs of portal stones to the symmetrically designed burial chamber within. Get is a short-horned cairn which was originally square with concave sides. Characteristically the cairn has been in-filled with earth, stones and burnt deposits at the end of its life. The stone fort of Garrywhin can be seen to the north while two brochs stand on the east of the Loch. The entire landscape around this area is a temple of interlinked sites.

CAMSTER

ND 2603 4390
ND 2601 4420

HER-Historic Environment Team, Highland Council

The Grey Cairns of Camster are considered to be the most outstanding ancient site in Caithness. Two chambered cairns near Lybster are open, fully excavated and restored, one round with a single chamber and the second nearby is a long or double-horned cairn with two chambers and projecting horns in its unique architectural design. Remarkable and grey in their Neolithic beauty, this is an "immense stately home for the ancestors", according to the popular Scottish archaeologist Anna Ritchie.

A recent re-interpretation of Camster titled *Monuments and Water: A re-interpretation of the Grey Cairns of Camster, Caithness* by Amelia Pannet can be accessed for further information on this curious site. See the Caithness.org website: http://www.caithness.org/history/archaeology/camsterbypannett/

It seems that the more we know on ancient places, the more there is to know.

CNOC FREICEADAIN

ND 0126 6531
ND 0130 6540

Iain Maclean

A pair of Neolithic long-horned burial cairns known as Cnoc Freiceadain are found along a muddy inclined hill a few miles west-southwest of Thurso at Shebster. Standing proud on the Caithness skyline, the cairns are 65yds/60m apart at right angles to each other along the crest of the hill, and 79–85yds/73–78m long. Never excavated, the burial chambers are invisible, but their multi-humped outline suggests a development from round to long cairn. Mysterious is the order of the day here.

DUNBEATH BROCH

ND 1553 3044

There are very many brochs in Caithness. At least 100 of them are found throughout the area and probably more to be discovered and excavated. One magical Caithness broch stands on a wooded hillside above the confluence of two burns and the Dunbeath Water, generally a good sign for a sacred site. Its wall rises up to 13ft/4m. A guard cell and a double cell are found within the broch wall from the doorway. As the Dunbeath Heritage Centre is nearby, more information can be found there.

YARROWS

ND 306 433

An archaeological trail has been created to explore the varied ancient landscape around the Loch of Yarrows south of Wick by Thrumster. Chambered cairns, a 2,000 year-old broch, and two impressive long cairns – the southern cairn being 79yds/73m long with horns at either end of the burial chamber – are some of the treasures found in this isolated moorland. The trail goes on to pass a small fort, a standing stone, cairns and hut circles.

On the archaeological trail.

The archaeological landscape by Loch of Yarrows.

The sites at Yarrows have had human occupation for 5,000 years beginning in the Stone Age/Neolithic period, starting with the building of the chambered burial cairns which comprise five sites on the circuit. These huge cairns were burial places for entire communities, in use for a thousand years with successive burials taking place. The Yarrows Broch, only half of its original height now, had thick windowless hollow walls containing stairs and passages and living areas within – all defended by a guard chamber at the narrow entranceway.

Of special interest around the broch are the tumbled remains of the earliest Pictish houses on the mainland. These were partially sunk into the ground with the roof supported on stone pillars propped along the inside wall called a *wag*, from the Gaelic 'little cave'. What remains visible here with much more lost, gives the traveller an impressive glimpse into what Caithness may have been like thousands of years ago. Timelessness pervades at Yarrows.

Recent excavations at Thrumster have produced evidence for the first time of even earlier occupation of Caithness in the Mesolithic Period.

WAG OF FORSE

ND 2048 3521

The Wag of Forse may look like a big pile of stones from a distance, but it is another significant archaeological landscape at Latheron. The wag name seems to be a Caithness version of *weem* used for Pictish cave dwelling in Southern Pictland territory like the East Wemyss Caves in Fife. This extended site is far more complex than the Yarrows with circular fortification being used over a succession of periods of history. Turf walled enclosures with small round houses in stone turned into larger circular dwellings – the broch morphing into a settlement of rectangular houses. This final stage of building was called a wag, *uamhag* in Gaelic, dated mid first millennium AD which is Pictish. The landscape around the Wag of Forse contains ancient field walls, cairns, hut circles, burnt mounds (cooking places) and a great mound to the north, likely to be another broch. The archaeological plan shows areas coded as Pre-Wag, Primary Wag, and Secondary Wag.

HILL O' MANY STANES

ND 295384

The Hill o' Many Stanes at Mid Clyth near Lybster is a Caithness 'speciality', that of a fan-shaped setting of standing stones. These are actually stone rows similar to those at Carnac in France but on a smaller scale. Described as "an oddly moving remnant of an ancient way of life", the stones are set on a gentle slope, all 200 of them. These are low stones no more than 3.3ft/1m high arranged in roughly twenty two rows running southwards downhill. As in the Achavanich stone setting, the stones here are also set side on, each broad face sitting on the axis of its row lining a parallel footpath. There could have been more than 600 stones here originally, it is thought. One theory is that this site was a complex lunar observatory but the jury is out on this one.

STONE LUD

ND 2216 6174

The Stone Lud is a wonderful name for a standing stone, which is located in the parish of Bower, better known as Upper Bowertower near Castletown, standing at 10ft/3m tall. This stone is said to mark the grave of Ljot Thorfinnsson, tenth Earl of Orkney (Lot or Loth was the mythic King of Orkney and

Iain Maclean

Stone Lud.

Highlands

Lothian in Arthurian legend). Other stories tell that this was the dragon that St Magnus turned into stone. However, being nearly the tallest standing stone in Caithness, comparable to the stones at Ring of Brodgar, it also has an astro-archaeological function. One of two stones on site originally, the pair marked the summer solstice sunset alignment. Ancient sites are found on every eminence in the parish of Bower including the Cairn of Heather Cow, Cross of Bower and Cairn of Ushally.

CASTLE SINCLAIR GIRNIGOE

ND 378 549

A most spectacular ruin dramatically totters on the cliffs projecting into Sinclair Bay three miles north of Wick, the only castle in Scotland on the World Monuments Record. This is Castle Sinclair Girnigoe, two castles in one, both built by the Sinclairs of Caithness and of Rosslyn Chapel in Midlothian. This fortress comprises Girnigoe, a tower house built around the fourteenth century, and Castle Sinclair from 1607, now thought to be part of the same structure more than likely built by the Norse Earls of Caithness. Numerous coastal castles in Caithness are Norse in their foundations as the Norsemen arrived during the tenth century when the county was still Pictish with Goidelic influences from the Celtic church. This stunning ruin is no longer falling into the sea as a restoration project is underway to rebuild it by the Clan Sinclair Trust.

CASTLE OF OLD WICK

ND 369 488

"The Old Man of Wick", as it is popularly known, is a castle complex perched on a promontory of the Caithness coastline just south of Wick. Another dramatic coastal ruin dating from the twelfth century on a spectacular site, it sits on a spine of rock that juts into the North Sea between two narrow deep gullies. Considered to be the best preserved Norse castle in Scotland, the Castle of Old Wick was probably built by the great Earl Harald Maddadson, half-Orcadian Earl of Caithness and Orkney at a time when the Kings of Norway held sway over all of the North including the Northern and Western Isles. It is dominated by a tall four-storey tower, the 'old man' look, not far off from the Old Man of Hoy and a double for Cubbie Roo's Castle on Orkney of the same period. Funnily enough the original entrance was via a door on the seaward side, long since collapsed. There was such a strong link between Caithness and Orkney at this time that the sea was the main highway from one shore to the other, Highland galleys and seafaring vessels being the motorcar of the day.

PICTISH STONES

Ulbster Stone original site ND 1256 6879
Skinnet Stone original site ND 1309 6205
Sandside Stone NC 9522 6518

The Caithness corpus of Pictish stones covers a spectrum of Pictish sculpture in the Northern kingdom of the Picts. Scattered throughout the region, they are found built into the gable end of a house, hidden away in old chapels, and some displayed with pride including the two great Caithness cross-slabs. These are the Ulbster Stone and the Skinnet Stone now united in a new home at Caithness Horizons in Thurso (ND 1186 6851). The **Ulbster Stone**, associated in some ancient way with Clan Gunn, is a Class II Pictish cross-slab circa eighth century and bears an interlace Celtic style cross on both sides surrounded by Pictish symbols and beasties of varying types. Curiously there is a kneeling man beside a cauldron with another figure opposite but mostly eroded away.

The **Skinnet Stone**, originally from Skinnet Chapel in Halkirk (ND 1309 6205) and of the same period as Ulbster, also bears a cross on both faces along with Pictish symbols including the triple oval symbol and a finely embellished crescent and V-rod on the reverse side. Another Early Christian stone with a delicate carved cross is still on site at the ruined chapel at Skinnet but very lichen-worn now.

Marianna Lines

The Skinnet Stone. Impression by Marianna Lines.

The **Sandside Stone** is an unusual triple-symbol early Class I stone found in the grounds of Sandside House and erected upside down as a 'curious antiquity of its day'. It shows the triple oval, a notched mirror case and mirror and comb.

The Sandside Stone.

Iain Maclean

Most of the other Pictish stones of Caithness are either in the National Museums in Edinburgh or lost. One intriguing entry in the National Monument Record for Caithness Pictish Stones (Royal Commission for Ancient Monuments of Scotland – RCAHMS) is Craig of Hattel. The 1873 Ordnance Survey recorded a six foot high standing stone "sculptured with a very crude drawing resembling a greyhound". Its fate is unknown. A few notable, if less monumental, exceptions include:

The Watenan fragment of a crescent and V-rod, now in Northlands Viking Centre at Auckengill.

Latheron stone (ND 1990 3343) This slab forms the lintel of a false window in the south gable of the farmhouse at Latheron and bears the Pictish crescent and V-rod symbol. It had been whitewashed over on last viewing.

Reay (NC 9691 6483) An Early Christian monument of grey sandstone is finely sculptured in relief with a cross, set into the west wall of the old church in Reay Old Burial Ground. The cross-slab is a large stone, 6.3ft/1.9m tall, that dates from the ninth century. In the Pictish style of sculptured stones, it is described as having square ends to the cross arms, round hollows in the angles and a ring connecting them: the shaft is short and the rectangular base is the width of the stone. The ornament on the right and left arms and the base is a key pattern: circular knotwork adorns the shaft. Though lacking the symbolism and animal features found in the Farr, the Ulbster and the Skinnet stones, the Reay stone is well placed in the list of northern sculptured monuments.

Another fragment of a Pictish stone, once built into the church at Reay and now in the National Museum of Scotland (NMS) in Edinburgh, is decorated on all four sides in flat relief. A cross on the front, various beasts on the right side, a spiral on the left, and a stag with interlace on the back are found on this eighth century stone.

The Eagle Stone, Strathpeffer.
Art by Marianna Lines, displayed on site.

10

THE NORTHERN ISLES

ORKNEY AND SHETLAND

ORKNEY

PRINCIPAL SITES

1	Maes Howe	11	Broch of Gurness
2	Stones of Stenness	12	Tomb of the Eagles
3	Barnhouse	13	Ladykirk
4	Ring of Brodgar	14	Minehowe
5	Unstan Cairn	15	Dwarfie Stane
6	Ness of Brodgar	16	Midhowe
7	Skara Brae	17	Taversoe Tuick
8	Borwick Broch	18	Stone of Setter
9	Brough of Birsay	19	Vinquoy chambered cairn
10	Quoybune Stone		

Previous page: 'The Bird Men'. From the Papil Stone, Shetland.
Natural dye art by Marianna Lines.

Orkney

THE NORTHERN ISLES
ORKNEY

SCOTLAND IS SAID to have over 2,000 islands around its coast. For many reasons the Scottish islands are the real essence of Scotland with a coastline offering 6,000 miles of a seascape of islands and all the rocky inlets and secret places along the way. Mysterious, remote, beautiful, uninterrupted for generations in their history, they have been mostly left untouched from modern pursuits such as development.

It is no surprise that the mythology of the Scottish islands lends a certain air of surreality and enchantment to this land. One such place is Hy-Brasil, a phantom island that, like Atlantis, could be anywhere in the western Atlantic. It is said that Hy-Brasil is cloaked in mist except for one day every seven years when it becomes visible but never can be reached. Other similar magical islands include the Island of Thule, somewhere north of Caithness or Orkney, and of course Tír nan Óg, that Celtic land of eternal youth which is always the place to strive for, the vision on the horizon, the ultimate paradise. An eighth century Gaelic tale of the Imrara, or sacred voyage, takes us to the Isles of the Blest, the Isle of Glass, where "…even the stones themselves are of the precious variety".

This 'otherworld' is a concept that can be found within the Pictish symbols and their inner message or within a stone circle that radiates a certain light. Islands of the mind, islands of the soul. And then there are the real islands that the traveller may visit. According to a reputable survey, there are some 165 islands listed that are forty hectares or over, which is 100 acres and sizeable enough to support some sort of habitation.

According to Hamish Haswell-Smith, an expert on Scottish islands:

"It should be remembered that the best-preserved and largest number of Neolithic remains in the whole of Europe are to be found on the Scottish islands, and many of these structures pre-dated the Egyptian pyramids."

Orkney

ORKNEY

"Beyond Britannia in the endless ocean..." is how a fifth century scribe wrote of Orkney. Closer to Norway than to London, Orkney is only fifty miles south of Greenland and begins where the North Sea meets the Atlantic Ocean.

Yet Orkney is a world of its own, so near and so far from Scotland. Only six miles across the Pentland Firth to the southern tip of Orkney, across some of the most dangerous waters ever, this fiercely independent 'nation state' whose Mainland means Orkney, not Scotland, has a personality that is enchantingly Orcadian. With a lilt of the tongue, Orcadians speak their own version of the Norse dialect of 'Norn' with a sing-song rhythm much like their indigenous music. Settled by the Norse, it has a Scandinavian flavour that persists, mixing in with a Scottish 'topping'. Like the rich Orcadian ice cream, it tastes and looks great, this archipelago of islands – a composite of sixteen inhabited islands, altogether about 70 low-lying islands, many being skerries or islets. The ancient world of Orkney is elemental no matter where you go, on the surface, deep down, a way of life that stretches back in time, a living history. The landscape is treeless, fertile, stony, sea-locked rather than land-locked, and intensely vibrational.

Old red sandstone is the bedrock of Orkney, the essential building material of virtually all of its ancient sites.

A pocket history of Orkney, post-megalithic Stone Age settlement and Pictish culture, will tell you that the backbone of Orkney is Viking. The history of the Norse Earldom of Orkney lies in the semi-mythical *Icelandic Sagas*, the most famous being the *Orkneyinga Saga* compiled around 1192–1206 by Icelandic scribes. This presents an interpretation of the first conquest of Orkney by Harold Fairhair, King of Norway, and the subsequent founding of the Earldom. The Norse settlers, who were no longer Viking raiders by that time, arrived in the ninth century and developed a powerful outpost of Norse culture both on Orkney, Shetland and throughout the Western Isles.

Orkney only became a part of Scotland by accident in 1468 when it was pawned to Scotland through a royal marriage agreement, along with Shetland. The Norse influence lives on in both of these archipelagoes after six centuries of Norse occupation.

WILDLIFE

Orkney is a wonderful place to experience wildlife close up and untamed by the twenty-first century. Home to some rare species of animals such as the Orkney vole, the blue mountain hare, and the elusive Eurasian otter, Orkney's cliffs are home to vast numbers of breeding seabirds during summer. With thirty six Sites of Special Scientific Interest (SSSI) and thirteen

Orkney

RSPB reserves, important birds in this area include the hen harrier, short-eared owl, kestrel, rare corncrake, snipe, oyster-catcher, curlew, red-throated diver, puffins, and an endless list of migrant birds. There is always something special to see at any time of the year, from sky dancing hen harriers to hunting orcas and dolphins.

In winter Orkney's coasts are home to internationally important populations of curlew, turnstone, purple sandpiper and redshank. Its seas support large numbers of long-tailed ducks, great northern divers and dainty Slavonian grebes.

Seals are a speciality as Orkney is an important breeding site for two species, the grey and the common seal. Although the number has declined recently, there are about 7,000 common seals in the islands, charismatic, friendly and curious, just like the people. Orkney folk legends tell of the magical race of *selkies*, or seals, in Orcadian dialect. They are said to shed their sealskins on Midsummer's Eve and become beautiful seal folk who bewitch humans. Could this be the mermaid story come true? Curiously, Orkney's name in Old Norse was 'Orkneyjar', meaning 'seal islands'.

LANGUAGE

THE ORCADIAN DIALECT survives today in many commonly used phrases and words although the dialect is dying out. Many of these words are closer to Norwegian than English. The dialect comes from Norn which was a mixture of Norse and Scots. This provides the Orcadian sing-song accent of the same tonality as Norwegian with an accent that could be heard as Welsh. Some favourite Orcadian words are:

peddie: small; *pugie*: stomach; *swadge*: rest after a meal; *gansey*: jumper; *throughby*: next door.

The meaning of Orkney the place name is as complicated as some of the ancient sites. The Old Gaelic name was *Insi Orc* meaning 'Island of the Orcs', or young pigs, i.e. Islands of the Wild Boar. This concept links with the theory that the Picts being the predominant tribe in the islands, used the boar as a tribal totem among other favourite symbols like the sea eagle. When the Norsemen settled in Orkney, they called it Old Norse for 'Seal Islands', interpreting the ancient 'orc' to be *orkn*, the Norse word for seal.

So whether it's pigs or seals, Orkney has both in one form or another.

Orkney

MAINLAND

ORKNEY is made up of 13 parishes with the West Mainland including Firth, Rendall, Evie, Birsay, Harray, Sandwick, Stenness, Orphir, and Stromness.

George Mackay Brown, the great Orcadian writer who lived in Stromness all his days, writes of Orkney: "In a sense we have never fully shrugged off the Stone Age. Within living memory people were sleeping in stone beds. The great mill-stones that gave the people their bread and ale have, only lately, lost their fruitful thunders. In spite of concrete and imported wood, the best new houses are still built of local stone... Stromness will always, to the end of its days, be a stone town like Skara Brae: its score of piers stone feet in the ebb."

East Mainland consists of Holm, St Andrews, Deerness, with St Ola surrounding Kirkwall, the capital.

Mainland Orkney has so many notable relics dating from the late Stone Age that one must assume there was a prosperous advanced social structure on the island. From Neolithic people to the broch builders to the Picts to the Norsemen to the modern 'white settlers', the melting pot of Orcadians may be annexed by Scotland but they are their own peculiar and unique race of people.

MAES HOWE

HY 3182 1276

Bill Boaden, geograph.org.uk

The landscape setting for Maes Howe.

The world famous Maes Howe displays an insight into prehistoric Orkney along with a later history of Viking invasion of these islands. The cairn is built so that sunlight will penetrate the passage at the time of the winter solstice sunset. The green tumulus of Maes Howe is Britain's largest chambered cairn – 'the finest Neolithic burial chamber in Europe' – with megalithic

Orkney

craftsmanship of the highest order. A long low passage leads into a large chamber with corbelled walls and small side chambers. The iconic, amusing runic-graffiti inscriptions are evidence of Norse crusaders in the twelfth century, mostly referring to treasures and women. One rune reads:

"These runes were incised by the best runester in the west, using the axe that Gauk Thrandisson once owned in south Iceland". A beautiful small carving of a dragon is also found there. As the dragon is made by the same hand and at the same time as the runes,

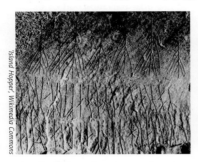

'Island Hopper', Wikimedia Commons

it suggests that this is a Christian motif in which the dragon represents paganism being slain by the sword of Christian belief. By the time these carvings were inscribed, Orkney was already settled by the Norse, so it is incorrect to describe their visitation to Maes Howe as 'raiders'. They were crusaders breaking into an ancient tomb, a bit of tomb-raiding on a night out.

Early Norwegian settlers in Orkney referred to Maes Howe (also written as Maeshowe) as *Orkahaugr* meaning the Mound of the Orcs, or Wild Boars.

Russel Wills, geograph.org.uk

'Island Hopper', Wikimedia Commons

Top: The entrance to the Maes Howe chambered cairn.
Above: The entrance corridor from within the chamber.

STONES OF STENNESS

HY 3068 1250

The Stones of Stenness are part of a megalithic walkway from Maes Howe to the Ring of Brodgar, located on a narrow isthmus. Only four slender tapering stones remain, all over 16.3ft/5m high, of an original twelve stones of a circle. The Watch Stone, standing on the causeway between the two lochs, is an outlier doing its job as the watchman stone. The area of Stenness is an extraordinary ceremonial landscape from 5,000 years ago in the heartland of Orkney, centred between the Lochs of Harray, which is freshwater, and Stenness which is saltwater.

Greg Willis, Wikimedia Commons

This can be seen as the spiritual centre of Orkney with its duality of earth and sky, land and water, sunrise and sunset. The earliest monuments were the chambered tombs of Unstan and the Stones of Stenness, all built before 3,000 BC. The Ring of Brodgar followed, then Maes Howe, and so the landscape

Andy Farrington, geograph.org.uk

The fallen stone.

began to be connected with burial mounds. The surface has only been scratched on Orkney to reveal the whole story of its past. So much more is still deep in the earth.

BARNHOUSE

HY 3075 1271

A short distance from Stenness is Barnhouse, a Stone Age village recently discovered which has close links with Skara Brae. Occupied from circa 3200–2800 BC the Barnhouse settlement

Orkney

consisted of drystone-built houses with stone-slab beds, dressers, hearths and drains. Two of the structures are of such a scale and complexity as to imply a non-domestic function, meaning this was a ritual complex.

The Barnhouse Stone is part of the ceremonial landscape complex. This solitary lichen-covered monolith 10ft/3m tall stands in a field southeast of Stenness, near Maes Howe, and has been found to be perfectly aligned to the entrance of the cairn at the winter solstice sunset.

RING OF BRODGAR

HY 294 133

The dramatic Ring of Brodgar is among the largest stone circles in all of Britain (beaten only by the outer circle of Avebury and the large circle of Stanton Drew) with twenty-seven standing stones still in position ringing a sacred site where originally sixty stones once stood. Built as a henge (a Neolithic earthwork) with a deep rock-cut ditch around the perfect circle, two entrances into the circle are located on the northwest and southeast, 113.6yds/104m in diameter. The site rests upon a great bed of heather between Loch Harray and Loch Stenness.

William Kempen

The Ring o' Brodgar was the ideal place to construct such a great ceremonial monument. The stone circle is in the centre of a massive natural cauldron formed by the hills of the surrounding landscape. While the site is accentuated by the water of twin lochs, originally Stenness Loch did not exist. Only a wet marshy bog and pools of water surrounded the stones. It is well known now that the Ring was part of an enormous prehistoric ritual complex, from Maes Howe to the Stones of Stenness to the southeast, Ring o' Bookan to the northwest, the Comet Stone to the east, the Ness of Brodgar on the west, and beyond to Skara Brae.

Orkney

Unknown photographer acknowledged

So much special energy is contained in this beautiful Ring of Brodgar site.

The best time to visit is at dawn or sunset, when the atmosphere reflects and echoes the past.

UNSTAN CAIRN

HY 2828 1172

The chambered cairn of Unstan stands on a promontory in the Loch of Stenness overlooking the Bay of Ireland. This is the tomb responsible for the type of Neolithic pottery known as Unstan Ware, as excavations yielded sherds of over thirty finely decorated bowls. An oval cairn is composed of a long passage, a stalled chamber, and a side chamber with three central compartments. The lintel into the side chamber has a lovely delicate carving of a bird and a faint runic inscription.

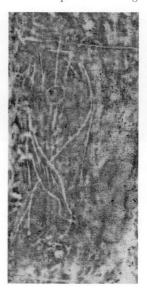

Above: The lintel stone.
Right: The Unstan lintel stone –
art by Marianna Lines.

Orkney

NESS OF BRODGAR

HY 2948 1304

Johyn Ireland, geograph.org.uk

The Ness of Brodgar looking west.

The Ness of Brodgar, a peninsula between two lochs linking the two great stone circles of Orkney, Brodgar and Stenness, has been under intense excavation since 2004 revealing what is believed to be a grand temple at the heart of this monumental Neolithic complex on Mainland Orkney. When archaeologists first glimpsed the Ness of Brodgar, after a farmer ploughed up a notched stone in 2003, they had never seen anything like it. The warren of interconnected stone buildings of various sizes remains unique in Europe in both size and construction.

Photo by Tme, Wikimedia Commons

Excavations in progress, 2014.

To date, Nick Card of the University of the Highlands and Islands and his team have excavated about 10% of the site's 29,900 square yards (25,000 square metres) uncovering about a dozen stone buildings. One large building footprint, thought to be a temple or meeting hall at the centre of the complex with a cross-shaped interior, has been dubbed 'the cathedral'. Walls up to 13ft/4m thick and internal divisions of stones incised with mysterious 'butterfly' patterns are featured, with the whole complex surrounded by an outer stone wall spanning nearly the entire width of the isthmus the site sits on.

So far over 600 panels of rock art decorations have been found, Grooved Ware pottery, a clay figurine, and endless structures in sandstone of both red and yellow variety. The red and yellow sandstone was reserved only for 'the cathedral' area. Finds such as shin bones from around 600 cattle show that feasting was done on a large scale. Such a ritual slaughter may have also been part of a closing down ceremony of the ancient site. An inverted cattle skull was found placed at the centre of the cathedral on a large stone.

The complex was first occupied about 3200 BC – circa 5,000 years ago, and was in use for a thousand years. These latest discoveries emphasise the importance of monuments as places where people came together to perform rituals. The Ness was 'the centre of the universe' for all of Orkney and beyond, it seems, a major ceremonial and ritual centre to serve the entire Neolithic population of the Northern Isles.

The dig on site is open during the excavation season in July and August and welcomes visitors. More information can be found on *Orkneyjar.com*. It is said that the Ness will change the entire picture of archaeology in Orkney with its stunning finds, with more to come.

According to project manager Nick Card, the discoveries are unparalleled in British prehistory, and the complexity of finds is changing the whole vision of what the landscape was like 5,000 years ago. "It's on a scale that's almost related to the classical period in the Mediterranean, with walled enclosure and walled precincts," he says.

Additionally, some archaeologists suggest that the site could be more important than Stonehenge.

SKARA BRAE

HY 230 187

The Bay of Skaill, north of Stromness on the west coast, harbours another of Orkney's exciting ancient sites, the 5,000 year-old Stone Age village of Skara Brae. A World Heritage Site, it only came to light in a great storm in 1850, the village having been buried in another sandstorm around 2450 BC which helped to

Helmut Zozmann, geograph.org.uk

Dresser in stone in a Skara Brae house.

Orkney

preserve the site. Everyday domestic life is exposed and illuminated here with tiny individual cellular houses linked by passages, each containing Stone Age furniture such as beds, dressers, hearth, fish larder pools, and personal effects made of pottery, stone and whalebone. As with important ancient sites of this type, there are many other satellite 'Skara Brae' type sites throughout Orkney and its many islands.

BORWICK BROCH

HY 2241 1677

Yesnaby headland is one of the most spectacular places on the islands, where cliffs of grandeur have eroded into a wild sculptural landscape of stacks and geos. This is where to find the Broch of Borwick, an Iron Age drystone tower rising to 10ft/3m on the landward side, a defensive site in its time. Traces of buildings between the broch and the headland wall indicate continuity of use into the Pictish period, mid-first millennium AD with a Pictish comb artefact discovered.

Top: A dramatic view of Skara Brae showing connecting passage.
Above: Another view of the site showing fireplace and panelled bed space.

David McGovern

BROUGH OF BIRSAY

HY 236 284

An island at the north-west corner of Mainland on a tidal isthmus at Brough Head is the magical Brough of Birsay, a tidal island with extensive remains of Pictish and Viking settlements, an early medieval chapel and a fine Pictish symbol stone. The Birsay Stone, composed of thin flagstone, dates from the eighth century AD giving a vivid picture of Pictish nobility at the time. Depicted are Pictish symbols of the mirror case, crescent and V-rod, the Pictish beastie and a

The Birsay symbol stone.

prominent (sea) eagle above a trio of warriors in relief carving. Clad in ankle length ceremonial robes, the procession of three warlords carry decorated square shields, spears, and swords in a hierarchical ranking.

Note the decorated hem and hairstyle of the crowned leading figure, no doubt the chieftain/king and main focus of the sculptured stone. Also interesting is the use of the eagle symbol on the Birsay Stone, as the famous Neolithic Tomb of the Eagles on South Ronaldsay is celebrated for its ritual hoard of sea eagle bones. This stone was found in fragments in 1935 beside the cemetery, conjecturally near a triple grave. The original is preserved in Edinburgh with a replica on site.

Orkney

The Brough, a defensive promontory/island, not to be confused with the stone 'broch' tower, was a power centre in its heyday from Pictish to Viking times. A small Pictish well is also found along with evidence of bronze-working craft nearby such as penannular brooches and finger-rings. A rich island in many ways, fertile on all counts, makes this sacred site one to relish or cherish. It is well documented in the famous *Orkneyinga Saga*.

QUOYBUNE STONE
HY 2532 2630

On the mainland by the village of Birsay is the Stane o'Quoybune, one of the tallest and most striking monoliths on Orkney. A standing stone of 13ft/4m tall, it stands guard over the Loch of Boardhouse. Legend tells that the stone represents a giant who was turned to stone but who comes alive at the turn of the year and goes down to the loch for a drink. Like other stories of vampires, he must return to his place before dawn breaks on New Year's Day and cannot be watched for dire peril.

BROCH OF GURNESS
HY 3818 2684

Petr Brož, Wikimedia Commons

In the parish of Evie where the swirling tide of Aiker Ness stirs the coast lies the haunting site of Gurness, the best-preserved broch on Orkney. A complex of surrounding ruins adds to the mystery of what this site is all about. Like many other ancient sites on Orkney, there is a long history of settlement at Gurness, an Iron Age village where original features of the houses are well preserved, leading on to the later Pictish and Viking building remains. As described by archaeologist Anna Ritchie who led many digs on Orkney: "The maze of walls, upright slabs, hearths and cubicles presents a mute but evocative image of

Orkney

teeming life around the chieftain's broch."

Gurness is just one of a series of brochs lining both sides of Eynhallow Sound, built at the narrowest point of the Sound. A small Pictish stone was also found within the broch complex on a wall at Gurness, showing a mirror case and two rectangular symbols, now kept in Edinburgh.

TOMB OF THE EAGLES

ND 4703 8451

Discovered by a local farmer in 1958, the tomb contained both human and eagle bones.

At the southeastern tip of South Ronaldsay is the Tomb of the Eagles, at Isbister. This is a chambered tomb with a special story. Discovered by the local farmer, it has been turned into a privately run family museum site where the visitor can handle the skulls of the ancients. Along with bones of 340 people found in this virtually intact tomb, the bones of sea eagles and their talons were also found, hence the name.

A fine example of a hybrid tomb with unusual design features, it is both stalled and has side chambers built sometime before 3000 BC. There is a personal connection when one enters the Tomb of the Eagles, a special atmosphere that allows the modern traveller to feel the spirit of those who once created this sacred space.

The 'Sea Eagle story' of Isbister may be deceptive. Although 641 sea eagle bones were found inside the cairn, giving the site its popular name of Tomb of the Eagles, this may be a misnomer. We would like to think that these magnificent birds, with their two-metre (6.5ft) wingspan, once

Orkney

common to Orkney, held some special significance to the cairn builders, being a totem animal also seen carved on the pre-Christian Pictish symbol stones around Orkney.

Recent research shows that the birds were not original to the tomb, but were actually placed in the cairn at least 1,000 years after it was built. Such is the divide between fact and fiction. From the archaeological standpoint it simply means that Orkney's chambered cairns remained a focus of activity for centuries after the construction and initial period of use. Thus the rise of the sea eagle and its symbolism may have come later in the history of this site, a change in belief system – maybe even with the arrival of the Picts who honoured this iconic bird throughout Pictland on the sculptured symbol stones. The joy of studying the past is that speculation and change is always there to intrigue us.

LADYKIRK

ND 4399 8425 church

Also on South Ronaldsay is a stone known as the Ladykirk Stone, located at St Mary's Church in Burwick, which bears footprints – the worn carved impression of two feet. This is part of a tradition of foot-imprinted stones that represent kingship, found in several other parts of Scotland such as Shetland, Argyll and Fife. The inauguration stone, its famous counterpart seen at Tara in Ireland, also links the sacred landscape of Orkney with other sites of regal power. The Ladykirk stone carries the legend that St Magnus used it to sail across the Pentland Firth. As also found in Shetland, this stone has two feet, while others on the mainland only show a single footprint. Another footprint stone has been reported on the Isle of Sanday but is not documented yet.

MINEHOWE

HY 510 060

One of the more mysterious sites on Orkney, Minehowe is all underground. Dating from the Iron Age, Minehowe is a stone-built chamber dug into a large earthen mound. Access is by a steep staircase of narrow stone steps, first into a landing with two low branching chambers. Further down into the darkness is a lower chamber at the bottom, 20ft/6m in depth. Once thought to be a well, or a broch, none of this is for certain. The obvious function was ritual/ religious, a symbolic entry into the underworld. A broken hammer stone was found during excavations along with a totemic dog skull. Minehowe is surrounded by a massive ditch similar to that at the Ring of Brodgar, perhaps marking the territory between sacred and secular.

Orkney

HOY

DWARFIE STANE

HY 2434 0043

The Dwarfie Stane on Hoy, the highest island of Orkney's archipelago, has a unique stance, being the only chambered tomb in Hoy and the only rock-cut tomb in Britain. A vast block of red sandstone 27.8ft/8.5m long on a hillside has been hollowed out with a short passage and small cell on either side along with a boulder nearby which once was fitted as an entrance door. Carved 'modern' graffiti includes a mystical Persian calligraphy reading, "I have sat two nights and so learnt patience".

Colin Smith, geograph.org.uk

This remarkable monument conjures up images of giants and dwarves. Sir Walter Scott wrote that it was the favourite residence of Trolld, a famous dwarf in the Norse sagas. An ancient Orcadian fable suggests that the Dwarfie Stane was the handiwork of a giant and his wife. A rival giant imprisoned the couple inside the stone but the giant within gnawed his way out through the roof of the chamber thus explaining the hole in the roof that can be found on site.

In modern times the famous composer and Master of the Queen's Music, Sir Peter Maxwell Davies lived on Hoy where he wrote some of his greatest works, including the favourites *Orkney Wedding* and *Farewell to Stromness*. He is the creator of the annual St Magnus Festival in Kirkwall. His music continues to beguile the world from this distant corner. After visiting Hoy the haunting melodies linger.

Orkney

* * *

ROUSAY

MIDHOWE

HY 3716 3060 broch, HY 3724 3048 tomb

Top: The remains of the great broch of Midhowe. Above: The chambered tomb lies within its protective shed, viewed from the Broch.

Photos Iain Maclean

The island of Rousay is a virtual ancient landscape with at least fifteen chambered tombs and five Iron Age brochs (stone towers), as well as significant Bronze Age artefacts and burials. The huge circuit of sites to visit includes Blackhammer chambered cairn (HY 4142 2760), Knowe of Yarso chambered cairn (HY 4048 2794) where the bones of thirty six red deer were found, and countless other sites. Midhowe broch and its chambered tomb is the highlight of all the sacred and historic sites on Rousay. The broch stands on a promontory between two geos, or steep-sided inlets and is architecturally powerful even at its current reduced height of 14ft/4.3m, once a very tall and imposing tower.

Midhowe broch is the midpoint of three brochs on this coast. The chambered tomb now encased in an enormous protective shed has a rather eerie atmosphere. A very long stalled cairn lies within, twelve burial compartments marked out by upright slabs along a chamber that stretches at least 75.5ft/23m long. Somehow it feels like entering the catacombs of Rome, a deep world of death and bones, a sanctuary to the ancestors. It is know as the *Great Ship of Death*.

Orkney

TAVERSOE TUICK

HY 4258 2760

Top: The north entrance of the Taversoe Tuick.
Above: The south entrance.

A most unusual monument, Taversoe Tuick, or 'Taiverso Tooack'
in Orcadian is found on the south side of Rousay overlooking
Wyre Sound. This is a chambered cairn built into a sloping
hillside. Dating from around 3000 BC, what is most interesting
about this Neolithic cairn is the fact that it is a two-storey
structure, a double chamber 'high rise'. One chamber actually
sits on top of the other, and each had its own entrance passage.
Today a ladder can be used to view the lower level chamber.

Taversoe Tuick has a spooky atmosphere about it, probably heightened by the claustrophobic feeling as you descend
the steel ladder to the dark recesses below. The two-tier system
may have been an indication of some form of hierarchy in the
Neolithic culture.

The only other cairn of this design is found on Eday.

Its discovery was quite Victorian: the owner thought this
heathery knoll would be a nice place to take in the view so he
ordered a seat to be constructed there, whereby a burial chamber was discovered, bones and all. It is said that his wife was
not too pleased. When the chamber was opened in the 1890s
the remains of three bodies were found in the upper chamber,
cremated remains in the lower.

Orkney

EDAY

STONE OF SETTER

HY 5645 3717

The Stone o' Setter on the Island of Eday is the tallest single standing stone in Orkney, 14.8ft/ 4.5m tall. Its distinctive profile caused by the deep weathering of the upper half makes it look like a great giant's hand. Its powerful presence stands guard over an ancient landscape dotted with chambered cairns in the northern half of Eday. An island blanketed in peat, more remnants from the past may lie below.

Becky Williamson, geograph.org.uk

VINQUOY CHAMBERED CAIRN

HY 5601 3811

Colin Park, geograph.org.uk

Top: The Stone of Setter. Above: Vinquoy chambered cairn.

Vinquoy Chambered Cairn is the most impressive burial tomb on Eday, a restored Maes Howe-type tomb made from red Eday sandstone. Nearby is Huntersquoy Chambered Cairn, an unusual design with two storeys, only two upright stones remaining of the upper chamber. More tombs are to be found on the Calf of Eday.

The Manse Stone, a drawing circa 1865.

Another significant stone that originates from Eday is the Eday Manse Stone, or the Eday 'sun stone', a Neolithic horned spiral sculptured slab fragment. This decorated stone was found at the site of a chambered cairn at Eday Manse, possibly used as a lintel to the entrance of a cell within the tomb, and dates from 3100 – 2500 BC. It bears an uncanny resemblance to the more well-known Westray stone and also to Newgrange in Ireland. The sun motif is a faintly carved spiral on the periphery of the deeply incised spirals.

Such symbols played a part in early beliefs. Designs on stone from tombs, monuments and early dwellings are also found on pottery and other items likely to have been used in rituals.

OTHER SITES

There are so many other sacred sites on Orkney's necklace of far-reaching islands that it is not possible to consider them all here in detail. A list to seek them out can bring further rewards of visionary conquest and inspiration. More discoveries are turning up every day in this quixotic land of the sea.
These include:

Quoyness chambered tomb on Sanday (HY 676 377)
Burroughston broch on Shapinsay (HY 540 210)
Cubbie Roo's Castle on Wyre (HY 441 263)
Knap of Howar Neolithic farmstead on Papa Westray
   (HY 483 518)
Chambered tombs on Holm of Papa Westray
   (HY 509 518)
Burrian broch on North Ronaldsay (HY 762 513)
   where there are seaweed-eating sheep on the foreshore and
   St Magnus Church of the twelfth century.
Round tower Viking church on Egilsay (HY46613039).

PICTISH STONES ON ORKNEY
Several important Pictish stones from Orkney have sadly migrated south to the NMS – National Museum of Scotland in Edinburgh, which include:

Flotta Stone – A Pictish cross-slab dating from the eighth century with an equal arm cross infilled with interlace, found on the site of a ruined ancient church, donated by George Petrie of Kirkwall in 1877. This is considered to be the Isle of Flotta's most cherished artefact.

St Peter's stone – Pictish symbol stone from South Ronaldsay, re-used as a windowsill in the church of St Peter until 1852, bears fine incised symbols on both faces. Side one: crescent and V-rod and mirror case. Side two: rectangle symbol and a crescent and V-rod with elegant curvilinear ornament. The crescent and V-rod resembles a 'happy face'.

Brough of Birsay Stone (discussed earlier)

Greens, St Andrews – Class I Pictish symbol stone with mirror case, crescent and V-rod and mirror, on flagstone.

Skaill cross-slab, Deerness (lost)

LATEST DISCOVERIES

A stunning Class II Pictish cross-slab has been discovered on the Isle of Sanday during renovation of a house near Lady village, lying under the floorboards. The stone shows a relief Pictish style cross with heavy interlace and the Pictish 'sea creature', a fish monster or sea horse symbol which dates from the eighth century when Christianity was arriving in Orkney. This is an exciting find for Orkney, a first of this kind. Sanday also claims the fame for the newly found Viking boat burial.

Burray Bone Hoard – Two Pictish carvings have been found on old ox bones recovered from the Bu Sands in Burray which show a figure of a man in a tunic walking with a staff or spear, in profile, typically Pictish (very similar to the Collessie man warrior stone, but dressed).

Viking Gaming Board – A perfect example of a Viking Gaming Board, known as a *Hnefatafl board* (combo of draughts and chess) has been found at the Brough of Deerness.

The Westray Stone has been returned to the Island of Westray to join the 'Westry Wife' figurine and others at the new Westray Heritage Centre. The Westray stone is from a Neolithic chambered cairn which is the finest example of prehistoric spiral carvings in Britain and bears a striking resemblance to the famous Newgrange stone in Ireland.

ST MAGNUS CATHEDRAL

HY 4493 1086

The great medieval St Magnus Cathedral (begun 1137) in Kirkwall is another important sacred site on the mainland that links with the modern era in its evolving use today, a welcome banner to all who enter its majestic sacred space. This red sandstone edifice embodies the spirit of Orkney's twelfth century Golden Age and is the finest medieval building in the north of Scotland.

Neil Irving, geograph.org.uk

The nave of St Magnus Cathedral, Kirkwall.

VIKING BOAT BURIAL

HY 6780 4584 (site of)

Orkney keeps turning up great discoveries. One of Orkney's most important archaeological finds of the late twentieth century came to light on the island of Sanday after a fearsome storm. A farmer found a number of bones in an exposed sandbank and a *peddie* (Orcadian for 'small') lead object. These turned out to be a Viking boat burial dated to AD 875–950. The lead object was a lead bullion weight used by Norse traders to weigh gold and silver. The boat is

Education Scotland, Wikimedia Commons

The Scar Dragon Plaque, whalebone carving.

called a *Viking Faering*, a wooden clinker-built boat. Three bodies were found along with a treasure trove of grave goods,

Orkney

including the Scar Dragon Plaque, a decorated whalebone plaque which is now in Tankerness House, the Orkney Museum in Kirkwall. Buried alongside the woman in the boat burial were also a comb, a gilded brooch, a sickle, a weaving sword, shears and two spindle whorls.

NEOLITHIC FIGURINES

The Island of Westray has unearthed three hand-carved figurines found during ongoing excavations at the Links of Noltland (HY 432 488).

First there was the 'Westray Wife', dubbed the *Orkney Venus*, a sandstone figure of a woman 1.6 inches/41mm high who is truly Neolithic. She is the earliest representation of a person ever found. The figure bears some resemblance to the prehistoric 'Venus' carvings from Mediterranean Europe with the rounded head, large breasts and hips. Two more figures have now emerged to join the rescue excavations to combat irreplaceable archaeological remains on the Island of Westray being lost to erosion. As a result, an extensive Neolithic and Bronze Age settlement has been found. All three Neolithic figures are on display in the Westray Heritage Centre, and are so popular that visitor numbers increased by 2,000 in one year, and shortbread biscuits made there in the shape of the original figurine are in great demand. Such is the power of a few 'magical' grave goods or votive offerings.

Now another buried figurine has turned up in the Ness of Brodgar excavations, dubbed the *Brodgar boy*, a clay figure of crude workmanship.

The Westray Wife.

S·HETLAND

PRINCIPAL SITES

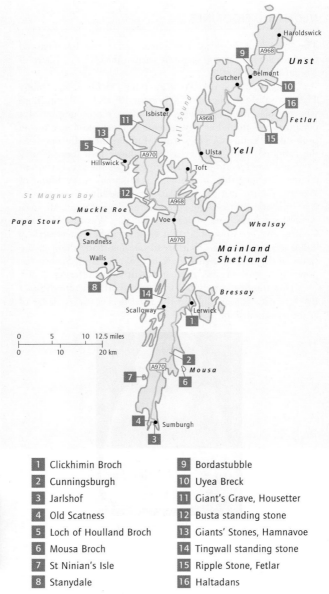

1 Clickhimin Broch	9 Bordastubble
2 Cunningsburgh	10 Uyea Breck
3 Jarlshof	11 Giant's Grave, Housetter
4 Old Scatness	12 Busta standing stone
5 Loch of Houlland Broch	13 Giants' Stones, Hamnavoe
6 Mousa Broch	14 Tingwall standing stone
7 St Ninian's Isle	15 Ripple Stone, Fetlar
8 Stanydale	16 Haltadans

Shetland

THE NORTHERN ISLES
SHETLAND

ALTHOUGH IT IS THE MOST northern part of Scotland, Shetland is a different country, beyond the horizon, and quite off the map from the mainland world of Scotland. Shetland has its own culture, its own dialect, its own music, and its own distinctive megalithic and ancient sites. The Picts were here and all who came before. Closer to Norway than Scotland, Shetland was once part of the Viking Scandinavian world, so aptly reflected in its place names. An archipelago of flat treeless islands like Orkney, there is a vast array of sacred sites to tantalise the traveller along with the best wildlife and scenery to discover. The sea is never more than three miles from anywhere in Shetland, its coastline a wild landscape of cliffs, caves, blowholes and stacks.

The distinctive flavour of Shetland's ancient past leans toward brochs and defensive settlements, all laced with the island mists and the 'simmer dim', that midsummer gloaming twilight when it never really gets dark in the summer months. Remarkably complete archaeological landscapes dating back 5,000 years are to be found in Shetland, perhaps due to their isolation from the rest of the world.

The continuing tradition of the *Up Helly Aa* spectacular Viking fire festival in January brings Shetland into the modern age of bonfire parties and fun. Many of its rituals reflect ancient history: boat-burning, guising (fancy dress), torches thrown about, processions, and indeed, drinking.

Speaking Shetland is to speak a form of Scots with a Shetland dialect and a strong Norse accent, but the old language was called Norn. Many Norn-derived words are still in common usage. Speaking Shetland is also playing the fiddle. Traditional music is a famous export and an integral part of the islands' lively culture, its music as enchanting as its people.

Unlike Orkney, Shetland is more Norse than it is ever Scottish. This is because it became ruled directly from Norway, whereas Orkney never was.

Shetland

Ultima Thule, referred to by early Roman writers as the 'end of the world', most certainly meant Shetland (but of course not everyone agrees). Out of the 100 islands of Shetland's archipelago, only about twenty are inhabited. The Northern Lights, the Aurora Borealis, is a phenomenon that is often seen in Shetland, a perfect setting with no city lights to drown them out. Shimmering Shetland, but not in the 'simmer dim' of summer.

WILDLIFE
Shetland has unique bird life. It is one of the few places in Britain where you can see breeding red-throated diver, whimbrel, red-necked phalarope, arctic and great skua. Huge seabird colonies can be found at Noss, Hermaness and Sumburgh Head, while the famous Iron Age broch in the Isle of Mousa is home to thousands of breeding storm petrels. Many of the birds have local dialect names such as Tammie Norrie for puffin, Whaup for curlew, Shalder for oystercatcher, Bonxie for great skua, and Tystie for black guillemot. The Shetland Isles are famous for the rare birds that appear, particularly during migration times, and seek refuge at places like Fair Isle, halfway between Orkney and the Shetland mainland.

Fetlar in the north isles may be the best place to see the red-necked phalarope and red-throated diver. Snowy owls were once a popular bird there but they are rare now. Always watch out for the dive-bombing 'bonxies', as well as the arctic tern, especially in nesting season. Both grey and common seals can be easily seen and sometimes killer whales in the summer.

Otters are found through the islands, and are regularly seen even in the busy capital of Lerwick. The Isle of Yell is known as the otter capital of Britain. Yell has a desirable environment for wandering families of otters because there is plenty of low-lying peat shoreline where they can excavate 'holts' with fresh water supply. These are the normal European river otters.

And don't forget the Shetland pony, one of Shetland's most beloved worldwide exports. They are still found roaming around the islands, often seen around Mousa Broch on the island of Mousa.

Panoramic view of Clickhimin Broch, Lerwick.

CLICKHIMIN BROCH

HU 4643 4081

On the road to the south near Lerwick stand the remains of a great round tower with a surrounding Pictish settlement which was flourishing around 700 BC. Clickhimin began life as a stone-walled ring fort with an unusual outer free-standing blockhouse, the first stage in its long history. The building of the massive and prestigious broch, originally up to 49.2ft/15m high, followed with a wheelhouse built within. Once an island broch in the Loch of Clickhimin, the well-preserved broch now stands 17.3ft/5.3m tall on a low promontory within the walled enclosure.

Several periods of occupation included a late Iron Age fort period, a broch period, a wheelhouse settlement both inside and outside of the broch, with occupation within the Pictish period. There is a footprint slab located at the island end of the approach causeway carved with two shod prints, this being associated with inauguration ceremonies. This tradition of the footprint stone and kingship ritual is found elsewhere in Scotland and its islands — Orkney, Dunadd hillfort in Argyll, and Dunino in Fife.

CUNNINGSBURGH

HU 4255 2709 to HU 4235 2705 steatite quarries

In the quarries of Cunningsburgh steatite, or soapstone, was used for domestic living to make vessels and weights from 2000 BC up to medieval times. Remains of bowls cut upside can still be seen on site. Cunningsburgh means *king's fort*, reflecting the importance of the steatite industry in both Pictish and Norse times.

Also found in this area is a striking Pictish stone called the *Mail Stone* (HU 4330 2790), depicting a dog-headed masked man – a transformational half-human, half-beast figure walking in the characteristic profile stance of the Pictish warrior.

Shetland

Dem Zwickelbert sei Frau, Wikimedia Commons

This style of composite figure is also found on Pictish stones on the Scottish mainland more often depicted with a bird head. The dog-like head may be a mask in the style of the guising

figures also seen on the birdman sculpture from Shetland, The Papil Stone, now in Edinburgh. The Mail Stone can be seen in all its strange originality in the new Shetland Museum in Lerwick. Like a modern fantasy figure drawn by a child or something out of a dream, this figure conjures up a cosmos we may never understand. Various theories include a wolf mask or even cetacean, an influence related to Shetland stories of seal men.

Shetland Museum

Left: Painting based on the Mail Stone. – dog-head figure by Marianna Lines. Right The original stone now in the Shetland Museum.

JARLSHOF

HU 398 095

On the very tip of mainland Shetland at Sumburgh, near the promontory fort on Sumburgh Head lies the famous site of Jarlshof, a rather organized jumble of buildings and stony bits. In this typical multi-period settlement, the Neolithic farm is the earliest from 2400 BC, an oval house sunk into the sand. Ruins of four later preserved houses include evidence of a bronze-working smith's workshop from 800 BC. Stone roundhouses from the Iron Age farm are complete with underground cellars.

© Crown Copyright reproduced courtesy of Historic Scotland
www.historicscotlandimages.gov.uk

A broch with courtyard and wheelhouses, the Iron Age settlement dwellings are the best-preserved and most inspiring part of the site, despite coastal erosion.

There was a Pictish period defined by smaller buildings and a further Norse settlement of interlocking walls along with a true Viking longhouse from the ninth century where people and cattle lived side by side. A late structure of the seventeenth century, ruins of the Laird's house, gives the site its name which was invented by Sir Walter Scott for his novel *The Pirate*.

© Crown Copyright reproduced courtesy of Historic Scotland www.historicscotlandimages.gov.uk

Jarlshof (meaning *Earl's temple*) has seen 4,000 years of occupation and is a key place for understanding aspects of the ancestral life of the Scandinavians who dominated the Northern Isles for centuries, and whose legacy lives on.

Among the many artefacts from Jarlshof is a small round stone disc bearing only a single Pictish symbol, the double disc and Z-rod. This may well be the earliest Pictish symbol to be recorded.

OLD SCATNESS

HU 389 106

Near Jarlshof in the South Mainland at Old Scatness there is an ongoing excavation where some exciting Pictish finds have been made including a Pictish carved stone of a bear. A mound of over 17.3ft/5m high and 87.5yds/80m diameter has revealed an Iron Age broch and earlier settlement structures from at least 3,000 years occupation. The broch-village, once a pristine time capsule, was discovered in 1975 when a road was put through the area. Twelve summers of the dig are showing that the broch had two doorways, one of which has a huge triangular lintel stone above, this being a characteristic feature seen in Caithness and elsewhere as a sign of prestige and power, which dates from 400–200 BC.

Shetland

A few years into the dig, broch and roundhouses plain to see. August 2000.

Five late Iron Age structures built on top of the earlier village show a cloverleaf structure added to the centre of the broch and cellular houses. Along with the discovery of the bear stone, now in the Shetland Museum, stones showing a Pictish boar, a salmon, several painted pebbles and a pebble with an arch and V-rod symbols have been excavated from the site. Viking soapstone artefacts

A wheelhouse, part of the archaeological site of Old Scatness.

were found in the Pictish houses with occupation continuing well into the Norse period offering a rare chance to understand the elusive Pictish-Viking transition in Shetland.

LOCH OF HOULLAND BROCH

HU 2139 7917

At the point of Eshaness Lighthouse can be found a fine island broch which actually sits on a promontory in the loch with a narrow neck of land connecting to the mainland. Unexcavated and half-submerged in fallen rubble, this is the best kind of broch to discover in order to envisage its former life without modern intervention, perhaps, with the dust of the past still hanging around. Traces of later buildings are seen between the broch and its outer defences that are likely to be Pictish. An unusual feature of the site is a causeway linking it to an adjacent island, also linked with a further causeway to the shore. Whether this was a ceremonial walkway or a path for livestock is unknown.

Shetland

MOUSA BROCH

HU 4573 2366

Both photos: Iain Maclean, Caithness Broch Project

On the western shore of the tiny island of Mousa, the world's finest, best-preserved and most complete broch can be seen from across the Sound. The Broch of Mousa, Iron Age in date, stands 42.5ft/13m tall, having only lost its upper courses. No settlement surrounds it in this case, an iconic lone tower that holds the magic of all Shetland. Climbing to the top lookout through six galleries shows many nooks and crannies in the double walls where storm petrels live, offering an exciting wildlife outing at midnight to see them swirl out. (Boat trips are laid on during the summer to witness this phenomenon.) Built of highest quality Mousa flagstone, the walls curve gracefully inwards as they rise to the top.

Brochs often go in tandem, and Mousa's sister broch stands on the mainland, the Broch of Burraland. Icelandic and Norse *Orkneyinga* Sagas both tell tales of young lovers finding refuge in the broch as a honeymoon winter home. The Saga recorded in 1153 tells that Erland the Young abducted Margaret to Mousa, but her captor found it 'an unhandy place to get at'. Such is the romance of a broch. Private, beautiful and protected, a broch with a view – perhaps this is the best ever.

There are several internal 'windows' as one climbs up the staircase between the inner and outer walls of the broch. This is the view through one such window, down the inside to the floor of the broch.

Rob Farrow, geograph.org.uk

Shetland

ST NINIAN'S ISLE

HU 3685 2091 chapel

"Shetland's answer to Mont St Michel" is one fanciful way to describe St Ninian's Isle, compared to that evocative monastery edifice on a tidal island in France. St Ninian's has a chapel built on ancient foundations with a great *Treasure Island* story and a sandy, tidal isthmus that has to be crossed to reach the sacred land. This is called a *tombolos* or *ayre*, a sand beach, spit or bar, characteristic of the inner coast and 'voes' (long narrow sheltered bays) of Shetland's submerging coast-line. The beautiful sandy beach and bar of St Ninian's leads to the ruin of a pre-twelfth century chapel built over an Early Christian monastic site.

This is where the treasure of St Ninian's Isle was found by Shetland schoolboy Douglas Coutts on the 4th of July 1958: a hoard of twenty eight exquisite Pictish silver and silver-gilt decorated objects – bowls, weaponry, jewellery – and the jaw bone of a porpoise. These were buried under a cross-marked slab near the altar in a box of Norwegian larch, probably hidden by the monks before a Viking raid. Considered to be of Pictish origin, they date from the late eighth to early ninth century.

Corner-post carved stone shrines were also found. South of the chapel is a holy well (HU 3666 2068), a spring of crystal-clear water.

STANYDALE

HU 2853 5024

Stanydale Temple is a horseshoe-shaped structure with a single entrance passage leading to a large oval hall lined by massive stones. This could have been the house of a chieftain or a communal meeting place for rituals. Along the footpath leading in to Stanydale are cairns and a group of Neolithic houses. This Neolithic site has been designated as a 'temple' because it most closely relates in plan to the Temples of Malta, well-built, oval in plan with a concave façade.

Large post-holes show it was timber-roofed and measures 39.3 x 29.5ft/12 x 9m with walls some 12ft/3.6m thick. Standing stones in double alignment, now only stumps, are located on the north side of the temple, perhaps part of Bronze Age stone circles. Located in the middle of West Mainland near the Bridge of Walls, a footpath over rough moorland allows a chance to slow down from the modern world before approaching this site.

Shetland

* * *

STANDING STONES

The northernmost island of the Shetland archipelago, Unst, has two major standing stones. **Bordastubble** (HP 5787 0334) is Shetland's largest standing stone, a huge chunk of gneiss rising to 11.8ft/3.6m. **Uyea Breck** standing stone (HP 6063 0070), near the desolate ruin of Muness Castle, is a slender monolith of schist 10ft/3m high.

On Shetland Mainland we have the **Giant's Grave** at Beorgs of Housetter in the north (HU 3617 8546) with three tombs found in a most dramatic setting by the Loch of Housetter on a rocky cliff face. The **Trowie Knowe**, or Fairy Mound, made of pink granite, has two upright portal stones before the chamber while the **Giant's Grave** has two tall standing stones over 6.5ft/2m high that stand guard over the cairn where two colours of granite outcrop, pink and white/grey are used in its construction. The standing stones are pink. A pretty picture, colour coded for the early settlers.

Busta Standing stone on North Mainland (HU 3487 6739) has a commanding view over Busta Voe, legend telling that this hefty stone, weighing some 20 tons was thrown there in anger by the devil.

Giant's Stones, Hamnavoe, West Mainland (HU 2430 8055) A pair of stones standing over 6.5ft/2m tall; originally there were three.

Tingwall Standing Stone, Central Mainland (HU 4123 4203). A tall 6.5ft/2m stone on the neck of land between Loch of Tingwall and Loch of Asta at the famous Ting site of this island parliament. Tingaholm in Tingwall was the later 'stone circle' community gathering place, also called a 'thing', ting, ding, or fing – derived from the Norse 'ping'... a bit of rhyming slang for the old ones?

Ripple stone on the Isle of Fetlar (HU 6269 9044) is also made of schist at 7.5ft/2.3m high. Also on Fetlar, one of the more distant islands of Shetland's world, are the **Fiddler's Crus** (HU 6180 9269), which is a site of three mysterious stone circles set in a triangular pattern, almost touching each other. Each circle is about 44.3ft/13.5m in diameter.

Another site, **Haltadans** ('limping dance' in Norse) at HU 6221 9241, is connected with a legend of dancing trolls who were literally petrified at the rising sun. There is also the **Giant's Grave** at Aith, which excavation has shown to be a Norse boat burial.

Giant legends were big in Shetland, especially on fertile Fetlar, known as the 'fat land'.

SHETLAND'S HOLY ISLANDS AND PLACES

'Papay' or 'papar' is a place name found in Shetland that means priest or hermit isle. Shetland has many such places which are interpreted as eremetical monastic settlements. These tend to be found in clusters which include Papa and Papa Stour facing Papil on the southwest Mainland.

The far northwest of Shetland also has clusters of monastic sites.

The monastic settlement of Kame of Isbister is another aspect of the 'papay' sites on Shetland. This is a rocky promontory located off an uninhabited coast today, joined to the mainland only by a knife-edged ridge. The Kame of Isbister on the Sound of Yell in the Northmavine peninsula is a virtually inaccessible rock stack. The site has clearly been selected for purposes of refuge and isolation, as it is effectively screened from the land and shows an obvious need for privacy. There is documentary evidence that Irish missionaries reached the Northern Isles in the seventh to eighth centuries AD. The organisation of the Celtic church at that time was primarily monastic in character, and the monasteries were located often in lonely inaccessible places such as off-shore islands (like Iona in the Hebrides) or headlands with a stout drywall, *vallum monasterii* which served not only to enclose the monastery but to act as a symbolic barrier excluding the outside world.

Other sites of this nature include North Roe and Birrier located opposite on a holm in West Sandwick. Birrier was an early Culdee monastery in the west of Yell which was almost certainly in contact with the Kame of Isbister directly opposite.

Yell has been inhabited since the Neolithic times.

A 'petrosomatoglyph' or stone footprint is found at North Yell that is known locally as the *Wartie*, as it was used as a healing stone: to wash in dew or rain water when standing in it was supposed to get rid of warts. In legend it was made by a giant placing one foot here and the other on the Westing of Unst.

PICTISH STONES OF SHETLAND

Several important Pictish stones which are moved away from their original Shetland locations deserve a mention.

The Papil Stone is an eighth century Pictish cross-slab found in the churchyard at Papil Kirk of St Lawrence in Papil, West Burra, Mainland.

This fine cross-slab shows two monks on either side of the central round-headed cross, the monks in typical hooded dress holding crosiers and satchels. A large lion, in the Pictish style, a symbol of St Mark, is below, with the most curious bird men as a third motif panel. The bird men, another symbol of transformation with masks of bird heads and human bodies, are holding axes and pecking at a human head between their long beaks.

Some say this is shamanic, others that the bird men are really puffins (Icelandic *papi* is a nickname for puffins and also churchmen) with the sculptor having a bit of a laugh at the clerics. A replica of the stone is on site at Papil, the original in the National Museums of Scotland (NMS), Edinburgh.

Replica of the Papil Stone, West Burra, showing two 'birdmen'.

A second fine carved stone from Papil is the Burra Monk's Stone which is a shrine side panel showing a procession of monks walking to the left, one riding a Shetland pony. The original is in the Shetland museum. This image is thought to signal the coming of Christianity to Shetland.

The Bressay Stone is a beautiful double-sided Pictish cross-slab from the island of Bressay opposite Lerwick. It was believed to be the memorial to the daughter of a Pictish chieftain, Naddod. Both sides of the stone are carved with similar designs: a roundel cross and interlace. The front is similar to that of the main Papil stone with a round cross head, confronting monks on either side, a lion beast along with further animal images and a bilingual ogham inscription along both narrow edges. The exceptional image on this stone is a pair of fish or sea monsters above the cross seen devouring a Jonah figure. This ninth century stone is now displayed in Edinburgh, NMS.

Shetland

Mail Stone – A number of carved stones have been discovered in the Mail Churchyard, Cunningsburgh, including the outstanding single figure Mail Stone described above of masked/dog-headed man with axe and staff, now in the Shetland Museum, Lerwick.

A second Pictish stone recently discovered is a sandstone fragment with interlace and inscribed symbols of a double disc and Z-rod, unusually infilled with crosses, also on view at the Shetland Museum in Lerwick.

Old Scatness – Small Ritual Objects – A steatite disc from Eswick shows Pictish symbols on both sides: double disc and Z-rod and triskele, now in Shetland Museum. One of many decorated discs which are unique to Shetland. Two votive figurines of hooded figures found in Mail and Scalloway.

The cross-head of the Bressay Stone – art by Marianna Lines.

Opposite page: Stags from the MacLeods' tomb, St Clement's Church, Rodel, Harris. Detail of monoprint by Marianna Lines.

11

THE WESTERN ISLES

THE OUTER HEBRIDES, THE INNER HEBRIDES, ARRAN AND BUTE

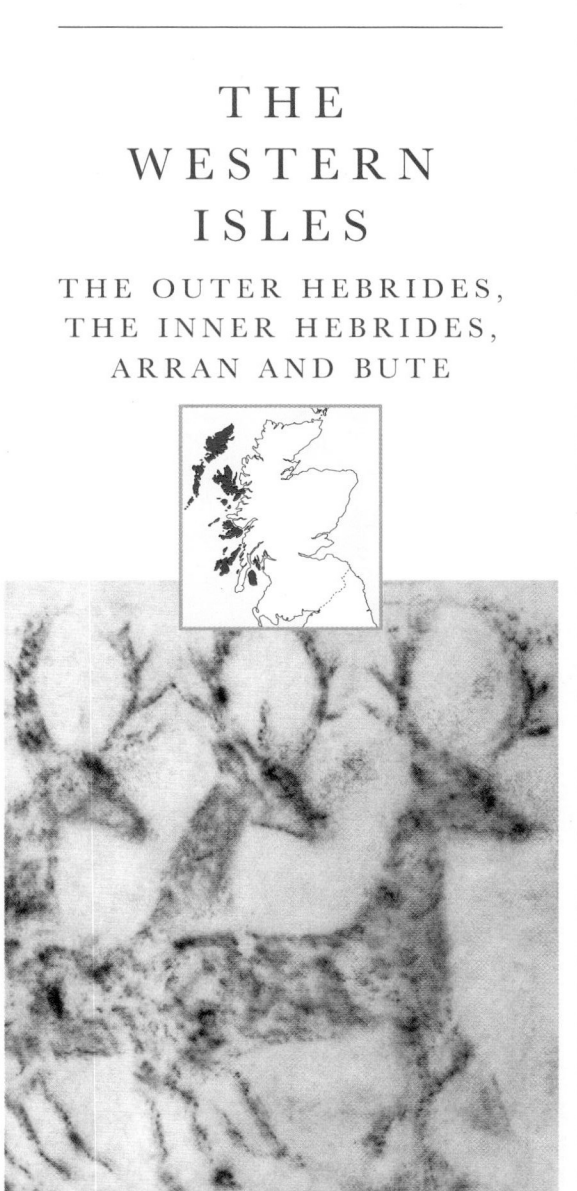

THE
OUTER HEBRIDES

PRINCIPAL SITES

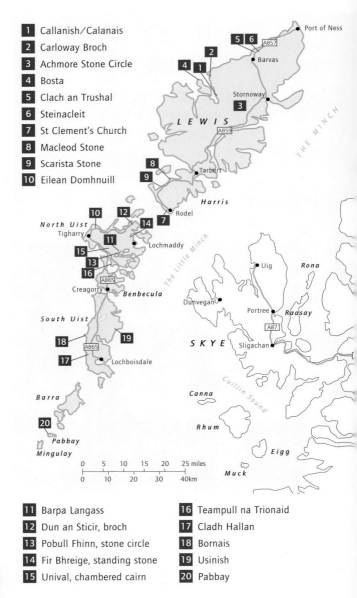

1. Callanish/Calanais
2. Carloway Broch
3. Achmore Stone Circle
4. Bosta
5. Clach an Trushal
6. Steinacleit
7. St Clement's Church
8. Macleod Stone
9. Scarista Stone
10. Eilean Domhnuill

11. Barpa Langass
12. Dun an Sticir, broch
13. Pobull Fhinn, stone circle
14. Fir Bhreige, standing stone
15. Unival, chambered cairn
16. Teampull na Trionaid
17. Cladh Hallan
18. Bornais
19. Usinish
20. Pabbay

Outer Hebrides

THE WESTERN ISLES
THE
OUTER HEBRIDES

THE ISLANDS OF SCOTLAND'S WEST COAST ARE KNOWN COLLECTIVELY AS THE HEBRIDES.

The Outer Hebrides, consisting of Lewis, Harris, North and South Uist, Barra, Berneray are separated from the Inner Hebrides by the Minch to the north and the Sea of the Hebrides to the south.

The Inner Hebrides consists of two groups. The northern group includes Skye, Raasay, and the Small Isles of Rum, Eigg, Muck, and Canna.

The southern group includes Mull, Iona, Coll, Tiree, Colonsay, Islay, Jura, Gigha.

THE OUTER HEBRIDES

The Outer Hebrides is the archipelago off the northwest coast of Scotland stretching from Lewis to Berneray that includes the outlying islands, like outliers of a stone circle, of the legendary St Kilda and the Shiant Isles. The Blue Men of the Minch are their guardians, the mythical spirits of the dark waters off the coast of Scotland that are as enigmatic in their presence as Nessie of Loch Ness. The Western Isles vary from peat-covered uplands on Lewis to the mountains of South Harris, the sandy beaches of Barra, the quiet beauty of the Uists to the breath-taking cliffs of Kilda.

The geological history tells of some of the oldest rock on the planet, Lewisian gneiss formed more than 500 million years ago, while the archaeological history reveals stone circles that predate the Pyramids in Egypt and rival even Stonehenge in their encrypted sacred geometry and setting. The Callanish Stones are the crown of the Hebrides but there are plenty of jewels to discover as well. Timelessness is the spell that these islands weave into our world today, something that is sought after but rarely found, like the Isles of the Blest. *Tír nan Óg* is just a stone's throw away when travelling through the islands of the West.

The beaches of these islands are described as creamy gold and silver, as they are formed by glacial deposits made up of tiny crushed shell fragments, skeletal marine life and algae. Coastal grasslands off the western seaboard make up the *machair*, a fertile ground for farming and grazing, and a flowering wonderland in spring and summer. Peat beds took over most of the island lands, treeless now but forested long ago. One might be forgiven for thinking they have been transported to the moon, such is the curvilinear 'out of this world' landscape of the Hebrides. Author Peter May has even written about the reality of this Hebridean moonscape, identifying the white rock called anorthosite rock, found in the Western Isles, rare in Britain but very common on the moon.

* * *

AN INSPIRED CONTRIBUTION ON THE WESTERN ISLES

by Alastair McIntosh

COMPASS POINTS WITHIN EILEANA BRIDE

THERE IS A TRADITION, reported by the great Alexander Carmichael in the Carmina Gadelica, that the Hebrides were once called Eileana Bride – the Isles of Bridgit or Bhrìghde. Scholars point out that there is scant written evidence, but then, this was an oral culture, and there is abundant evidence of the veneration of this most lovely and powerful Celtic saint and goddess in the place names of the isles. Most striking is the fact – and I have confirmed it from estate legal documents – that the whole of the Isle of Harris was the Parish of Kilbride – the cille – the anchorite's cell or church, of Bhrìghde.

It is my visceral experience that the Hebrides are a holy place, a sacred landscape that remains redolent with meaning. These isles have known the *drùidheachd* or 'Druid' lore and still sustain the standing stones and cup-marks of pre-history. They knew the Celtic monks at a time when the Irish Sea, flowing into the Sea of the Hebrides and up from the monastic cells of North Africa, was the information superhighway of Europe's otherwise 'Dark Age'. Then came the humble monasticism of the Culdees, the *Célé Dé* 'Companions of God' and after that, the feudal forms

that came in with Norman influence leading to the Roman-
isation of the church followed by the Reformation.

The moors and coastlines ripple with long-treasured hints
of holiness, whether stone circles, the healing wells or the
pre-Reformation teampallan or "temple" ruins. If I take just
my own home area Lochs, there are names like Loch Thobhta
Brìdein (the Loch of Bridget's Ruin) near Achmore, and the
little-known cluster of tranquil "beehive" or bothan stone
hut circles out at Loch Ariaigh an t'Sagairt (the Loch of the
Sheiling of the Priest) between the Grimshader road and
Leurbost. What is more, some of these places are still visited by
indigenous islanders, and in a spirit of veneration. A crofter
friend who goes back to my earliest school days in Leurbost
is, in my mind, the keeper of the Ariaigh an t'Sagairt ruins.
He regularly walks out to sit there, and was interested to hear
that my late father, the village doctor, had been told by
elderly patients of a tradition that there had once been a
monastic community on the island on the immediately neighbouring Loch Orasaigh, and that the monks had stocked the
loch with Arctic char because these were said to be in prime
condition at Lent. Undoubtedly this tradition would have
been linked to my friend's sheilings, and they say that these
traditions are dying out, but I say: they won't die out, if we
hand them on, just as there's a line in an R. S. Thomas poem:
"The parish has a saint's name time cannot unfrock."

I would only want to add that in our enthusiasm for looking back to see where we have come from, we must not
neglect to stand our ground today, and to see forward into
time. Although much misunderstood and often caricatured,
there is rich spiritual life to be found in the Catholic,
Episcopalian and Presbyterian traditions of the Outer and
Inner Hebrides. Collectively I think they reaffirm us in the
underlying undivided church, better known today through
eastern Orthodox traditions with their profound nature
spirituality. I have come to think of each of these denomi-
nations as windows in God's house of many mansions. None
of them is perfectly placed. Each has problems of draft,
damp and rot. Some were caringly crafted by the whisper-
ings of the Spirit. Others, blown through by canon ball and
executioner. But at the end of the day, irrespective of their
history, these are windows nonetheless into the spiritual
world that is the interiority of the material world. God
comes shining through them, God as Goddess, God as Christ
in whom, as Paul affirmed, there is no male nor female; for
are we not in equal measure made "in the image of God"?

Our task today is to open those windows more widely,
to polish their glass, to repair their damage and to heal
what has been hurt. We are heirs to all that Alexander
Carmichael documented, all to which these antique ruins
testify, and so much more.

We are heirs and must claim a spirituality that is rooted in nature as the Creation, in its love, its wisdom, its providential joy.

"God's Providence is our Inheritance" is the town motto of Stornoway. These are times for us to relax our bygone tensions, to breathe deep, to settle our souls' compass to the magnetic pull of the islands' spiritual field. They are times for us to take fresh bearings, to navigate new courses in our lives, to live a life that's not just any old life, but the spiritually promised "life abundant". Make no mistake of what it is we're speaking here. Places of rock and heather, fleeting skies and streams of running water, for sure. But underlying all of these, the meanings of love in all its passion.

Alastair McIntosh is author of *Soil and Soul* and *Island Spirituality*, as well as the forthcoming *Poacher's Pilgrimage* on which this contribution for his artist friend, Marianna Lines, is based.

* * *

ISLE OF LEWIS

CALLANISH/CALANAIS

NB 213 330

Calanais, the name in Gaelic for Callanish, is far more than a stone circle. It is the most important prehistoric monument in Britain along with Stonehenge, referred to as the 'Stonehenge of the Hebrides'. A central monolith, an inner chambered cairn, a circle of thirteen stones and avenues that run north, south, east and west make up the stone heart of the site, laid out in the shape of a Celtic cross. Yet the complex of Callanish is a wider landscape temple embracing more than twenty satellite sites of stone settings and circles. This is a lunar observatory created as an ancient power centre to witness the major lunar standstill that occurs only once every 18.6 years. The hills of Harris to the south are part of the dramatic tableau that has taken place for over 5,000 years. The next lunar standstill will be staged by the moon in 2025.

Clachan Chalanais or *Tursachan Chalanais* in Gaelic, the Stones of Callanish are situated near the village of Callanish on the west coast of Lewis on a low ridge beside Loch Roag with the Great Bernera hills and the mountains of Harris as a backdrop in either direction. The Lewisian gneiss stone of Calanais is the oldest rock in the British Isles, three billion years old. This black and white crystal banding gives a stark whiteness in colour and texture that enhances every stone as a work of art, allowing the stones to stand out in the landscape from a great distance. The inclusion of black hornblende crystal in the 15.6ft/4.8m tall central stone gives the appearance of a great eye, a purposeful and magical choice for this great monolith. The Classical historian, Diodorus Siculus, may have been describing Callanish when he wrote,

This island...is situated North and is inhabited by the Hyperboreans... And there is also on the island both a magnificent sacred precinct of Apollo and a notable temple which is adorned with many votive offerings and spherical in shape.... They say that the Moon, as viewed from this island, appears to be but a little distance from the Earth and to have upon it prominences like those of the Earth, which are visible to the eye. The account is also given that the God visits the island every nineteen years, the period in which the return of the stars to the same place in the heavens is accomplished.

Calanais stones overlooking Loch Roag.

Salli Shand

Loch Roag is the setting for this great site. This sea loch bites deeply into the northwest coast of Lewis, part of which envelops the island of Great Bernera. On the east shore of the loch is the headland that is home to the small settlement of Calanais, while on land between the village and its jetty lie the Standing Stones of Calanais.

At the heart of Calanais is a circle of 13 stones that range from 8 to 13ft/2.4 to 4m tall surrounding the tallest monolith which is 16ft/4.5m high and weighing about 5.5 tonnes. A chambered tomb was added to the centre of the circle later. Extending north from the main circle is an avenue formed by a double row of stones, with single rows extending east, west and south. It is thought that the alignments of the various stones were used to mark significant points in the lunar cycle. The stone circle inner ring and the north avenue were built around 2900–2600 BC making Calanais earlier than Stonehenge. The three single lines of stones and the tomb were added around 1500 BC, although the dating is variable and new theories often will push this back even further.

Aerial view clearly shows the double stone row avenue and cross shape.

Calanais stone avenue.

Around 3000 BC the climate in the Western Isles was warmer than it is today and the sea level lower. Salmon ran in the rivers, animals grazed on the hills and barley grew on the broad ridge where Calanais stands. A religious cult seems to have swept through the British Isles at this time which involved the building of large earthen enclosures, called henge monuments and impressive circles of timber and later stone. That was the beginning of Calanais.

The site had probably lost its special significance by 800 BC and was abandoned when a small settlement was built close by. Climate change meant peat had been growing across the site for over 500 years causing many stones to be lost from view, disappeared. The peat was cleared on site in 1857 when it was approaching six feet in depth. Around that time one stone in the north avenue was broken, its missing tip found later in a wall and replaced. Other stones had gone astray as well, but are now re-instated. A veil had been drawn over this ancient power centre. Renewed interest in the ancient circles emerged in the seventeenth century and the standing stones were called *fir bhreige* or 'false men'. A more scientific attitude gradually prevailed and the main circle was taken into State care by 1885.

The magnificence of the main site at Calanais I does not overshadow the many other satellite monuments in the area. Calanais III is just off the main road to the southeast where a collection of twenty stones form a double ring with an outside diameter of 52.5ft/16m. This site has a remarkable atmosphere, as quiet as the wind with less visitors. A few hundred yards to the west of this site is Calanais II, a 59ft/18m diameter circle comprising ten stones of which five are still standing.

Looking further at the purpose of Calanais by the ancestors, the lunar observatory rides high in the sky. The moon that skims low over the southern hills every 18.6 years is a great god visiting the earth, and certainly to be able to predict this heavenly event afforded power to the chief priests of the site. This event of the Lunar Standstill is attended with reverence today and once again Calanais has regained its status as a magical power centre for all time.

CARLOWAY BROCH

NB 1899 4122

Dun Carloway, down the road from Calanais as the curlew flies, is a stunning Iron Age Broch, the best-preserved example in the Western Isles. Looking something like a Roman amphitheatre in its ruined state, it lies open spreadeagled to the sky, its galleried walls running down the sides, a massive lintel over the doorway protecting the entrance.

Tess Darwin

The broch is a defensive stone tower unique to Scotland which developed during the first century BC from strong circular houses into tall imposing buildings. The drystone structure is built with two concentric walls, a narrow entrance passage and a corkscrew stone stair. Dun Carloway stands close to its original height, rising up to 29.5ft/9m high. The collapse of part of the wall provides a perfect cross-section of the design with two tiers of internal galleries formed by flat slabs. Little is known of its use, but it is safe to say that the brochs were a high-status dwelling of their time.

ACHMORE STONE CIRCLE

NB 3174 2926

Above the village of Achmore on a lonely peat moor lies the fallen stone circle of Achmore, only discovered in 1981. Nineteen megaliths, only one now standing, have been found in the peaty golden pools around the fallen giants, in a circle of 134.5ft/41m diameter. As the site is a currently worked peat bank, it provides a useful example of how peat on Lewis is a real growing entity that has the ability to bury the past, as indeed it did in past centuries around the main Callanish circle. The views from the elevation around the site show a clear view of the 'Sleeping Beauty' mountain of Clisham to the south in North Harris, which is the highest mountain at 2621ft/799m in the Outer Hebrides. There may be many more circles on Lewis that remain buried in the peat which grows across most of the island, and is the mainstay of island fuel supply. Achmore has been dubbed *Callanish 22* in the greater plan of the Callanish complex of ancient sites on Lewis.

UIG: The Chessmen

The historic significance of Uig on the Atlantic west coast of Lewis cannot be overestimated. Uig beach was where the discovery was made of a Viking chess set in a small stone chamber at the edge of the beach. Inside were ninety three chess pieces made of Norse ivory from the tusks of walrus and whale teeth. The pieces were probably crafted in Trondheim in Norway around AD 1150–1200. The Western Isles were ruled by Norway at this time, so they may have been treasure hidden for safe-keeping or a hoard, or an offering as is more consistent with Dark Age finds in recent thinking.

Known world-wide as the Lewis Chessmen, these iconic gaming miniature warriors have travelled the world, recently seen in New York and housed both in Edinburgh (11 in NMS) and London (82 in the British Museum). Replicas may be seen locally on the island in the Uig Heritage Centre in Timsgearraidh.

Although full of life and character, these are not figures of fun. They are meant to represent the feudal order of society, to convey the qualities of king, bishop, knight and soldier through the language of gesture. Despite their miniature size, they embody truly monumental values of the human condition. Chess is a game of war between two opposing sides, and the twelfth century of Norwegian society is portrayed here. All of the pieces are sculptures of human figures, with the exception of the pawn shapes. The knights are mounted on diminutive horses and shown holding spears and shields, while the rooks are standing soldiers, four shown as wild eyed berserkers biting their shields with battle fury. The queen may represent the Virgin Mary, the King is strength and power, such as the human condition demands in roles of state.

A group of Lewis Chessmen replicas.

Marianna Lines

Scholars have observed that to the modern eye, the figural pieces with their bulging eyes and glum expressions have a distinct comical character. It is believed however that these expressions were not intended by the makers; rather these images instead displayed strength, ferocity or, in the case of the queens who hold their heads with a hand, 'contemplation, repose and possibly wisdom'.

BOSTA

NB 1373 4010

Bosta, or Bostadh, is a brilliant Pictish village on the north coast of Great Bernera off the west coast of Lewis dating from the seventh to eighth century. Like many of these archaeological discoveries, weather was the chief archaeologist. The site was exposed following gales in 1993 and excavated to reveal a Norse settlement in a remarkable state of preservation. This was built over earlier houses dating from the late Iron Age, AD 400–800, the age of the Picts. A network of nine stone buildings found at Bosta were all connected by tunnels. This is said to be the most completely preserved late Iron Age village ever found in this country.

The actual village has been back-filled to preserve it for future generations, and a replica Iron Age house has been created on site in the beautiful little bay. The tops of the original walls of two houses can still be seen. The design of this house is called a 'jelly bean house' due to its ground plan, with a low-slung thatched roof held down with stones in the Hebridean 'blackhouse' style. The remains of many of these abandoned blackhouses can be seen around Bosta.

Bosta Blackhouse.

Some wonderful finds have come out of Bosta including a number of bone combs of Pictish origin as clearly seen on the symbol stones. These fine composite bone combs consisted of multiple delicate bone teeth and a handle of decorated bone held together with iron rivets. A number of bone pins were also found for dress fastening. The wide range of finds and environmental reports gives a vivid picture of the lifestyle of the villagers of Bosta who lived by mixed farming, fishing, hunting and collecting seafood and seabirds.

The setting on the beach with its pure turquoise water is very special.

CLACH AN TRUSHAL

NB 3755 5377

The tallest standing stone in Scotland is found in a remote corner of the island but it is hard to miss at 19ft/5.8m tall. Sited in the village of Ballantrushal on the west side – on the way to nowhere – stands the Trushal Stone, Clach an Trushal, 'stone of compassion'. Legends say that it marks the site of a

Salli Shand

Trushal Stone.

great battle fought between the feuding clans of MacAulay (also spelt Maccaulay) and Morrison, but in fact it is much older than that. The Trushal is the solitary upright stone remaining from a stone circle built about 5,000 years ago. The second last standing stone was removed from the site in 1914 to be used as a lintel. They were known as 'blue stones'... perhaps a link to Stonehenge?

STEINACLEIT

NB 3963 5408

Visible to the northeast from Clach an Trushal is the stone circle at Steinacleit, identified officially as 'the remains of an enigmatic structure of early prehistoric date'. That should be enough to entice the traveller to explore this jumble of old stones as the site consists of an array of boulders that mark what is left of a chambered cairn. Ten large stone slabs surround the central mound, or cairn. A stone circle is another possibility with five stones left standing, or perhaps a combination of both once stood proudly here at the south end of Loch an Duin by Shader, en route to Ness in the north of the island since 1500 BC.

HARRIS

Although Lewis and Harris are parts of a single island, there is a natural six-mile barrier of high mountains and forbidding moorland between the great sea lochs of Seaforth and Resort. This landform separated the two communities throughout history so well that they were considered entirely separate islands. The two island regions speak Gaelic with a distinctly different dialect.

ST. CLEMENTS CHURCH, RODEL

NG 0476 8317

A distinctive landmark of Harris and the Western Isles is the medieval church of St Clements at the old port of Rodel, or Roghadal. It was built by Alasdair Crotach (the humpback), the eighth Chief of the MacLeod Clan around AD 1500 using sandstone imported from Carsaig on Mull. Its solid rectangular tower is unique to the Isles but the real treasures lie within. MacLeod's Tomb is one of the most beautifully carved memorial tombs in all of Scotland, the finest example of late medieval sculpture in the Western Isles. The weathered effigy of MacLeod of Harris* lies beneath a canopy of sculptured reliefs depicting elemental representations of a stag hunt, the Holy Trinity, St Michael and the devil, an angel weighing the souls of the dead, and St Clement himself holding an orb.

Ruari Halford-MacLeod

Detail of MacLeod's Tomb, a magnificent display of sculpture in St Clement's Church, Rodel. The birlinn is seen upper right.

One of the finest panels is that of a West Highland galley, or *birlinn*, which has been the template for modern wooden boat-building. The birlinn was the smaller West Highland version of the Viking long boat, the symbol of the MacLeods, and represented the Lord of the Isles period of Hebridean medieval history.

There is a stunning significant carving of a 'Sheela-na-Gig', not only an Irish fertility goddess figure but also found in England and further afield, on the upper south side of the church tower with a companion carving of a male version on the west face, also displaying his genitalia. These pagan images are thought to have been placed outside the church walls as high as possible to ward off evil. The symbolism of the Sheela-na-Gig appears throughout Scotland in the most unlikely places, and perhaps most importantly on the Island of Iona at the Nunnery. It is also said that this female religious carving was placed on churches to remind those with the ability to see that entering a sacred space is to enter the Womb of the Goddess. Universally she is seen as a protective symbol.

St Clement's Church, Rodel, seen from the east end.

The churchyard at Rodel is the burial place of the MacLeods of Harris who were the ruling clan of the Isles for generations. There is also a curious headstone dedicated to one who was drowned on the Titanic.

* * *

THE STORY OF ALASDAIR CROTACH OF RODEL AND THE MACLEOD TOMB

The *Bannatyne Manuscript* records the history of the Clan MacLeod, and states that while the Western Isles were now nominally under the direct rule of the Scottish Crown, that the chiefs took the law into their own hands and in consequence anarchy descended across the West Highlands and Isles. The manuscript states that the most vicious acts were carried out between the MacLeods and MacDonalds of Clanranald. The manuscript gives several examples of feuding between the clans. One such example is a story of a birlinn which was driven ashore on the island of Eigg. The crew were refused provisions and in consequence they slaughtered some local livestock to sustain themselves. The locals then put the majority of the crew to death and set three others to sea, where they miraculously washed ashore on Skye. When Alasdair Crotach heard of the treatment of the crew he swore he would not change his clothes until every soul on the islands of Eigg, Rum, and Canna was put to death. The chief ordered six large galleys to be made ready, and together with his son, William, and several hundred armed men, sailed for the Small Isles. The inhabitants of the islands knew the intentions of the MacLeods and attempted to escape their fury by hiding themselves in a large cave on Eigg. When the MacLeods reached the island they waited for three days before discovering the cave and the inhabitants within.

The manuscript states that Alasdair Crotach was a religious man; so before the massacre of all the local inhabitants, he prayed for six hours incessantly. Before his prayers, he declared that if the wind was blowing off the mouth of the cave at the end of the six hours, then the people should be spared; however, if the wind was blowing on the mouth of the cave, they should be put to death. While Alasdair Crotach prayed, the wind blew sideways across the mouth of the cave, but at the last moment it shifted to blowing hard upon the mouth of the cave. Alasdair Crotach took this as a sign from heaven and ordered the massacre.

* * *

MACLEOD STONE

NG 0408 9719

SIAR, Western Isles Council © Deborah Anderson

A massive standing stone guards the shore by Horgabost, Clach Macleoid, Neolithic in origin but named for the MacLeods who ruled the islands and perhaps became their gathering place. The stone stands 13ft/4m tall, 5ft/1.5m wide and has a fine growth of hairy green lichen on the seaward side. The MacLeod Stone serves another function in its setting by the sea, looking out to Taransay, for it sets off the captivating scenery of Harris, considered by some to be the most beautiful island ever with its turquoise crystal clear water, white sandy beaches, and splendid isolation.

The 15th century Kisimul Castle in the bay off Castlebay, Barra, was built by the MacNeils, probably Gilleonan MacNeil, the first Lord of Barra. It fell into disuse in 1838 but was purchased in 1937 by Robert MacNeil.

Chris Downer, geograph.org.uk

THE UISTS

The Scarista Stone, also known as Borvemore, stands in a field south of Horgabost in a possible alignment with the MacLeod Stone. Scarista has two fallen stones close by. Like Clach Macleoid, this stone has a flat face and points out to sea. Alignments have been studied between the two stones and the Celtic festival year suggesting that Scarista has a Beltane (May) and Lammas (August) alignment for the sunset, while MacLeod is positioned for the setting sun at the equinoxes.

The Scarista Stone - Clach Sternigeadh: This stone is almost the only one still standing of a stone circle which archaeologists believe to be a complex ritual site of Neolithic age. Beyond is Tràigh Mhòr or Scarista Beach. The hills of North Harris are in the background.

Anne Burgess, geograph.org.uk

SCARISTA STONE
NG 0202 9392

South of the Sound of Harris lie the islands of North and South Uist, with Benbecula as the stepping stone between the two. These have a magic all of their own and a hidden wealth of ancient sites.

The Hebrides were originally settled in the Mesolithic era and have a diversity of important pre-historic sites. Beyond the Uists and Benbecula are the islands of Eriskay, famous for its Eriskay ponies, Barra, famous for its medieval fortress, Kisimul Castle, Vatersay, Pabbay, the priest/hermit island famed for the only Pictish stone found in the Outer Hebrides, and Mingulay. This string of islands reads like a Gaelic song and has indeed inspired many.

The Uists have the highest density of breeding waders in Britain and many rare bird species. The native British graylag goose uses South Uist at Loch Druidibeg for its

Fae, Wikimedia Commons

Cille Bharra (Kilbarr or St Barr's) was a significant religious settlement dedicated to St Barr founded in the 7th century. One of many ruined chapels on the site, this burial chapel is 16th century built by the Barra MacNeil chiefs and houses the cast of the Clach Chille Bharra, a late 10th or early 11th century cross-slab discovered here. The original is in NMS, Edinburgh. Several fine late medieval sculptured stones are found at the chapel site as well and are attributed to the Iona School and the Oronsay School of carvers. Local customs are associated with St Barr who was held in great veneration here that testify to an entwining of pagan and Christian beliefs. This melding of superstition and religion endures in these island communities throughout Scotland.

main breeding grounds, and no wonder as it is so quiet in these environmentally sensitive islands. The corncrake is here from mid April. Even the place names tell tales of sacred sites.

An early chronicler wrote of the Hebrides in a poetic fashion that seems to describe the essence of them all: "...low sandy islands of small size without remarkable features, but of graceful form, and for the most part covered with luxuriant pasture richly besprinkled with the variegated hues of the hyacinth, clover, daisy, buttercup, thrift or sea pink, and sweet-smelling rue." Such floral carpets on the machairs, the fertile common land of the shoreline of the Hebrides, adorn the meadows throughout all these islands.

NORTH UIST

North Uist is extraordinarily rich in prehistoric remains with chambered cairns more plentiful here than in any other part of the Western Isles. The fertility of the island has attracted settlement over the centuries, being low-lying and sprinkled with lochs which are teeming with salmon and trout. An early chronicler wrote of North Uist: "...when the wind blows, the sea swells to a prodigious height and rolls with inexpressible violence against the shores, exhibiting a prospect awfully grand beyond description." Beinn Mhor, at 623.6ft/190m in height rewards the climber with a superb view of the Sound of Harris and the enchanted landscape below.

EILEAN DOMHNUILL crannog

NF 7468 7533

Within Loch Olabhat is an ancient crannog that dates from 3200–2800 BC, an artificial island dwelling that may be Scotland's earliest crannog. It even predates Ireland's earliest known crannogs by 2000 years.

BARPA LANGASS chambered cairn

NF 8376 6573

Heather Richard

Barpa Langass, on the road to Lochmaddy, is visible from the road on a hill slope. This great bare cairn of stone gives a good impression of how the Neolithic landscape appeared with numerous cairns dotted around. A round cairn of 82ft/25m diameter and 13ft/4m high, it has survived virtually intact, a low kerb of pointed stones and V-shaped forecourt at the entrance. It can be entered through a tunnel passage. Another cairn of about the same size can be seen from the entranceway to the tomb, Tigh Cloiche on the slopes of Mharrogh Hill to the north.

Outer Hebrides

DUN AN STICIR broch

NF 8971 7767

Dun an Sticir, located in Loch an Sticir near Balranald, is one of the best preserved brochs in the Western Isles, its walls more than 10ft/3m high. From Newtonferry one must walk to the end of Loch Sticir and cross two islands from the causeway, a wee pilgrimage journey to the sacred place. A rectangular house was built within the broch and robbed of its stones in the Middle Ages by Hugh MacDonald, the failed chief who was later imprisoned in Duntulm Castle on Skye.

POBULL FHINN stone circle

NF 8427 6501

Anne Burgess, geograph.org.uk

'Finn's People', the stone circle of Pobull Fhinn, is one of the most magic remote stone circles ever, standing on the south side of Beinn Langais with scenic views to the south over Loch Langais and to the east over the peak of Li a Deas. This is pure Hebridean bliss with white sands and turquoise sea below. The ring, a flattened ellipse, is 124.6 x 92.8ft/38 x 28m. At either end of the long axis, which runs east-west, are pairs of tall portal stones forming the two entrances. A total of twenty four stones make up the circle of Pobull Fhinn, also translated as the 'White People' or the 'Holy People'

FIR BHREIGE standing stones

NF 887 717

On the western slope of Blashaval are three standing stones called Na Fir Bhreige, which translates as 'the false men'. They are reputed to mark the graves of three traitors who were buried alive. Another story is that they are three men from Skye who were turned to stone for deserting their wives. Local legends are often attached to these poor innocent ancient stones which were probably standing there long before humans had such problems, merely watching the heavens to mark another solstice.

UNIVAL chambered cairn

NF 8003 6685

A chambered cairn and a standing stone beckon from a prominent hill above moorland lochans. Unival is a square cairn with tall stones marking the kerb of the cairn which increase in size to 8.2ft/2.5m at the entrance. The Unival standing stone is near the south west corner of the cairn and is 10ft/3m high. Later use of the site is evident from the Iron Age when the chamber was turned into a cooking pit.

TEAMPULL NA TRIONAID

NF 8162 6028

Zenit, Wikimedia Commons

Trinity Temple is a curious ruin of twin churches founded by Somerled's daughter Beathag about 1200 on an earlier Celtic site. A seat of learning similar to Iona, it was attended by Duns Scotus (circa 1265) who earned the label 'dunce' for the high English language, but that is another story.

SOUTH UIST

South Uist is a stunningly beautiful island of the Hebridean chain. Crystal clear blue waters, white powder beaches to the west, and heather uplands crowned by Beinn Mhor to the east. Along the sand dunes a generous length of twenty miles of machair carpeted with wild flowers in the spring provides habitat for the rare corncrake with its raspy call. Golden eagles, red grouse and red deer can be seen on the mountain slopes to the east. South Uist is one of the last surviving strongholds of the Gaelic language in Scotland with crofting industries like peat cutting and seaweed gathering still an important part of everyday life. After the Norse occupation South Uist was held by the MacDonalds of Clan Ranald. Famously this is the home of the romantic Jacobite heroine Flora Macdonald who was born in a farmhouse north of Milton. She is remembered for helping Bonnie Prince Charlie escape to Skye in 1746 when she was only twenty three years old.

CLADH HALLAN

NF 73138 21977

Cladh Hallan is the only site in the British Isles where prehistoric mummies have been found. This Bronze Age/Iron Age settlement on South Uist, found in deep sand on the machair near Daliburgh, began around 2200 BC with the small U-shaped house form. This was replaced with a row of seven roundhouses, up to 197ft/60m square, around 1250 BC, a new type of house built with a low stone wall and a timber roof covered in thick reed thatch, its floors sunken below ground level. So far three roundhouses have been excavated along with more houses built after 700 BC. Daily activities and life cycles were arranged in a sun-wise or clockwise fashion around these houses. Reconstruction can be seen on site along with some wheelhouse remains.

Heather Richard

The big story of Cladh Hallan is incredible, as two human burials were found, male and female, which had been mummified. They were buried in peat bogs for preservation like the bog bodies found in England, but then retrieved and set up inside the dwelling. Only the skeletons remained, a religious rite that speaks strongly of ancestor worship. The dating of these mummies correlates with the time of King Tutankhamun of Egypt.

BORNAIS

The Bornish machair, looking east, Beinn Mhor rising in the distance.

Excavation has revealed the site of Bornais to be possibly the largest Viking settlement in Scotland. Three artificial settlement mounds (NF 729 302) dominate the machair plain east of Dun Dulan (NF 7140 2981). A late Iron Age wheelhouse with a rectangular building added later on top was found at the first mound – a central hearth surrounded by cattle leg bones up-ended, a symbolic statement perhaps. Many 'midden' finds of occupation were also discovered, like bone dice and a whalebone axe. The other two mounds revealed the remains of a much larger Norse period settlement of over twenty buildings.

Dun Dulan, a broch located west of the Bornais machair.

This represents one of the largest and most important Norse settlements in Scotland. These halls indicate the home of an important Viking lord and his family. Again a central hearth and raised beach with large quantities of antler, ivory, tools, cooking vessels, and ornaments include a bone cylinder in the distinctive Norse 'Ringerike' style. The large size of the settlement is unusual suggesting it was an important centre for other Norse communities in South Uist. It was also a rich trading centre based on the varied finds, perhaps the 'Asda' of the Hebrides linking the west coast with southwest England, Ireland, Shetland, Norway, Greenland, and beyond to Greece.

Outer Hebrides

USINISH

NF 8434 3326

An earth-house, or souterrain hides in the township of Usinish Bay on the north side of Glen Usinish on a steep hillside south of the precipitous face of a mountain known as Maoladh na h-Uamha, a spur of Hecia, which towers above it. Found in a dilapidated condition in 1915, there are ruined sheilings, circular buildings and beehive cells all tucked among the bracken. Maybe one of the most remote places on earth, some say, but worth a visit for the sheer magic of it all if one is not put off by inaccessibility.

More sites on South Uist include a chambered cairn west of Lochboisdale, an early Norse church and settlement at Loch Kildonnan (similar to Finlaggan on Islay), Dun Roauill, the best fort (dun) on this island, 'Our Lady of the Isles' giant granite sculpture (modern) by Hew Lorimer on the Hill of Miracles at Rueval.

A SPECIAL SITE IN
THE WESTERN ISLES

PABBAY

NL 6072 8745 pictish stone

Marc Calhoun, geograph.org.uk

The Fort of Dunan Ruadh, a galleried broch ruin on the Isle of Pabbay. The Pictish stone and crosses are a short distance west of this site.

The tiny island of Pabbay, part of the Bishop's Isles group, is known as the Priest Island, of which there are many *papar* place name islands dotted around the Hebrides. Here on the edge of a steep sandy slope, running up from Bagh Ban on the eastern shore of Pabbay, is the site of a prehistoric midden, an Early Christian burial ground and a medieval chapel. Surviving monuments include three weathered slabs of the sixth to ninth century with Christian crosses superscribed over earlier pagan markings.

**Outer
Hebrides**

Most important is the Pabbay Stone, the only Pictish symbol stone still to be seen in the Western Isles. Dating from the sixth century, it is marked with the crescent and V-rod and the flower symbol (or possibly a helmet in profile) with a crude cross added later at the top of the stone. The stone lay horizontal for over a hundred years until it was re-erected in 2008 on its original location at the base of the chapel/ burial mound. It may not be an easy sacred site to visit, but like similar 'hermit' sites around the British Isles, especially in Ireland, it is one worth visiting.

Keith Brannigan, Archaeology Hebrides

The Pabbay Stone, a Pictish symbol stone prior to re-erection on its original site.

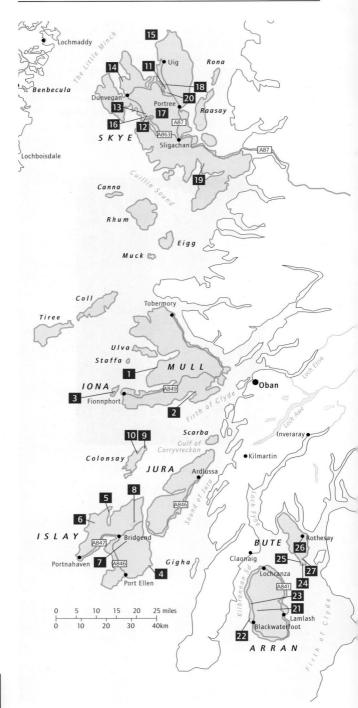

Lochmaddy

The Little Minch

15

14

11   Uig

Rona

18

Dunvegan   20

13   Portree

17

16   12   A87

A863

SKYE

Sligachan   A87

Lochboisdale

Cuillin Sound

19

Canna

Rhum

Eigg

Muck

Coll

Tiree   Tobermory

Ulva

Staffa

1   *MULL*

IONA   A849   ●Oban

3   Fionnphort

2   *Firth of Clyde*

Scarba

10   9   *Gulf of Corryvreckan*

Colonsay

JURA   Ardlussa   ●Inveraray

8   ●Kilmartin

5

A846   *Sound of Jura*

6   *Loch Awe*

ISLAY   Bridgend   *BUTE*   Rothesay

A847   *Loch Fyne*   26

Portnahaven   7   A846   Claonaig   25

4   Lochranza   27

Port Ellen   *Gigha*   A841   24

23

21

22   Blackwaterfoot   Lamlash

ARRAN   *Firth of Clyde*

Benbecula

Raasay

Loch Etive

Kilbrannan Sd.

0	5	10	15	20	25 miles
0	10	20	30	40km	

Inner
Hebrides

THE WESTERN ISLES
THE INNER HEBRIDES
WITH ARRAN AND BUTE

PRINCIPAL SITES

MULL
1. MacKinnon's Cave
2. Lochbuie stone circle

IONA
3. Abbey; Museum; Nunnery; Hermit Cell

ISLAY
4. Kildalton Cross
5. Kilnave Cross
6. Ballinaby standing stones
7. Dun Nosebridge
8. Finlaggan

COLONSAY
9. Kilcatrine Chapel
10. Riasg Buidhe Cross

SKYE
11. Carn Liath
12. Dun Beag

13. Dun Mor
14. Claigan souterrain
15. Kilvaxter souterrain
16. Knock Ullinish souterrain
17. Tungadale souterrain
18. Sornaichean Coir' Fhinn
19. Uamh an ard Achadh
20. Clach Ard

ARRAN
21. Machrie Moor
22. King's Cave
23. Auchagallon

BUTE
24. St Blane's, Kingarth
25. Dunagoil
26. St Mary's Chapel, Rothesay
27. Blackpark stone circle

HYPERBOLES ARE HARDLY OUT OF PLACE when it comes to talking about the Inner Hebrides, the southern islands of the west of Scotland. The jewel in the crown of course is the Isle of Iona, the cradle of Christianity in Scotland and a place of pilgrimage and sacredness for people of all faiths or none, pagan or Christian. "The veil is thin on Iona like nowhere else" said Lord George MacLeod of Fuinary. This 'otherworld' has a soft doorway so tread lightly when you enter.

The Island of Mull, the gateway to the tiny island of Iona, has endless peat moors of heather and mountainous peaks, home to sea eagles and ancient sites. The surrounding islands are hidden gems of the Hebrides, highlights including Lismore, Inch Kenneth, Coll, Tiree, the Dutchman's Cap, and the famed Treshnish Isles.

Inner Hebrides

The Inner Hebrides are separated from the Outer Hebrides by the Minch, a treacherous strait of water on the northwest coast. The most famous inhabitants are the Blue Men of the Minch who are said to inhabit this stretch of water between Lewis and the Shiant Islands, and the Long Island. Something like 'mermen', the blue men tribe lived in deep underwater caves and would swim alongside ships passing the Sound of Shiant, conjuring sailors into the sea and creating storms to wreck ships. Like other supernatural creatures they enjoyed a good riddle and pitted their wits against many an intrepid sea captain. Some say they are fallen angels or a folk memory of Moorish slaves marooned in Ireland in the ninth century by Viking pirates. The Vikings get blamed for a lot. Perhaps they are simply lost Picts. There are also eyewitness accounts of seeing these rubbery blue forms floating in the sea, and like the Bermuda Triangle, the Minch has taken its toll on ships.

ISLE OF MULL

Marianna Lines

Mull, a general view.

Shrouded in mist or bathed in sunshine, Mull has its own special story of sacred sites and deep history to share. The third largest of the Hebridean islands, measuring 26miles/48km East–West x 24miles/38.5km North–South, Mull is teeming with wildlife and wildflowers. This is the place to see sea eagles at their best, as recently many have taken up residence here from the east coast in a new breeding programme. The seas bring whales, dolphins, porpoises and basking sharks to the area for exciting viewing. Bird watching, stag hunting, whale watching are all an essential part of the Mull experience.

Mull has one stone circle, fourteen stone settings, and thirteen single standing stones along with a number of significant castles such as Torosay, Duart, Glengorm, and some of the most spectacular coastal scenery anywhere. The fort of Dun Ara is one of four medieval hillforts on the island.

Perched on the summit close to Some Point looking out to the Ardnamurchan peninsula, the remaining walls are all that is left of three buildings, once the stronghold of the MacKinnon clan.

Dun Ara sits majestically guarding the approaches to the Sound of Mull.

Mick Garrett, geograph.org.uk

South Mull, dominated by Ben More, on the road to Fionnphort and the Isle of Iona, contains the famous stone circle of Lochbuie. On the way is MacKinnon's Cave which takes you back into the earth for 100 yards under the sea cliffs, and a fossilised tree, MacCullough's Tree, takes you back 50 million years. The Lochbuie Stone Circle, near the shores of Loch Buie overlooked by the majestic Ben Buie, stands in boggy meadowland in a 39.3ft/12m diameter ring of nine granite slabs. Three outlier stones are set apart from the circle, a processional way perhaps, the second one being a spectacular monolith over 10ft/3m high. The Bronze Age circle relates to the Nine Maidens tradition that is found throughout the British Isles. Nine stones always seem to conjure up nine maidens, usually having been turned to stone for dancing on the Sabbath. The legend associated with Nine Maidens is found from Cornwall to the islands of Scotland and beyond, and of course has magical significance to any who visit these sites.

Ben More.

Marianna Lines

Stone circle near Loch Buie. View northeast from one of three outlier stones.

The Standing Stones of Mull are unique to the Western Isles and to Scotland. These are often arranged in the form of a small row of three to five stones. Some of the best known groups include Kilmore or Cnoc Fada near Dervaig, the Maol Mor linear setting of four stones in forestry on the ridge of Maol Mor, Dervaig cemetery with three stones now rebuilt into a drystone wall, and the Quinish stones, a row of four or five originally with only one tall stone remaining.

Nine crannogs, the ancient loch dwellings from the Iron Age period are located on Mull in various lochs.

IONA

I Chaluim Chille, the isle of Colm Cille, is the island of the Irish princely priest who became revered as St Columba. The beautiful Hebridean island of Iona holds a unique place in the story of Scotland, its history and its spiritual beginnings. A place of pilgrimage since the Iron Age of the first millennium AD, its shores have seen monks, pilgrims, clan chiefs, kings, artists, craftsmen, farmers and fishermen come and go.

A rich artistic legacy survives in the intricately carved stones and crosses and the finest illuminated manuscripts ever created, *The Book of Kells* (*circa* AD 800). What was lost is impossible to reconcile when the Vikings sacked the island and its monastery in the late eighth and early ninth centuries. The monks took *The Book of Kells* off to safety in Ireland, but presumably an entire library of knowledge went under the sea. Yet what remains is a great sense of peace, beauty and infinite oneness with everything.

Inner Hebrides

This tiny island, three miles long and one and a half miles wide, off the southwest coast of Mull in the Inner Hebrides is now a Western 'mecca' for the whole world. The label 'Cradle of Christianity' could apply to both Iona and even earlier to Whithorn, but taking aside from taking history beyond reality it is not possible to claim any one place as being the first berth of Christianity in the Western world, much less in Scotland. The importance of Iona lies in its brilliant monastic centre of faith, learning and art whose influence spread across Europe, thanks to Columba and his successors.

Iona Abbey looking towards Mull.

Marion Leigh

Iona, originally the Latin 'Ioua', was for some the Yew Island of the Druids or the Sacred Isle of the Blest, 'Tìr nan Òg', the land of youth, the 'otherworld'. Such a lot of expectations to live up to when this fertile land was given to St Columba in AD 563 as a place for prayer and meditation. His monastic community thrived with a simple church, beehive type of drystone cells for the monks, and an enclosure with bank and ditch to define the monastic area. A corner of this earthwork can be seen to the northwest of the restored Iona Abbey we see today. Also, west of the Abbey the foundations of a small building, Columba's cell, have been unearthed. One can even see 'Columba's pillow', a small oval stone inscribed with a cross, in the Abbey Museum. Yet nothing of the Columban or Early Christian monastery building survives; only the later medieval buildings and remains.

The high crosses that survive from the eighth century include St John's Cross (a replica on site, the original in the Abbey Museum) in front of the Abbey showing its high Celtic style of ringed cross with panels of serpents and boss motifs and interlace illuminating the eternal journey of life in stone. Also seen by the Abbey is St Martin's Cross with classic Biblical scenes of the Virgin and Child and Daniel in the Lion's Den.

The Abbey Museum, in a stunning new interpretive display, presents the original three high crosses re-erected: St Oran's Cross, St Matthew's, and St John's along with elaborate West Highland sculptured stones of the Lords of the Isles period from the fourteenth to the sixteenth century. The very fine sixteenth century memorial stone to Anna Maclean, Prioress of the Nunnery, includes the Pictish mirror and comb symbol among her symbolic attributes – symbols also associated with mermaids who may also have been part of the deeper Iona story. The green pebbles on the shore of Iona are known as 'mermaid's tears'.

Top: St Martin's cross; West Highland sculptured stone; Maclean's cross.
Above: Memorial stone to Anna Maclean; West Highland stone with birlinn.

The ruins of the thirteenth century Nunnery weave their own gentle history in stone among the wildflowers in the open rockery garden presentation. A lintel over the arched window on the road leading to the Abbey has the worn ancient carving of the Sheela-na-Gig fertility motif, a symbol of the Mother Goddess wor-

The weathered image of Sheela-na-Gig.

ship in the islands. This image is also found on the islands of Harris, Eigg, and on the western mainland.

Following the Viking raids Iona experienced a phoenix rising by the medieval period when the Benedictine Abbey was established by Reginald of the MacDonalds of the Isles in 1200. The Reformation may have wrought its destruction after which the buildings fell into disuse and crumbled into disrepair. In two periods of restoration the Abbey Church was restored and rebuilt by the Iona Cathedral Trust in the first decade of the twentieth century, followed by the adjoining cloister and buildings by the Iona Community later in the mid century. Pilgrimage became a modern buzz word for spiritual travel.

Sacred spots around the Abbey include St Columba's Shrine, a beautiful tiny shrine-chapel located outside the west front of the Abbey reputed to be the site of the saint's grave and St Oran's Chapel, the oldest part of the Abbey complex beside the Reilig Odhrain, the sacred burial ground. This burial ground was used mostly for the monastic orders, perhaps for some early Scottish and Irish kings (although the evidence is scant), for the clan chiefs of medieval Gaeldom and for the local crofting population over at least four centuries.

Further around the island is the Hermit Cell, a small ring of stones in the peat bog near Dun I, the highest hill where the Well of Eternal Youth is also located, the marble quarry, St Columba's Bay where the saint first landed, Sithean Mor, the hill of the faeries, and the most perfect beaches and coves at the Bay at the Back of the Ocean.

The depth of the Iona story cannot be told, only experienced on the island. The Celtic blessing, "Deep Peace of the running wave to you" is recalled upon arriving on Iona.

Griffin and vine scroll detail –
art by Marianna Lines.

Inner Hebrides

STAFFA

Marion Leigh

The very tiny uninhabited island of Staffa which lies off the coast of Mull to the north of Iona is one of the most spectacular sights in the world, not just Scotland. Fingal's Cave is a sacred site not to be missed – to experience the echoing sounds of the sea as well as the basalt lava columns that are only found on Staffa and on the Giant's Causeway in Northern Ireland. These immense hexagonal pillars rise up like a giant sea serpent dressed like a pipe organ. The famous German composer Felix Mendelssohn wrote his famous overture *The Hebrides* in 1829 inspired by the weird echoes in the sea cave, and you will never forget it, especially if you go inside the cave.

THE GARVELLACHS

There are a number of islands in the Garvellachs chain which can be seen from the ferry that sails past from Oban, but the most important is the southern island of Eileach an Naoimh, the Isle of the Saints which shelters early ecclesiastical buildings of the Celtic Church. It is said that St Brendan the Navigator, the famed Irish missionary/explorer who sailed his coracle to the New World, established this monastery in AD 542.

Eileach an Naoimh is famous for being the burial place of Columba's mother Eithne. St Columba retreated to the island for solitude from the demands of Iona – that 'New York of the monastic world'. A roughly carved stone overlooks the monastery marking the grave of Eithne. The spirituality of the sixth century Irish Christian missionaries seems to have been embedded in their lives and daily routines while building their chapels and cells as seats of learning. Like Columba and Brendan, they sought out the most remote of places to continue their work, places like The Garvellachs and Iona.

One of the beehive cells recorded as part of the monastery established on Eilach an Naoimh.

A visit to Eileach an Naoimh is a remarkable chance to experience the solitude of the life of the hermit in the setting of the natural grandeur of the surrounding islands.

ISLAY

Yula was a Norse princess who is reputed to be buried under a standing stone on Islay, thus the island was named after her – *Yula's Isle*. This overture to Norse rule tells some of the story of the Queen of the Hebrides, as Islay is known. Islay was once the 'capital' of the Western Isles when the powerful Clan Donald ruled as Lord of the Isles. Dunyvaig Castle, fourteenth century 'fort of the little ships' at Lagavulin Bay was the stronghold, war galleys at anchor. Before the twelfth century Islay was part of the Scots Kingdom of Dálriada settled by the Irish for 300 years. There are many elements that make this island so popular; a turbulent history belied by peaceful surroundings; the whisky and the incredibly rich bird life including the famous wintering geese; and finally the ancient sites and ruins dotted around the landscape. Monastic chapels, fine medieval carved grave slabs and high crosses define the sophistication of Islay life during the rich medieval period.

Inner Hebrides

The eighth century high cross at Kildalton.

Marianna Lines

The Galley Stone, Kildalton church-yard. Art on site by Marianna Lines.

Marianna Lines

The Kildalton Cross

(NR 4580 5083) is one of the greatest achievements of Early Christian art of Dalriada. A high cross of the later eighth century, it stands alongside the Iona crosses in excellence, a splendid ringed cross with sculpture of great skill. Located in the churchyard of the ruined Kildalton church on the southern end of the island, it is carved out of local bluestone, reputedly created by a sculptor from Iona. The west face shows four lions around the central high relief boss of the cross along with entwined serpent and boss ornament, with the east face, toward the sea, showing figurative Biblical scenes including the Virgin and Child protected by angels. There are a number of distinctive fifteenth century West Highland grave-slabs throughout the churchyard dating from the medieval period including a beautiful carving of a 'birlinn' or galley that belonged to the Lords of the Isles. A sanctuary cross, the 'Thieves' Cross, is found on a knoll on a knoll oppo-site the church outside the churchyard wall.

The Kilnave Cross (NR 28513 71519) on Loch Gruinart is another eighth century cross on Islay with fine decoration linking it with Iona and the illuminated manuscript art of the period. Although somewhat fragmented and worn, it holds an evocative place in the landscape. An elegant high cross is also found at Kilchoman on the Rhinns where there is a wishing stone in the base of the cross.

Robert Liston, geograph.org.uk

The 'Blue Knight', from a stone in Kilchoman churchyard, Islay. With peaked helmet, the Medieval Warrior is a powerful motif in West Highland stone art of the 14th and 15th centuries. Natural dye fabric art by Marianna Lines.

Ballinaby Standing Stones (NR 2199 6719, NR 2210 6739) include two surviving tall slabs, a third stone now missing. One of the uprights, a tall and narrow stone measuring 16.4ft/5m in height is one of the most impressive standing stones in western Scotland, a testimony to the skills of the early inhabitants in the

Inner Hebrides

Bronze Age. Ballinaby is a Norse-derived name with Norse settlements, burials and artefacts found in this area. The only stone circle on Islay and one of the few in Argyll is at Cultoon on the Rhinns of Islay (NR 1956 5697) with three stones standing and another twelve lying prone in the elliptical setting.

Dun Nosebridge (NR 3713 6011) is a fortified ridge, a spectacular monument with extensive earthworks near Neriby from Bridgend.

Finlaggan (NR388 681) was the parliament and council isle of the Lords of the Isles, and is one of the most atmospheric sacred sites on the island as well as being the most important archaeological site. Located on Loch Finlaggan at Ballygrant, this island complex within an island contains the chapel, dwelling houses, burial ground with some of the finest West Highland decorated slabs and effigies, a great hall, and a crannog.

The Council Isle of Lord of the Isles on Loch Finlaggan, Islay.

JURA

Jura is the neighbouring island to Islay, but as wild as Islay is civilised. In fact, Jura has been declared the wildest island in the Inner Hebrides. The author George Orwell wrote *Nineteen Eighty-Four* in his island retreat on Jura. The triple peaks of the Paps of Jura are a landmark throughout the west of Scotland from the Mull of Kintyre and Firth of Lorn to every vantage point and standing stone on the mainland and islands. The name Jura means *udder island* in Old Norse. Heavy peat content and red deer mean the land is poor and depopulation during the Clearances has left the island with little but great scenery and a haunting presence of the past. The score reads 200 people and 6,000 red deer on Jura. In fact, Hamish Haswell-Smith in his impeccable book on *Scottish Islands* (1998) says, "On Jura it is easy to believe that there is no such thing as the human race..."

The Paps of Jura from Bunnahabhain.

Isolation is the essence of Jura.

Off the north end of Jura between Jura and Scarba is the famed legendary notorious **Gulf of Corryvreckan** whirlpool, its name in Gaelic meaning 'the speckled cauldron', or *Coire Bhreacain*. It is said that this dangerous spring tidal race of waters, sometimes called the Great Race, was named after Breacan, a Norse Prince or King who foundered with his entire fleet of fifty ships. First he had to prove his courage to win the maiden, anchoring his boat in the whirlpool using three ropes, one of hemp, one of wool, one of virgin's hair. All three ropes gave way and Breachan was drowned.

An underwater basalt pillar known as *The Old Hag* forms part of the mechanics that forces the water upwards into its bottleneck maelstrom. The Corryvreckan is one of the largest whirlpools in the world. It is sometimes known as the Gateway to Hell, so many sailors drowned and ships wrecked trying to navigate a passage through. It has also been an inspiration to artists, musicians, writers, mystics and storytellers the world over.

COLONSAY AND ORONSAY

Colonsay means *Columba's island* in Old Norse. The twin islands of Colonsay and Oronsay have been inhabited for 7,000 years. The beautiful Kiloran Bay, the 'cave of the grave-dust', has revealed bones of domestic animals and Neolithic flint tools as well as pre-Christian and Early Christian relics. A Viking warrior with a ship burial from AD 855 was found in the sand dunes by the Bay, a pagan burial with cross-inscribed slab added for extra measure.

The chapel ruin of **Kilcatrine** (NR 4216 9989) is marked by a standing stone and a cross in the north of the island, the site of an eleventh century convent.

Inner Hebrides

A most unusual rather strange carved stone is found in the gardens of Colonsay House, the ancestral home of the Clan MacNeil built by Malcolm MacNeil in 1722. **Riasg Buidhe Cross** dates from the eighth century, a figurative cross/ human statuette carving that is as pagan as it is Christian. The solemn face with distinctive eyebrows and ears rests its chin on top of a Latin cross, with cross arms in the form of double spirals and the lower shaft ending in a fishtail. Found in 1870 at Kiloran on a chapel site, it now lives beside Tobar Oran, a covered well dedicated to St Oran (NR 3957 9679). It wouldn't be too out of place on Easter Island with its sculptured exaggerated 'face-cross'.

Top; Riasg Buidhe cross. Above: Tobar Odhrai well chamber dedicated to St. Oran, with Riasg Buidhe cross, east of Colonsay House.

This anthropomorphic cross has a virtual double in Ireland. The Island of Boa in Lough Erne, Fermanagh, has two stone statues of the same period and the same rough triangular face thought to be pagan deities and possibly a precursor to the Sheela-na-Gig fertility figure.

Other carved stones at the site were built into neighbouring houses and a rock cut basin with a round hole, classed as a 'knocking stone', can be seen.

Colonsay can boast of a Piper's Cave that carries the same legends as found on other islands of the Hebrides like Mull, Skye, Barra, and Gigha. The Piper's Cave at Port Ban is named after the story of a piper and his dog who go into the cave in search of a treasure and disappear, with only the dog reappearing later four miles south of the cave with all of its hair burnt off. The ghost of the piper can still be heard playing his pipes on a quiet evening. This curious legend occurs throughout the country from Edinburgh to Oban with differing stories but always the same theme, and nobody knows why. The Paps of Jura glow in the evening sun as witnessed from Colonsay.

Inner Hebrides

ORONSAY

The tiny tidal island of Oronsay seems to have a much bigger history than its neighbour in many ways, much like that of Iona and Mull. Oronsay means 'Oran's Island', derived from St Oran who was one of Columba's twelve disciples on Iona. A simple sanctuary cross separates the two islands on the Strand, a wide expanse of shell sand. Any Colonsay fugitive who reached the Sanctuary Cross was immune from punishment. Such is the role of the Celtic icon of a sanctuary cross which can be found throughout these islands, especially on Iona and Islay.

St Oran's original monastery, circa AD 563 was considered second only to Iona in importance. An Augustinian priory was later built on the same site, its ruins dating from 1380, a fine group of buildings well preserved on the island. Within the cloisters is a collection of around thirty West Highland sculptured stones from the Lord of the Isles period, fourteenth to fifteenth century, their craftsmanship rivaling the great carved stone slabs on Iona. The Oronsay Cross (12ft/3.7m high) seen outside the cloisters, is a splendidly carved high cross of late medieval artistry.

SKYE AND THE SMALL ISLES
EIGG, MUCK, RUM, CANNA

The Isle of Skye is the most famous of all the islands in Scotland, the essence of 'Bonnie Scotland', Bonnie Prince Charlie and his Jacobite history, and 'chocolate box' tourism. However, there is more to Skye than its rampant jagged mountain beauty and its misty reputation. There is a bridge to Skye, a modern development for the traveller, no more 'over the sea' journey required. Symbolic and practical, it has changed the island and made it more accessible.

The Gaelic name for the Isle of Skye is *An t-Eilean Sgitheanach* meaning 'the winged isle' or 'the notched isle'. *Skitis*, an early Celtic word for 'winged' may describe the island's peninsulas that radiate out from a mountainous centre, giving the appearance of a wing of land. Another derivation comes from the Norse word for cloud, *skuy*, giving it the name *Eilean a' Cheo*, the 'Misty Isle'. From the surreal rock formations of the Trotternish Peninsula to the strange hummocks of Fairy Glen to the Red and Black Cuillins in the epicentre of the island, Skye can claim the greatest concentration of peaks in Britain. These are also the most challenging. It is said that the Cuillins name is derived from Cu Chulainn, a legendary hunter who crossed from Ireland to Skye in two mighty strides.

The Old Man of Storr is the best known pinnacle in the Trotternish Peninsula north of Portree, part of a twenty mile-long escarpment of sheer cliffs and stone towers. The Quiraing at Staffin Bay is another famous jumble of strange shaped hills

Glendale Harper, Skye: Located near Dunvegan Castle the clan seat of the MacLeods, the Glendale stone of medieval period shows the kneeling figure of a man playing a harp, likely to have been a famous harper to the MacLeods. The grave-slab also depicts a Claymore sword with foliaceous design and a mitred priest figure with a chalice. Art by Maranna Lines.

and rocks, perhaps one of nature's best stone circles. The Fairy Glen is even more of a wild, magical secret place located along a track outside the village of Uig. Here you enter an eerie mysterious world of perfect conical hills, some up to 60ft/18.3m high, a natural formation that defies belief. The dramatic scenery of Skye is enchanted if not enhanced by such powerful rock formations, always better on a misty day with the *haar* (the foggy mist of Scotland) for atmosphere thick enough to bottle. Further enchantment is found at Dunvegan where the mighty fifteenth century castle of Clan MacLeod of Dunvegan holds a relic that is revered as the Fairy Flag. This charm is said to have been given to the clan by a fairy to ensure victory in battle three times and it has done its job twice. The delicate silk is dated from the fourth century AD. Legends of change-lings are associated with the Flag, when a fairy child would replace the stolen human child.

The Old Man of Storr.

Wojsyl, Wikimedia Commons

The ancient sites of Skye tell the story of the landscape of early man as he developed his spiritual settings, his sacred geometry in stone. A plethora of archaeology including duns, brochs, souterrains, standing stones, burial cairns and sculptured stones are the earliest records to be found.

Carn Liath (NG 4201 5139) is the largest of a cluster of cairns beside the River Haultin at the head of Loch Eyre near to Uig. This tall Neolithic chambered cairn rises up to 13ft/4m in height, a striking presence on the horizon from a distance. The stones covering the cairn appear to glow in their whiteness as they are covered with white lichen. A large stone stands beside the cairn pointing towards the centre of the cairn with another large slab nearby, likely to be part of the entrance passage. A short cist was also exposed, the burial cairn. The landscape is breathtaking.

Dun Beag (NG 3395 3863) is Skye's chief broch, the best known, best preserved, most accessible on the island. Dun Beag means 'small fort', and the ruined but atmospheric broch is located near the Dunvegan to Sligachan road.

Highland Council

The massive walls rise up more than 6.5ft/2m high. Within a gallery space, entrance passage, security cell and a stone stairway the traveller may be encouraged to imagine life in a broch around 200 BC. This defensive site offers amazing views over Loch Bracadale to the Cuillins.

Dun Mor (NG 3398 3907) is the diminutive double to Dun Beag, now only a big pile of stones but it is only a short distance further down the road from its big brother. This was the big fort originally.

Claigan Souterrain (NG 2382 5394) is an underground chamber in use from 800 BC up to AD 200 lined and roofed with stone. It is located north of Dunvegan Castle at Claigan. Being underground, souterrains can be a challenge to find.

MORE SKYE SOUTERRAINS

Kilvaxter Souterrain (NG 3899 6961) opened up in a field, literally, after a rainstorm in 2000. A long trench of 65.5ft/20m lined with drystone walling, capped with massive lintel slabs, and a chamber were exposed on that day, having been covered with just a few feet of earth. Souterrains were believed to be underground chambers in the Iron Age period but no one really knows of their real usage.

Knock Ullinish Souterrain (NG 3330 3848) is an earth house, as souterrains are also called, located at the foot of Knock Ullinish near Struan which is near the broch of Dun Beag. To find this may be a bit of an adventure.

Knock Ullinish.

Tungadale Souterrain (NG 4075 4006) is one of the most interesting of ancient sites on Skye near Sligachan. Located in a remote spot, there is a long walk of 9.9 miles/16km through some dense forest, but the reward is great. The Tungadale Souterrain is part of a large Bronze Age construction consisting of possibly two underground houses built of stone and terraced into the hillside. Its entrance lies on a steep slope through a wall from one of these earth houses requiring a good 10ft/3m of crawling to get inside.

Inside Tungadale Souterrian.

Inner
Hebrides

Sornaichean Coir' Fhinn (NG 4142 5251) is a pair of standing stones near Kensaleyre overlooking Loch Eyre. The story is told that the stones were erected here by Fingal the legendary warrior and his fellow hunters in order to suspend a cooking pot to make venison stew.

Fingal place names are common around Scotland, such as Fingal's Cave on Staffa by Iona. In Irish mythology, the hero Fingal is known as Fionn mac Cumhaill and the eighteenth century writer James Macpherson featured him in his *Ossian* cycle of poems. The name Fingal derives from 'white stranger' in old Gaelic. Fionn is also said to have built the great Giant's Causeway that was meant to bridge Ireland and Scotland.

Uamh an ard Achadh (NG 5943 1971) is a High Pasture Cave which was discovered by London cavers, located near Torrin in a valley by Beinn an Dubhaich. This limestone cave is one of the longest caves on Skye with around 382.6yds/350m of accessible passages.

John Allan, geograph.org.uk

Uamh an ard Achadh - 'High Pasture Cave'.

Clach Ard, a Pictish symbol stone of the Class I early period, circa seventh century, stands in its original location (NG 4210 4908) at Tote by Portree. A similar Pictish stone is kept in the dungeons of Dunvegan. A third Pictish symbol stone is found on the nearby small island of Raasay, also the home of the great Gaelic poet Sorley Maclean.

Wildlife on Skye offers great delights with golden eagles and otters, the Atlantic salmon as well as the

Clach Ard Pictish stone [detail].
Art impression by Marianna Lines.

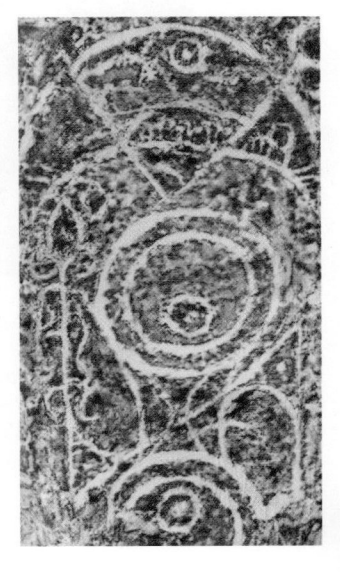

outstanding seabird population found throughout the Hebrides. *Ring of Bright Water,* the classic story of the otter by Gavin Maxwell, was written at Kylerhea where there is an Otter Sanctuary.

Martin Martin, a native of Skye, wrote about stones of a different kind in his native land in his famous *Description of the Western Islands of Scotland* in the seventeenth century:

> There are marcasites black and white, resembling silver ore, near the village Sartle: there are likewise in the same place several stones, which in bigness, shape, &c., resemble nutmegs, and many rivulets here afford variegated stones of all colours. The Applesglen near Loch-Fallart has agate growing in it of different sizes and colours; some are green on the outside, some are of a pale sky colour, and they all strike fire as well as flint: I have one of them by me, which for shape and bigness is proper for a sword handle. Stones of a purple colour flow down the rivulets here after great rains.

Marianna Lines

'The Crusader', medieval gravestone, Skeabost, Isle of Skye.
Skeabost is probably the most important religious site on Skye.
The island is occupied by a burial ground and the remains of two
churches dating from the 11th to 15th centuries when the island was the
seat of the bishops of the Southern Isles. The larger of the two churches
now survives as a grass covered mound and traditional burying place of
the Clan Nicolson. Medieval gravestones include the effigy of a West
Highland knight of the late 15th century known as The Crusader,
depicted with his ship, a West Highland birlinn, at his feet.

RUM, EIGG, MUCK AND CANNA

The Small Isles of Rum, Eigg, Muck and Canna are places of discovery well beyond the beaten track.

Rum is an especially spectacular island and contains evidence of the earliest settlements of the Mesolithic period to be found in Scotland, which date from 7000 BC. Vast herds of red deer live on Rum which has also been a breeding ground for the reintroduction of the white-tailed sea eagle. The eccentric folly of Kinloch Castle, a merchant build in 1900, brought a rather bizarre flavour to the island that has never really recovered. Rum is also a paradise for the naturalist. As an SSSI (Site of Special Scientific Interest), Rum has plant life that has been undisturbed since the Ice Age, rare spotted orchids unique to Rum, Rum ponies descended from the Spanish galleons, nineteen species of butterfly and breeding corncrakes.

CANNA

Canna belonged to the Benedictine Monastery of Iona, and was the granary of Iona for food supplies, in part. It was taken over, like much of the Hebrides, by Norwegian suzerainty but the monks continued to cultivate the island up to the Reformation although piracy was a great problem in those days. Again like the rest of the Scottish islands in the west, Canna became part of the Kingdom of Scotland under the rule of the Lord of the Isles, the ruling body of the west with the MacDonalds of Clanranald in charge. Later the world's biggest Gaelic library of Celtic language and culture was established on Canna under the auspices of the historian John Lorne Campbell.

Historic remains include A'Chill, the seventh century St Columba's chapel and an exquisite sculptured cross along with an earlier period standing stone on the same site. A Viking ship burial was uncovered in Camas Thairbearnais on the north side of the island where there are steep rocky dangerous cliffs. More signs of Norse occupation and burials have been found around the island and on the adjoining tidal isle of Sanday. Sir Walter Scott wrote of Canna:

> *Seek not the giddy crag to climb*
> *to view the turret scathed by time*
> *it is a task of doubt and fear*
> *to aught but goat or mountain deer.*

EIGG

Eigg is a community-owned island, a great success in the modern world of island life. St Donan set up a monastery on Eigg in the seventh century, leaving a number of relics and

Above: Sheela-na-Gig from Eigg.
Art by Marianna Lines.
Left: The Kildonnan cross.

carved stones, but was murdered on the island with fifty two of his monks in AD 617. Kildonnan is the sacred site on the island with an ancient Celtic cross-slab. A Pictish stone has also been found and is now located at the Lodge, the main house on Eigg. Another smaller portable stone showing an unusual carving of a Sheela-na-Gig, the fertility goddess figure, is also part of the Eigg heritage. The crannog of Loch nam Ban Mora, the loch of the mighty women, provides further insights on some of Eigg's dark past.

An Sgurr is the prominent landmark, a strange wedge-shaped conical hill rising 492ft/150m above sea level, its sugar-loaf crag dominating the island. Puffins and Manx shearwaters colonise on Eigg in large numbers.

ISLE OF ARRAN

THE POPULAR ISLE OF ARRAN, dubbed *Scotland in minia-ture*, lies south of the Hebridean islands and is easliy reached from Glasgow. The Isle of Arran's unique profile owes much to the fact that it was once part of a string of volcanoes running from Antrim in Ireland to Skye. Separated from the mainland by a few miles of water, Arran's highly distinctive and welcom-ing climate make it the most accessible island in Scotland and the most southerly as it lies off the coast of Ayrshire in the Firth of Clyde. Only 20 miles long by 10 miles wide (32 x 16km), it packs a lot in.

Inner
Hebrides

Many place names are derived from the Norse who were early settlers on the island: Brodick, the capital (*broad bay*) and Goatfell, (*goat mountain*), the highest mountain peak at 2,953ft/900m and the home of the 'sleeping warrior' as he appears in profile in the mountain range. Strong Gaelic influences are also found with place names like Machrie, *low-lying plain* and Cir Mhor, *the mountain of the Great Comb*.

The spectacular standing stones of Machrie Moor are found on Arran's west coast looking across to the Kintyre Peninsula. The King's Caves contain a mysterious record of early people's graffiti. From Whiting Bay toward Lamlash, the distinctive shape of Holy Isle can be seen, historically sacred to the medieval Irish saint, St Mo Las or Molaise (born AD 566) with remains of carvings and caves. It is now a sacred retreat for the Tibetan Samye Ling community. St Molaise's Cave (NS 0586 2972) was the saint's seventh century 'well kitted-out' dwelling on the isle with runic and Early Christian inscriptions decorating the walls and the holy Well of St Molaise. 'St Molaise's Table', a flat sandstone boulder, also contains rock-cut crosses. The saint lived to a ripe old age of one hundred and twenty. The cave became a place of pilgrimage thereafter. Golden eagles, red deer, otters, take your pick; wildlife is everywhere on Arran and even the salmon fishing is great. Wild goats roam only on Holy Isle.

MACHRIE MOOR

NR 900 324 to NR 924 322 (W-E)

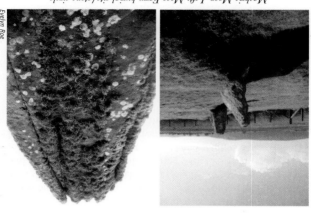

Machrie Moor. Left: Moss Farm burial site/stone circle.
Right: Red sandstone pillar stone on the Moor, encrusted with lichen.

Evelyn Roe

Alice Simpson

The ceremonial landscape of Machrie Moor is far more than a few tall stones. A walk of 3.1miles/5km leads you through a prehistoric complex of stone circles and chambered tombs of

Machrie Moor – photo by Evelyn Roe.

the Neolithic period, cairns and hut-circles of the Bronze Age and standing stones on a timeline from 3500 BC to 1000 BC. There are six stone circles in Machrie Moor, some complete with up to nine or ten stones, others in a ruined state. The resonant trio of three tall, elegant pillar stones within the moorland setting dominate the landscape. These iconic red sandstone slabs soar to a height of 18ft/5.5m. The final stone circle on the circuit, Circle 1, originally consisted of 12 stones with tall sandstone slabs alternating with low granite boulders.

A great deal of research has been conducted on Machrie Moor as to its archaeo-astronomical meanings by the well-known archaeologist Aubrey Burl.

KING'S CAVE

NR 8844 3092

King's Cave at Blackwaterfoot on the west side near Machrie Moor is a large and deep dry sandstone cave. Its massive entrance can be seen high up on the cliffs from the sea on the approach into Kilbrannan Sound. It was said to have been occupied by Fingal, or Finn McCool, the legendary Irish warrior-king who we have met many times in legend around these isles. Both Early Christian and Viking wall carvings of hunting scenes and fascinating images are found here but badly damaged by modern graffiti now. The most significant carving in the cave is the schematic outline of a human figure in the *orans* or prayer position. His arms are raised up in praise fashion and a pair of horns or antenna spout from the top of his head. This is surely a godlike figure that has not been properly studied. King's Cave is one of the reputed sites of Robert the Bruce's famous 'spiritual' encounter with the spider.

Storytelling time:

> It is told that in the early days of Bruce's reign he was defeated by the English and driven into exile. He was on the run and sought refuge in a small dark cave where he sat and watched a little spider trying to make a web. Time and time again the spider would fall and then climb slowly back up to try again. Finally as the Bruce looked on the spider managed to stick a strand of silk to the cave wall and began to weave a web. Robert the Bruce was inspired by the spider and went on to defeat the English at the Battle of Bannockburn. The legend was first published by Sir Walter Scott in *Tales of a Grandfather* in 1828, some 500 years later. Caves across Scotland are legendary as the real cave of Bruce and the spider, including Kings Cave at Drumadoon on Arran, Kirkpatrick Fleming near Lockerbie, Balquhidder Glen and on Rathlin Island. The fact is Robert the Bruce did make a visit to Arran in 1307.

There are other versions of this tale with a royal prerogative, including one about a Mongolian warlord and an ant.

AUCHAGALLON

NR 8928 3464

Wendy Kirkwood, geograph.org.uk

The cairn of Auchagallon is found on the west coast of Arran, a low cairn of stones, elliptical in shape 47.5 x 42.6ft/14.5 x 13m, looking across the Sound to Kintyre. It is an unusual monument, a cross between a stone circle and a cairn. Its kerb of upright

Inner
Hebrides

stones are graded with the higher stones along the seaward side with a low broad stone flanked by two taller stones. It resembles the recumbent stone circles so prevalent in Aberdeenshire.

OTHER SITES ON ARRAN
Carn Ban Chambered Tomb at Kilmory (NR 9909 2619) – a spectacular site high up in the hills.
Monamore Chambered Tomb (NS 0175 2889) known as a 'Clyde tomb' like Carn Ban, a long chamber of 46ft/14m divided into four compartments.
Torr a' Chaisteil dun or fort (NR 9219 2326) with thick walls and substantial earthworks on a grassy knoll above a burn.
Torrylinn Chambered Tomb at Kilmory near Lagg (NR 9551 2107, visible east side, NR95202114 west side) on the southern shore of the island where two chambered tombs and a cairn are located on either side of the Kilmory Water, only the single Torrylinn now visible.

ISLE OF BUTE

The island of Bute is situated among some of the lushest scenery of the west coast nestling beneath the Cowal Peninsula in the Firth of Clyde looking out to Arran. Bute is rich in prehistoric sacred remains: cup and ring Neolithic sites, chambered cairns, stone circles, forts and crannogs. The Early Christian sites are extremely important monastic centres on Bute with St Blane's Church/Monastery and related carved stones a sacred treasure to discover. Bute has been a popular resort since Victorian and Edwardian days as it was known to be 'doun the water' from Glasgow, and a destination for the iconic *Waverley* paddle steamer that still paddles the Kyles of Bute and the Clyde coast. The *Waverley* is the last seagoing paddle steamer in the world.

Historically, Bute has been inhabited for at least 6,000 years. Post Roman Bute, along with neighbouring Arran, was part of the Kingdom of Strathclyde and ruled by the Britons who spoke a Brythonic or Welsh type of language. It then became part of the Royal Stuart family holdings under the Marquess of Bute.

The wildlife of Bute is not distinctive except for the presence of a unique long-tailed field mouse. The botanical world is exceptional, as the Victorian collection of ferns in the sunken fernery glass house at Ascog holds some of the rarest subtropical ferns in the British Isles, one species being over 1,000 years old.

Mount Stuart, the great Gothic mansion of the Marquess of Bute, although not an ancient site, is the curious relic of a mystic's creation, and for those with a bent for mysticism, not to be missed. Astrological painted ceilings and a mirrored floor private chapel create an experience beyond the sacred.

ST BLANE'S, Kingarth

NS 094 534

The view across to the Isle of Arran from St Blane's.

The ruins of St Blane's Church and monastic site have a spectacular view looking out to the Isle of Arran, Holy Isle and the West, and on a sunny day this offers an atmosphere beyond description. Some say that the feeling evoked by the setting of an ancient site can almost be more important than the surviving remains, and that rings true for St Blane's.

St Blane's with tiered earthworks.

St Blane, a native of Bute, founded his monastic community at Kingarth in the sixth century. St Blane was the child of a virgin, and his story is part of Celtic legend. There was a Celtic custom to expose frail maids and their offspring in a skiff made of single hide to the mercy of the sea as punishment, for a 'virgin birth' was not part of accepted local tradition. As he grew, it was believed that the young Blaan, or Blane, would 'sanctify the decayed grandeur of pagan civilisation' with his mission work.

The Early Christian monastic centre that began at Kingarth links with Iona of the same era and other important ecclesiastical sites at Govan, Lismore, and Whithorn to the south. The raised circular earthworks, known as a 'caiseal' or 'rath', form the enclosure of the site. Simple Early Christian crosses mark the graves of the early community. The well-preserved ruin of the later twelfth century Romanesque or Norman church stands at the top of the site, along with fine carvings and grave slabs from the medieval period with enigmatic images. Running dogs, stags, a monkey creature and worn and eroded leaping figures can just be made out on these stones. These motifs are echoed in some of the finds from St Blane's including decorated slates with Irish script and inter-lace now kept in Edinburgh. A separate male and female burial ground are seen along with the various historic gravestones.

The Devil's Cauldron.

Near the cliffs below the site of the church and monastic ruins is the Devil's Cauldron, a curious large circular stone-lined chamber that has no explanation or connection to the monastery site. This prehistoric ring, 32.8ft/10m in diameter, is reminiscent of the open-chambered cairns at Clava, by Inverness. St Blane's Well, situated near the foot of the cliff west of the church was a wishing well to cure sterility, now rather overgrown. A large stone font for bathing pilgrims' feet lies near the western approach to the site.

DUNAGOIL

NS 085 530

Dunagoil is an Iron Age fort dating from 100 BC that domi-nates the rocky headland west of St Blane's. Timber-laced walls set afire in its heyday have created a vitrified fort clearly visible from its glassy molten rock appearance in the northwest corner of the fort. There was also a fortified site in prehistoric times at Little Dunagoil with a large stone cist or burial cham-ber found on the way. With the wide views from this lofty point, it is possible to consider the trading route that would have been active in Dunagoil Bay with the waterways of the

Firth of Clyde and beyond. These coastal waters with long sea lochs were the highways of the past.

This whole area of tumbled landscape is said to be bristling with antiquities. Surrounded by the great expanse of the Firth of Clyde, it is a traveller's delight.

Dunagoil hillfort from St Blane's.

ST MARY'S CHAPEL, Rothesay

NS 0862 6370

The medieval ruin of St Mary's or Lady Kirk Chapel in Rothesay has many remains dating from the thirteenth century located on the site of a much earlier Christian foundation. This was the site of a Picto-Scotic style sculptured stone, the MacAlister Stone, which has now been removed to the Bute Museum. Dated to the eighth century, it shows the central image of a cat with arched back, a winged animal or fantastic 'beastie', and a confronting pair of birds with crests carved in relief above a Latin cross with a Pictish-style horseman and eroded knotwork on the reverse. MacAlister's Stone had been misappropriated for a MacAlister family burial plot for many years until it was re-erected in the Rothesay churchyard. The stone is actually the remaining shaft of a composite free-standing cross. There are other fine carved stones of this period to be seen in the Bute Museum, including the intricate cross-slab from Rothesay Castle.

The MacAlister Stone, in the Bute Museum.

Effigies of a fourteenth century Menteith warrior and an eroded, diminished female figure are found in the chapel's canopied wall tombs. The chapel has a dual dedication to St Mary and St Bruoc (also written as Brioc or Brieuc), said to be the sixth century aunt of the Irish Brigit, or St Bride. Ancient sites often weave the spirits of the saints and the old Celtic goddesses together. A holy well is found within the grounds.

BLACKPARK STONE CIRCLE

NS 091 556

Photos: Marianna Lines

Blackpark stone circle, Kingarth.
Inset: Split stone, also on right of main picture.

The Blackpark site near Kingarth contains three stones set in an arc, the remains of a stone circle of seven stones, now surrounded by a forestry plantation. These sturdy conglomerates, most containing quartz, include one cross-incised stone and another split in two by frost. This is an incredibly atmospheric site.

OTHER SITES INCLUDE:
Stone circle by **Ettrick Bay** (NS 044668).
Standing stones at **St Ninian's Bay** (NS 036626).
A crannog – ancient artificial island – on **Loch Quien**, the smaller loch beside Loch Fad, and a row of three standing stones at Largizean farm near the golf links. These are only some of the ancient sites to discover on the island.
On the western shore of Bute near Scarrel Point there is a cave known as the **Piper's Cave** which the natives believed to be the opening into a subterranean passage through Eanan Hill to Achavulig. Supernatural beings inhabited this dark retreat. A bold piper disappeared piping gaily, soon to be hushed in the depths of the mountain... then the music ceased forever.

Inner Hebrides

Detail of the MacAlister Stone (see page 313) showing the arched-back cat above two love birds. Flower impression by Marianna Lines.

SELECTED
BIBLIOGRAPHY

Allen, J.R. and **Anderson J.** – ECMS, *The Early Christian Monuments of Scotland*, Pinkfoot Press, Angus 1993

Badcock, Anna (ed.) – *Ancient Uists: Archaeology of the Outer Hebrides*, Comhairle Nan Eilean Siar, Isle of Lewis, 2013

Balfour, Michael – *Mysterious Scotland*, Mainstream Publishing, Edinburgh, 1997

Bradley, Richard – *The Moon and the Bonfire*, Society of Antiquaries of Scotland, Edinburgh, 2005

Brown, George Mackay – *Portrait of Orkney*, The Hogarth Press, London 1981

Butter, Rachel – *Kilmartin*, Kilmartin House Trust 1999

Byrne, Kevin – *Lonely Colonsay: Island at the Edge*, House of Lochar, Colonsay 2010

Caldwell, David H. – *Islay, Jura and Colonsay*, Birlinn, 2001

Campbell, Marion – *Argyll: The Enduring Heartland*, House of Lochar, Colonsay 2001

Clarke, David; Blackwell, Alice; Goldberg, Martin – *Early Medieval Scotland*, National Museums Scotland, Edinburgh 2012

Clifford, John – *Perth and Kinross*, Yale University Press, London 2007

Davis, Graeme – *The Early English Settlement of Orkney and Shetland*, John Donald, Edinburgh 2007

Fisher, Ian – *Early Medieval Sculpture in the West Highlands and Islands*, RCAHMS, 2001

Fraser, Iain, (ed.) – *The Pictish Symbol Stones of Scotland*, RCAHMS Royal Commission on the Ancient and Historical Monuments of Scotland 2008

Fraser, James E. – *From Caledonia to Pictland*, Edinburgh University Press 2009

Geddes, George and **Hale, Alex** – *The Archaeological Landscape of Bute*, RCAHMS 2010

Haswell-Smith, Hamish – *The Scottish Islands*, Canongate, Edinburgh, 1998

Hedderwick, Mairi – *Sea Change*, Canongate, Edinburgh 1999

Henderson, George and Isabel – *The Art of the Picts*, Thames & Hudson, London 2004

Henry, David (ed.) – *The Worm the Germ and the Thorn: Pictish and Related Studies*, The Pinkfoot Press, Angus 1997

Humphreys, Rob *The Rough Guide to Scotland*, Rough Guides 2011

Hunter, James – *Last of the Free: A History of the Highlands and Islands of Scotland*, Mainstream, 2000

Lines, Marianna – *Sacred Stones Sacred Places*, Saint Andrew Press, Edinburgh 1992

MacArthur, E. Mairi – *Columba's Island: Iona from Past to Present*, Edinburgh University Press, 2007

Mack, Alastair – *Field Guide to the Pictish Symbol Stones*, The Pinkfoot Press, Angus 1997

MacDonald, Murdo (ed.) – *Highland Art, a Window to the West*, Royal Scottish Academy, Edinburgh 2008

MacLeod, Innes – *Discovering Galloway*, John Donald Publishers, Edinburgh 1986

McHardy, Stuart – *The Quest for Arthur*, Luath Press, Edinburgh 2001

McHardy, Stuart – *A New History of the Picts*, Luath Press, Edinburgh 2011

McIntosh, Alastair – *Island Spirituality*, Islands Book Trust, Isle of Lewis, 2013

McIntosh, Alastair – *Soil and Soul*, Aurum Press, London 2001

MacSween, Ann – *Wee Guide to Prehistoric Scotland*, Goblinshead, Musselburgh, 2011

Martin Martin – *A Description of the Western Islands of Scotland*, London 1703

Modeen, Mary (ed.) – *Invisible Scotland*, Moray School of Art Press, University of the Highlands and Islands, 2013

Moffat, Alastair – *Arthur and the Lost Kingdoms*, Birlinn, Edinburgh 2012

Moffat, Alastair – *The Borders*, Birlinn 2007

Moffat, Alastair – *The Faded Map: Lost Kingdoms of Scotland*, Birlinn 2011

Moncreiff, The Hon. Rhoderick & Alison (ed.) – *The Annals of Kinross-shire*, Fossoway & District Community Council, 1990

Morrison, Elizabeth – *Beasts: Factual & Fantastic*, The British Library, London 2007

Munro, David – *Where Poets Dream'd: Michael Bruce Way*, Kinross 2013

Murphy, Alan (ed.) – *Scottish Highlands and Islands*, Footprint, 2011

Myatt, Leslie J. – *The Standing Stones of Caithness*, author published, Halkirk, Caithness 2003

Omand, Donald (ed.) – *The Argyll Book*, Birlinn 2006

Omand, Donald (ed.) – *The Fife Book*, Birlinn 2000

Omand, Donald (ed.) – *The Perthshire Book*, Birlinn 1999

Ordnance Survey – *Scottish Highlands and Islands*, 1999

Paterson, Raymond Campbell – *The Lords of the Isles*, Birlinn 2001

Ritchie, Anna and **Ritchie, Graham** – *Scotland: An Oxford Archaeological Guide*, Oxford University Press, 2004

Ritchie, Anna – *Shetland*, RCAHMS, 1997

Ritchie, Anna – *Picts*, HMSO, Edinburgh 1989

Ritchie, Graham and **Mary Hannan** – *Exploring Scotland's Heritage: Argyll and the Western Isles*, RCAHMS, Royal Commission on the Ancient and Historical Monuments of Scotland, Edinburgh 1985

Ritchie, David Alan – *We - The Skythians*, The Skythian Society Press, Skye 2012

Scott, Ian G. and **Ritchie, Anna** – *Pictish and Viking-Age Carvings from Shetland*, RCAHMS 2009

Smith, Roff – The First Stonehenge, National Geographic Vol. 226, August 2014

Society of Antiquaries of Scotland, Proceedings of the, Vol 141, 2011

Stevenson, J.B. – *Exploring Scotland's Heritage: The Clyde Estuary and Central Region*, RCAHMS 1985

Taylor, Kenny – *'Around the Scottish Islands in 80 Monuments'*, Historic Scotland project (online and book forthcoming) 2013

Taylor, Simon, with **Gilbert, Márkus** – *The Place-Names of Fife Vol I-V*, Shaun Tyas, Donington 2012

Ward, Anne – *Nothing to See Here: Guide to Hidden Joys of Scotland*, Pocket Mountains Ltd, Moffat 2006

Webb, Sharon – *In the Footsteps of Kings: Kilmartin Glen*, Kilmartin House Trust, Kilmartin 2012

Welfare, Adam – *Great Crowns of Stone: The Recumbent Stone Circles of Scotland*, RCAHMS 2011

White, Gary and **Aviva, Elyn** – *Powerful Places in Scotland*, Pilgrims Process Santa Fe, NM 2010

Wickham-Jones, Caroline – *Monuments of Orkney*, Historic Scotland, 2012

Williams, Ronald – *Lords of the Isles: The Clan Donald and the early Kingdom of the Scots*, House of Lochar, Colonsay, 2000

* * *

SELECTED WEBSITES:

Pictish Arts Society:
www.thepictishartssociety.org.uk

The Northern Antiquarian:
www.northernantiquarian.forumotion.net

Orkneyjar: www.orkneyjar.com

Canmore: Royal Commission RCAHMS:
http://canmore.rcahms.gov.uk/en/search/

Caithness Broch Project:
www.facebook.com/CaithnessBrochProject

Marianna Lines at the Aberlemno Stone, Angus.

INDEX